Giant Killers, War Heroes, & Sp

Published by Mission Point Press
2554 Chandler Rd.
Traverse City, MI 49696
(231) 421-9513
MissionPointPress.com

ISBN: 978-1-958363-81-2
Library of Congress Control Number upon request.
Printed in the United States of America

GIANT KILLERS
WAR HEROES &
SPECIAL FORCES LEGENDS

DAVID A. YUZUK

MISSION POINT PRESS

"And the truth is that all veterans pay with their lives. Some pay all at once, while others pay over a lifetime..."
—J.M. Storm

Contents

A hidden SOG recon team took this photo of North Vietnamese troops
on the Ho Chi Minh trail in Laos.

Michael E. Thornton at the Army-Navy football game on December 2, 2006.

Author and Aventura Officer David A. Yuzuk with Officer Kevin Bascle, 2016.

INTRODUCTION

My name is David Yuzuk and I'm a retired Aventura, Florida, police officer. My journey into researching war heroes started when a tiny homeless man named Richard Flaherty uttered the words, "It's time I tell you who I really am." Ten days later that man would be killed, and I would spend the next four years investigating his incredible life.

After I published the book on his life, *The Giant Killer*, I needed a way to get the story out to the world. I started with a small Facebook page made up of only a handful of followers. As I posted stories about my project, an amazing thing started to happen.

More followers, which I now call members, started to come on board and share their own stories of war heroes. As the members continued to grow, so did my education on these extraordinary soldiers who fought with gallantry and heroics above and beyond anything even Hollywood could dream of.

Every week on our page we would add more and more war heroes from all different times, military branches, and countries. The members loved these stories so much that we started getting requests to make a compilation book.

Great idea! But how do you make a book of the greatest heroes? Who judges who are the greatest? What's the criteria? Most medals? Time served? Enemy killed? Men saved? Medal of Honor only recipients?

The truth is, when it comes to the question of choosing the greatest military heroes, it's always going to be subjective. I also believe we will never truly know the greatest acts of valor on a battlefield because what about all the stories that were lost because a whole platoon was wiped out and there was nobody left to tell the incredible tales of heroism that occurred in that last stand?

My idea for this first book, delving into the subject, was to leave it up to you, the public, and our social media pages. This book, therefore, is the compilation of many of the most talked about, shared, and liked heroes we have featured on our pages.

As a side note, several histories of the greatest heroes that have had considerable amounts of media coverage are not in this book because their stories are already so well known. Those would include Audie Murphy, Daniel Daly, Chris Kyle, Alvin York, Desmond Doss, George Patton, Richard Marcinko, Pat Tillman, etc.

To be part of our team to help select the next group of Giant Killer heroes, please join our The Giant Killer social media pages on Facebook, Instagram, YouTube, and several other well-known platforms. Please tell us about the heroes you think we missed and the new ones we may haven't yet heard of. God bless you all for keeping the memories of these heroes alive.

DAVID A. YUZUK

Giant Killers, War Heroes, & Special Forces Legends

Specialist Fourth Class Gary G. Wetzel

US ARMY

Medal of Honor
Purple Heart
Air Medal

Born September 29, 1947

Gary G. Wetzel risked his life and sacrificed his limb in the name of saving as many men as he could. Despite suffering extensive wounds that might've killed another, when duty called, he answered.

Soldiers in Vietnam were not in a rush to become door gunners. Compared to most other occupations, hanging part way out the door of a helicopter as a living target seemed like a bad career path to most. What's the life span of a door gunner? Five minutes — or so said the popular legend at the time. While the real life span of a door gunner in Vietnam was longer than five minutes, within every legend is a kernel of truth, and being a door gunner meant your machine gun was the only thing between you and the enemy. But those odds never stopped Gary Wetzel.

It was January 8, 1968, and then-Pfc. Gary G. Wetzel was on duty and onboard a helicopter near Ap Dong An in the Republic of Vietnam. According to his interview from the Library of Congress Veterans History Project, they were on an "eagle flight," named because of how they'd fly over an area waiting to catch something happening on the ground or something looking off and then react to it. They had already made a few stops: dropping off their deadly cargo of seven or eight troops, scanning the area, scooping them up again and leaving. Nothing had happened so far — until the first bad omen reared its head. While grounded at an old French fort to meet with a ground commander, a group of Australian helicopters joined them, a number of them shot nearly to pieces. After that, decisions were made by the higher-ups, and Wetzel was back on the helicopter as part of an insertion force of both American and Australian choppers.

A short time later, Wetzel's helicopter was flying over the area of the air strike, getting ready to open up its doors and let the machine gun rip. In his interview with the Library of Congress, Wetzel described the job of the door gunner as laying down enough covering fire that enemies can't fire back at you or your brothers-in-arms. "You try and keep Charlie's head down to eliminate, you know, casualties as much as you can. And anyone with any common sense, you hear — you hear a *bang-bang-bang* — you're not going to stick your head up and look; you're going to duck." Wetzel was ready to do his job, but nobody was prepared for what happened next.

The standard procedure for a mission like this was to have more than one set of gunships closely staggered so they could cover each other. You can imagine how thick the tension felt in the hot Vietnamese air when Wetzel's helicopter was already starting to drop into the treetops, committing to the fight — and their backup was a quarter mile behind them. Wetzel states that this was the moment he realized the situation was a "big god-damn mistake." Now 15–20 feet off the ground, a barrage of gunfire immediately erupted as numerous Viet Cong stood up from their hiding places, Wetzel describing it feeling like there "must have been eight million of 'em stood up." In an instant they were caught in a hailstorm of gunfire — and then came the rocket-propelled grenade. From ahead and left of the helicopter, the RPG made a direct hit, blowing out the front of the ship.

What Wetzel did afterward was extraordinary, but the scenario he and the rest of the crew found themselves in was unfortunately very common. According to the Vietnam Helicopter Pilots Association, of the more than 12,000 helicopters operating in Vietnam, over 5,000 were destroyed by combat or accidents. But dig into the stats and the stories, and you'll find out why Vietnam was "the helicopter war," as retired Maj. Gen. Carl H. McNair described it. In addition to their incredible offensive capabilities, helicopters were used in more than 850,000 medical evacuation missions conducted during that war and they did incredible work boosting the survival rates of wounded soldiers.

Right now, though, it was Wetzel and his crew that needed rescuing. After scraping to a halt on the ground and being lit up by withering crossfire — all in the span of a few seconds — two of the men were already dead. Snapping into action, Wetzel was determined to save as many as he could, and he decided to start by making sure his aircraft commander was safe. When he threw open the door separating them, his commander was in terrible shape — but alive. He and his crew chief managed to get the commander out of the devastated helicopter. Then disaster struck. "And we got him about half-way up, and then Bart says duck, and then he goes like this — and I hear a bang." Before he knew what had happened, he was blown into a rice paddy by two enemy explosives that went off just inches from his location.

His left arm — gone. Severe wounds in his right arm, chest, and left leg. Profuse bleeding. War is hell, and Wetzel was in the ninth circle of it. Despite all of this he had no chance for hesitation; looking over his left side, he spotted a VC gripping another grenade, his body betraying his intention to toss it right at Wetzel. One-armed yet single-minded, Wetzel whipped his Thompson around and zippered him up. The stunned VC fell back, his explosive going off and killing multiple hostiles clustered around him. More explosives went off. It was a spectacular, chaotic light show of lethality.

"It's like July 4th but it's on the ground. And you don't get to see the colors, you don't get to say ooh and ah; you just shit in your pants."

Wetzel and another man raced to their aircraft commander and put tourniquets on his legs, staunching the flow of blood.

At that moment, Bart, the other conscious man, warned Wetzel that the Vietnamese were flooding the area and killing the wounded. Knowing his limits, knowing he couldn't take them all with brute force, Wetzel and the two other men opted to feign death. They certainly looked the part: Wetzel was missing an arm and sprawled out in muddy water, Bart with holes in his head and missing part of his jaw from shrapnel, the aircraft commander being so close to the light at the end of the tunnel he just rolled over. Wetzel heard footfalls ... a boot stomped down in front of him, his one eye peeking out of the muddy water being the only sense he had of his surroundings.

He's just waiting for the shot to come, making his peace, thinking the VC should just get it over with. The shot comes, but it goes through his foot. We can only speculate why the enemy would shoot Wetzel anywhere but the head, but what we do know is that he wouldn't live to know the error of his ways. Shots rang out, these now from Americans, and the VC hurried away. Wetzel figured he'd had enough rest and was ready for more action; he snatched his Thompson and crawled around the chopper. He saw the VC trying to unfix the machine gun from the helicopter — his machine gun — and raising up his Thompson, blew the six enemies off their feet and into their graves. Wetzel returned to his aircraft commander who said one of the hardest things a man can hear: to tell his wife he loves her.

"I'm like 'shut up, you tell her yourself, we'll get out of this shit, you know.'" The anger started welling up inside Wetzel, but he didn't have time to cry; he reacted with action — with vengeance. He tucked his useless, mangled arm into his waistband to keep it from flopping around and did what he described as his "John Wayne run," putting bursts of .45 rounds into anyone in his way as he dashed for the helicopter. He took some lead in the leg and went down on one knee ... and the next thing he remembers was having miraculously staggered back to his original position in the helicopter's gun-well. Fueled by sheer willpower and making use of what little blood he had left running through his veins, he overcame the shock and wracking pain of his injuries and full-pulled the trigger. At that moment his machine gun was the only weapon being used effectively against the enemy. Wetzel remained in place, pouring bullets onto the enemy weapons emplacement until they stopped firing back.

There was no time to stop. Refusing to tend to his own grievous wounds, he attempted to return to the aid of his aircraft commander. Unfortunately, the body has its limits, and Wetzel's was long past the breaking point. Massive blood loss left him passed out on the ground. But not for long. Regaining consciousness, he snapped back into doing what he believed to be his duty, dragging himself to the aid of his fellow crewman. After agonizing effort, he came to the side of the crew chief who was attempting to drag the wounded aircraft commander to a nearby dike, the safest place they could find. Amid all this, Wetzel passed out again, and again he pulled himself up to his feet, unwavering in his devotion to his brothers. He continued on, grabbing other wounded soldiers and pulling them across the rice paddy. It would be more than 10 hours before reinforcements would begin to evacuate the wounded.

Wetzel survived, but his left arm had to be amputated. After six months in the hospital, he made his transition back into civilian life. While working as an expeditor in Wisconsin sometime later, he had some unusual guests show up to his workplace. A colonel, a major, and a first sergeant all had a message to deliver: he'd be going on a trip soon. At the time Wetzel brushed it off — he'd already gotten some medals and didn't think this request was for anything important. After two weeks of prodding by the officers, he relented and agreed to the "trip." That flight ended up taking him to the White House to receive the Medal of Honor from President Lyndon Johnson.

When asked what the medal meant to him, Wetzel replied,

"When I was in the Tokyo hospital, where the doctors took out more than four hundred stitches, some of the guys I pulled out who were recovering from their wounds found out I was there. They would walk up to my bed and ask, 'Are you Gary Wetzel?' And I'd say, 'Yeah,' and they would pull out pictures of their wives, kids, or girlfriends and say, 'Hey, man, because of you, this is what I've got to go back to.'" Wetzel would reply, "I'm not Superman. I was just a guy doing his job."

Gary G. Wetzel was born September 29, 1947, in Milwaukee, Wisconsin, and continues to live in South Milwaukee. In 2015 he was named Milwaukee County Veteran of the Year and was the first recipient of the Milwaukee County Purple Heart Pass. Wetzel is a frequent visitor and honored guest of the War Memorial Center.

November 19, 1968: Wetzel (left) receiving the Medal of Honor from President Lyndon B. Johnson along with fellow recipients Sammy L. Davis, Dwight H. Johnson, James Allen Taylor, and Angelo Liteky. (White House Photograph Office)

Private First Class Herbert Kailieha Pilila'au

US ARMY

Medal of Honor
Purple Heart

October 10, 1928–September 17, 1951 (22 years)

At only 22 years old, Herbert Pilila'au would cement his legacy as the first Hawaiian to receive the Medal of Honor. Though his life would end in one of the bloodiest battles of the Korean War, his legendary last stand using hand-to-hand combat in the face of enemy gunfire and bayonets will forever remain a story of unbridled courage.

Herbert Pilila'au considered refusing the draft. As a devout Christian, he had a deep uneasiness about killing other human beings; to him life was precious and war was not to be taken lightly. Pilila'au was the quiet type, introverted, and an avid reader. But beneath his gentle demeanor there existed a deep-seated sense of justice and respect for humanity.

Pilila'au was born on October 10, 1928, on the island of O'ahu. He was born into a family of 14 children — five sisters and eight brothers. His family was a happy, tight-knit, working-class family living in the suburbs of the Leeward coast, in what was then a Territory of Hawaii. His parents, William Kaluhi Pilila'au and Abigail Keolalani Kailieha, were both Native Hawaiians and his mother spoke both English and Hawaiian. In those days, Pilila'au had a great love and talent for both singing and playing the ukulele. Pilila'au graduated from Waipahu High School in 1948 and then enrolled at Cannon Business School where he studied administration, secretarial work, and accounting. But the calm surrounding his life was about to be shattered; the United States was about to go to war.

On June 27, 1950, President Harry Truman publicly declared his support for South Korea in fending off a North Korean invasion — and so it was that the United States officially entered the Korean War alongside the United Kingdom and with the support of the United Nations. During the first year of the war, the opposing armies fought back and forth all up and down the Korean peninsula. By July of 1951, troops on both sides were exhausted by the bloodshed and the war moved into a stalemate.

When Pilila'au found out he had been drafted into the military, his nonviolent convictions remained strong and he considered declaring himself a conscientious objector. But after deep soul searching, he decided that serving his country was just as important as his personal beliefs. Ultimately, he saw standing proudly alongside his peers as his duty. Shortly after finishing basic training in March of 1952, he was sent to Korea to fight.

Pilila'au was now Private First Class with Company C, 23rd Infantry Regiment, 2nd Infantry Division, and he volunteered to be his squad's automatic rifleman. His primary weapon: the Browning Automatic rifle (BAR). Measuring 47 inches long with a 20-round magazine and weighing a whopping 19.4 pounds, the BAR was a beastly terror on the battlefield. Its ability to fire up to 650 rounds per minute gave it massive firepower, and high accuracy was possible through the use of single shots or bursts of two or three. Col. David Hackworth praised the BAR as "the best weapon of the Korean War" in his autobiography.

In September of 1951, the bloody stalemate on the Korean Peninsula showed no signs of ceasing, but that would soon change. The commander of the 2nd Infantry Division ordered the 23rd Infantry Regiment and an allied French battalion to attack the slopes of a strategically important ridge named Pia-ri or Hill 931, just to the north of their location. It was during this fierce fight that Herbert Pilila'au, the quiet, studious Native Hawaiian, earned his Medal of Honor. This battle would go down in history as the Battle at Heartbreak Ridge — a month-long slugfest that took place from September 13 to October 15, 1951.

On September 17, 1951, near Pia-ri and just a few miles north of the boundary between North and South Korea, Company C and two others were tasked with capturing Hill 931 — one of two identifiable peaks in east central Korea. When Company C's attack was thwarted by the ferocious North Koreans and allied Chinese, it was up to Pilila'au's platoon to stave off the enemy. A defensive perimeter was set up that mid-afternoon, and using artillery, mortar, and heavy machine gunfire, the platoon successfully held off a series of grueling assaults. At approximately 10 p.m., two battalions of the Korean People's Army began an aggressive attack on their position. Both sides fought forcefully, but as time wore on, their ammunition began to run out. That was only the start of their problems; the other platoon was caught in the ferocious crossfire right in the middle of the rice paddies. This platoon obtained permission to begin a withdrawal; Pilila'au's squad was assigned to cover their retreat.

As the retreating platoon pulled out, the fighting continued until, eventually, only Pilila'au and his squad leader remained in their original position. The squad leader and forward observer Lt. Richard Hagar called in artillery fire ahead of Pilila'au to cover him as he moved, but when it hit, it was so close to Pilila'au that Hagar thought he had killed him. His heart sank as shells pounded the position. By some miracle Pilila'au was unscathed, and when Hagar called out to him, he responded with a "keep going, I'm fine!" He really wasn't fine. When the ammunition for his BAR ran dry, he began throwing hand grenades until those too ran out. But he was not about to back down; if his weapons failed him, he would just make his own. He began to throw the nastiest rocks he could find and then, surprising friends and enemies alike, he charged directly at the enemy forces with his trench knife in one hand, punching with the other.

Some of his comrades could see what was happening from their positions down the ridge — Pilila'au's squad leader recalled years later his amazement at what he witnessed that day: "There was Herb standing up, fighting a lot of the enemy. It was hand-to-hand and just Herb against all of them. We all wanted to go back up to help him, but the captain said 'No.' We tried to help Herb by firing a few shots, but they didn't do any good. All of a sudden, they shot him, and when he went down, they bayoneted him. That was it." The next morning when his platoon went back to retake the position, they found a stunning forty dead North Korean soldiers surrounding his body.

And so it was that on September 17, 1951, in the mountains of North Korea, this quiet Christian boy from O'ahu lost his life on Heartbreak Ridge. He died a brave soldier and a hero to his country. Pilila'au was only 22 when he became the first Hawaiian to receive the Medal of Honor. On June 18, 1952, President Harry Truman presented his parents with their son's medal. The citation on his Medal of Honor reads: "His heroic devotion to duty, indomitable fighting spirit, and gallant self-sacrifice reflect the highest credit upon himself, the infantry, and the US Army. ... he closed with the foe in hand-to-hand combat, courageously fighting with his trench knife and bare fists until finally overcome and mortally wounded."

Pilia'au is buried at the National Memorial Cemetery of the Pacific. In January of 2000, the Navy named a Military Sealift Command cargo ship, the USNS *Pililaau* (T-AKR-340) in his honor. Thirty-one members of his family were given a tour when the boat first docked in Hawaii.

Chase Pilila'au said her uncle was a humble man to his core. "My uncle was a real quiet person. He studied music. ... But when the call came and they needed people to serve, he volunteered," she told the *Honolulu Advertiser* in 2009. Herbert Pilila'au had wanted to be a police officer, and that's why

Herbert's bravery wasn't so surprising to those who knew him.

"To be a police officer, you have to have a lot of guts," Chase said. The live-fire range at the Makua Military Reservation in his hometown and the Pilila'au Army Recreation Center also bear his name. Pilila'au's courage in the face of certain death will never be forgotten.

The USNS *Pililaau* off the coast of Camp Pendleton, CA, 2008. (www.army.mil)

14

Staff Sergeant William Hart Pitsenbarger

US AIR FORCE

Medal of Honor
Airman's Medal
Purple Heart
Air Medal (10)
Good Conduct Medal
National Defense Service Medal
Vietnam Service Medal
Republic of Vietnam Gallantry Cross w/ Bronze Palm
Republic of Vietnam Medal of Military Merit

July 8, 1944–April 11, 1966 (21 years)

Pitsenbarger hacked splints out of gnarled jungle vines and crafted stretchers out of nothing but saplings, his bare hands, and lots of ingenuity. Repeatedly he exposed himself to enemy fire, and repeatedly he suffered for his bravery.

William Hart Pitsenbarger, born and raised in the small town of Piqua, Ohio, had no doubts about what he wanted to do when he grew up. As a junior in high school, he already had his sights set sky high: he would join the US Air Force and become a Green Beret. Unfortunately, when he told his parents about his dream, they adamantly refused. Not that that would stop someone with the grit of William "Pits" Pitsenbarger for long. On New Year's Eve of 1962, shortly after his graduation, he said goodbye to his hometown and jumped on the first train headed for basic training in San Antonio to join up with the US Air Force.

Pitsenbarger was not one to scrape by with passing grades. After volunteering for Air Rescue and Recovery Squadron in San Antonio, he went on to become one of the first airmen to make it into the pararescue program straight out of basic training. His training was intense and extensive, taking him through the US Army Airborne School, US Navy Dive School, survival school, and both rescue and survival medical courses. More Air Force rescue training and jungle survival school was included for good measure. If that wasn't enough, he finished up by becoming proficient in air crash rescue and firefighting. Pitsenbarger's excellence in training wasn't a fluke — his profound skills in every one of those abilities he'd learned would be seen in action two years later in one of the most daring rescues in Air Force history.

After a stint with the Rescue Squadron stationed at the Hamilton AFB, California, the moment he'd been waiting for finally came: Pitsenbarger got sent on Temporary Duty to Vietnam. He hadn't fought this hard and come this far for just a Temporary Duty assignment, however, so after completing the assignment, he volunteered to return. In 1965, he reported to 38th Air Rescue and Recovery Squadron at Bien Hoa Air Base near Saigon, and it's here where Pitsenbarger would make one of the best friends he'd ever have: the Kaman HH-43 Husky helicopter. During the war, the two-pilot HH-43 Huskie flew more rescue missions than all other aircraft combined; the Husky was the first rescue helicopter to arrive in Vietnam and the last to leave, a legacy that it shares with Pitsenbarger. HH-43 aircrews saved more lives in combat than crews flying any other USAF helicopter, and Pitsenbarger saved more lives than almost anyone.

By the young age of 21, Pitsenbarger had already flown nearly 300 missions, risking his life almost daily during the war rescuing downed airmen and soldiers. Sometimes fact is stranger than fiction, and some accounts of Pitsenbarger's rescues sound more like scenes out of action films than textbook history. Take for example the time when he hung from a cable out of a flying Husky to rescue a dying South Vietnamese soldier from an active, burning minefield. His bravery didn't go unnoticed — that extraordinary valor earned him a trio of medals, one from Vietnam and two from the US. His commander, Maj. Maurice Kessler, said of Pitsenbarger: "One of a special breed. Alert and always ready to go on any mission."

On April 11, 1966, Pitsenbarger boarded one of two Huskies ordered to rescue a half-dozen or more American casualties pinned down by constant attacks from Viet Cong. After rushing across 35 kilometers of thick jungle to the scene of the ambush, he volunteered to be lowered — with complete disregard for personal safety — 100 feet through a dense canopy to a live firefight on the ground. Moving into action, Pitsenbarger dressed the wounds of the soldiers before getting them lifted to the safety of the Huskies by cable. After saving the lives of six men, the two helicopters had to return to a nearby aid station to make room for another load of wounded. This continued multiple times, always with Pitsenbarger refusing his own evacuation "in order to get one more wounded soldier to safety."

After several pickups, any luck they had left ran out. As they swooped in for a final evacuation, one of the Huskies began to lower its cable to Pitsenbarger. That's when the bullets started. A hail of small-arms fire peppered the helicopter, ripping into the Husky which began to show signs of engine failure. The pilot inside, realizing he had to fly out of harm's way as soon as possible or go down like a fireball, began to retreat. Back on the ground, Pitsenbarger had already made his decision. Believing that the troops still under fire needed him now more than ever, he gave the helicopter pilot the "wave-off," allowing it to fly to safety. Over the next hour and a half, constant, heavy mortar and small-arms fire kept the helicopters from being able to return safely.

Pitsenbarger did not wait idly by for his rescue. Focusing on the task at hand, he used everything at his disposal to save every last man he could. With firefights continuing on, Pitsenbarger hacked splints out of gnarled jungle vines and crafted stretchers out of nothing but saplings, his bare hands, and lots of ingenuity. Repeatedly he exposed himself to enemy fire, and repeatedly he suffered for his bravery. Despite receiving three bullet wounds, he valiantly kept risking his own life to save the lives of his fellow soldiers. As the battle raged on to the point of desperation, the soldiers' ammunition — the only thing keeping them alive — began to run dangerously low. Pitsenbarger saw the problem and knew the stakes. He gathered ammunition from the dead amid torrents of fire and gave it back to those still living. With the wounded taken care of and ammunition to spare, he took up a rifle to help hold the Viet Cong off the position.

The sun set with the men stranded deep in the jungle, no rescue in sight, and no choice but to fight on into the night. Viet Cong snipers had no intention of letting the soldiers sleep. In the vicious combat that ensued, American forces suffered a devastating 80 percent casualty rate as their perimeter buckled under the pressure of the enveloping enemy.

The next day, while evaluating the crushing losses, Pitsenbarger's body was found, having been killed by sniper fire in the middle of the night. Even in death he was defiant: He had one arm wrapped around a rifle, while his other hand gripped a medical kit. Pitsenbarger never made it out of that ambush, but thanks to his help, 60 other men who'd spent that night out in the jungle did.

This is not where his story ends. After his death, Air Force commanders heard the accounts, which led to his nomination to receive the Medal of Honor, the highest military decoration, reserved only for distinguished acts of valor. But before the nomination went through, an Army general recommended a downgrade to the Air Force Cross, explaining that there wasn't enough documentation of the staff sergeant's actions to award him the highest honor. Had that been the end

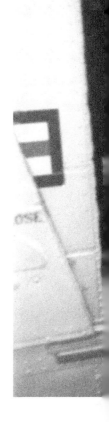

A1C William Pitsenbarger with an M16 outside the HH-43. (National Museum of the Air Force)

of it, Pitsenbarger's story may never have gotten the recognition it deserved.

Thirty-five years later, after much review, the decision to downgrade Pitsenbarger's award was reversed, to much celebration. On December 8, 2000, his mother and father, along with battle survivors and hundreds of pararescue airmen, accepted the Medal of Honor from Secretary of the Air Force Whit Peters on behalf of William "Pits" Pitsenbarger at the National Museum of the United States Air Force.

The Medal of Honor found a worthy man in the 21-year-old from Ohio; after all, it's due to the efforts of people like S.Sgt. Pitsenbarger that men and women on the battlefield know they will never be left behind, at any cost.

Paul Galanti (circled) among others in an article titled "42 North Carolinans are prisoners of war." (*The Gastonia Gazette*, 19 March 1972)

Lieutenant Paul Galanti

US NAVY

Silver Star
Legion of Merit with Combat w/ "V" Device (2)
Bronze Start with Combat w/ "V" Device
Purple Heart (2)
Air Medal (9)
Prisoner of War Medal

Born July 11, 1939

"There's no such thing as a bad day when there's a doorknob on the inside of the door." — Paul Galanti

Lt. Paul Galanti had been on cruise for nine months with the USS *Hancock*, and while it wasn't exactly a five-star hotel — they were stationed in Southeast Asia with no air conditioning — Galanti was alive and rumors were circulating through the halls of the ship that they were going home soon. He was relieved, excited: with over 90 missions under his belt, he was practically bursting with combat experience and needed to blow off some steam in the States. He and his flight leader, a former Blue Angel, made plans to fly to Pensacola so that Galanti could try out for the legendary Blue Angels himself.

Despite all the horrors and casualties of the Vietnam War, Galanti and the rest of the pilots on the USS *Hancock* had performed with flying colors: a few planes had been destroyed, which was to be expected, but not a single American soul had been lost, a truly remarkable feat.

Galanti was in the aircraft division, and he knew every single airplane in his squadron. On this particular day there was one bad seed, a Douglas A-4 Skyhawk, that Galanti knew was broken, and he wasn't about to let anyone else fly it.

"The A-4 was the only active-duty jet airplane that you could disconnect the hydraulic controls and actually fly it manually ... It was like driving a Mack truck with no power steering."

Day broke and the first flight off the *Hancock* had seen all hell break loose on their run over the land; they weren't going home any time soon. Everyone got briefed and suited up for another flight.

Galanti, not wanting any other pilot to risk their lives, decided he would fly the Douglas A-4 Skyhawk with the busted hydraulics. As he suited up and looked over the crippled A-4, he began calculating how he could land the bird in the water if he had to. After all the combat missions he had been on, he knew how vital it was to be prepared, but he could never have imagined that as soon as his wheels had lifted off the safety of the carrier, he was headed for disaster.

"Scratch that target you're going to, you can't get to it, the weather's too bad," Galanti recalled the skipper saying to him in an interview with the Stockdale Center.

The target had shifted, and now Galanti and his squadron were off to hit a railroad yard that they'd struck many times before. "This'll be a piece of cake," Galanti thought. As they neared the target, they pulled into their dive-bomb formation. The first plane rolled in, then the second, then the third ... but when Galanti went up to bat he found his gun sights to be so faulty that it'd take a miracle to hit a barn on his own. Thinking quickly, he used his fellow pilot's plane as a tool to stay on track, tucking himself just behind the aircraft's wing as they flew down in formation together.

His partner dropped his payload over the target, and just after Galanti "hit the pickle" — pressing the button to release his own bombs on the railroad yard— he felt the explosion in all its terrible glory. Only it wasn't hundreds of meters on the ground below, but directly behind his own head. Galanti instinctively yanked the stick back; the nose popped up and every red-flag warning went off like angry fireworks on all the instruments in the cabin. Electricity failed. Galanti heard a sound he'd never heard before, a "rap rap *rap rap*" of metal screaming. Galanti had a good guess of the cause: the turbine blades were tearing themselves off and slicing into the skin of the plane.

"This is not good," Galanti said out loud as the oil gauges stared back at him, rapidly dropping to zero.

When he'd flown the malfunctioning A-4 plane at 180 knots for the test flight, it was as easy to control as an angry bull; now he was going 600 knots. Galanti had no time for a radio call — he pulled the eject handle.

The plane folded in on itself like origami before tearing apart. The Douglas A-4 Skyhawk, nicknamed the "Tinker Toy Bomber" for its diminutive size, was obliterated like a child's toy in a wood chipper. Galanti had survived by a degree of seconds — perhaps milliseconds — his parachute catching the wind as he wafted down against the backdrop of an airborne explosion.

Stinging sensations pricked the back of Galanti's neck as he floated downward. His eyes caught what looked like high-speed insects whipping past him, but they weren't; they were tracer rounds fired from enemy weapons. A mass of enemy troops gathered below him while Galanti watched his airplane's final descent into its watery grave. He finally managed to make it to the ground, hitting earth in a messy clump of bruised flesh and ripped fabric, bleeding profusely from a bullet wound on his neck, and alone in North Vietnam.

"This is not good, this is not going to be a good day," Galanti said to himself in the understatement of the year.

He knew the cards he was dealt but tried to make a gamble anyway, weak as his hand was. He hid in a nearby bush, hoping they'd somehow pass him by. Instead, a young Vietnamese boy approached him with a grown-man's rifle in his hands, shaking like a leaf from fear, anticipation, or both.

Galanti had made a plan in his mind long ago for what he would do in this situation. In his holster was a pistol with six rounds. Five of those rounds would be gifted to his enemies.

One would be saved for himself. However, that plan had been hatched before looking his own death straight in the eyes, and before he'd been forced to consider leaving his wife a widow. He was going to do whatever it took to stay alive.

Galanti gave his pistol to the boy and stepped out of the bush with his hands raised. And then he laughed. In the darkest times, one can either choose to laugh or cry, and Galanti's mind sided with comedy rather than tragedy. "You know about that Italian war hero?" the old joke went. "Yeah, his hands were in the air and his pistol was on the ground."

"And there I was standing there, Italian, hands in the air and pistol on the ground and I said, 'I'm a fracking Italian war hero.'" After relinquishing his pistol, he was tied to a tree and left wondering whether he'd get to see the bullet that would kill him. Galanti had flown countless flights over Vietnam but had never stepped foot on this little country in Southeast Asia; his first footfalls on this war-torn land would be as a prisoner of war. Finally, he was led a few hours away to an old schoolhouse, where a Vietnamese soldier with an ounce of English at his disposal interrogated him. Galanti played dumb, shrugging and feigning ignorance to all of the questions aimed at him.

After a few rounds of beatings and torture, Galanti heard an American voice pipe up through the din of Vietnamese. He spotted two air force pilots, and even though he couldn't speak to them, Galanti knew they were all in this together. That night the three Americans were stuck in solitary confinement until dawn broke and the arduous trek continued. For 12 days they traveled blindfolded through the thick, sweltering jungle, arriving at their final destination of Hanoi on June 29. Galanti only knew that because it was the first time the US bombed the city.

"The Vietnamese were not real happy with that turn of events," Galanti stated matter-of-factly in his interview with the Stockdale Center.

Once in Hanoi, he was thrown into a cell drenched in the

stench of death and painted in blood. Three days passed without seeing another human — without a morsel of food or a splash of water. Some nights he would jolt awake from the scratching claws of a rat the size of a cat sitting on his chest. Galanti eventually felt the life evaporating out of his body, and he decided to scream and yell to get something — anything — to keep him from wasting away. A guard came rushing to his cell, and by the way he looked at Galanti, it was clear they'd forgotten he was even there. Now that they'd rediscovered their captive, four days of interrogation began.

Galanti was relentlessly abused by the "torture sergeant," getting strung up and mangled with ropes until he gave his name, rank, Social Security number, and date of birth. After four horrific days, they forced him into ancient, blood-stained rags and threw him a single crust of bread before tossing him back into his cell. That night, they blindfolded him and stuck him in the back of a Jeep, then handcuffed him to another prisoner.

As the vehicle bounced along the war-torn terrain, the blindfolded man handcuffed to him leaned over and whispered his name — Robbie Risner — and that he was air force. Galanti was shocked out of speech. As it turned out, Risner had been a Korean War ace pilot — featured in *TIME* magazine — and had been an idol to Galanti from his childhood. Risner talked to Galanti until a soldier battered him over the head to shut him up, but Risner just kept talking and giving Galanti the lowdown of all he knew.

It was June 1966 when a telegram arrived from the US military to the Virginia household of Phyllis Galanti. She began to read from the top: "I deeply regret to confirm on behalf of the United States Navy that your husband, Lt. Paul Edward Galanti ... is missing in action in North Vietnam."

Phyllis's worst fears had been realized; her husband had been taken from her, perhaps forever. Phyllis was a humble and unassuming young woman, never one to seek out the spotlight, and she did not submit to defeat. The shy Phyllis Galanti took her message of justice for prisoners of war onto the greatest stage imaginable and shouted her message from the mountaintops. In February of 1971 she spoke before the Senate of Virginia and became a national hero for the benefit of her husband and the hundreds of other men trapped and tortured in the jungle prisons of Vietnam.

"As you sit here today, in this heated room, in your nice clothes, with your well-fed and well-cared-for bodies, can you really comprehend what our men are going through, sitting in a prison camp for six or seven years? I think not," Phyllis Galanti began her speech, as recorded by *WSLS 10*.

She would go on to appear on *Today*, *60 Minutes*, and *NBC Nightly News*, as well as lead the "Write Hanoi" campaign. According to *WCVE News*, with Phyllis at the helm of the campaign, more than 750,000 letters were sent to the North Vietnamese government, and when the time came she even flew to Stockholm to meet with North Vietnamese officials. She fought day and night, and although it would be years before she was reunited with her husband, the beauty of husband and wife both fighting their battles to see one another again is a story that will never be forgotten.

While a POW, Paul Galanti never found out the full extent to which his wife was fighting for him, but he did receive a hint one day in prison. In an interview with *WCVE News*, Galanti recounted the moment he realized his wife had been doing something extraordinary. "The camp commander says, 'According to you, what are your wife's activities?' And I said, 'how do I know they are activities, I don't get any mail.' He said, 'Ah! Maybe that is why you get no mail.' So, I wasn't sure what she was doing, but he didn't like it, so therefore, I did."

Days stretched into weeks and weeks grew into years. Even through countless beatings, Risner was able to teach Galanti the "tap code" which American POWs would use to communicate with each other without speech. They swept the floors in code, shoveled dirt in code, and coughed in code. For many POWs, isolation was the last step to becoming a shattered man, and the ingenious "tap code" was their lifeline to sanity. Beyond sharing that priceless language with him, Risner was also able to impart the necessary truth of surviving endless torture.

"They've broken everybody," Galanti recalled Risner saying in his interview with the Stockdale Center. "Put this in your mind. You tolerate torture only to the point of permanent physical disability. When you can't take any more, you start lying, and keep lying and lying and lying ..." What Risner was describing had been standard practice in the Air Force, but since Galanti was Navy, he'd been taught differently. In the Navy he was taught never to say anything at all. But after discovering what torture was really like, and how dedicated torturers can squeeze something out of even the toughest man, Galanti found Risner's advice to be more realistic, and it served as a far better compass when braving the endless horrific abuse that awaited him. "It was like the weight of the world being lifted off my shoulders."

At one point the interrogators had given Galanti a package, supposedly from home, with Life Savers candies among other things. This wasn't a random act of kindness by the Vietnamese, it was a clever ploy to set the prisoners at each other's throats from unequal treatment. Galanti, knowing none of the other prisoners had received any packages, attempted to hand them off to the others to defy the Vietnamese's setup. He tossed the little package of candies to the neighboring cell in the showers, and then peeked over — there was a prisoner and a guard on the other side looking right at him. In retaliation the guards stripped him naked, tied him to a stool and left him in the freezing January weather for ten days. Galanti didn't get a wink of sleep. Shivering and hallucinating that he was seeing ghosts, he listened to the wind chimes on an old

French building across the way. Galanti's brain was so fried from the sleep deprivation that the vivid, technicolor hallucinations continued for months after he was released from the stool. For a period stretching over more than a year, he was in solitary confinement with nothing but the occasional "tap code" from fellow prisoners to break the deadly monotony.

Galanti was one of many American soldiers used as a human prop in the Hanoi March of 1966, where the North Vietnamese Army paraded 52 POWs through the streets of Hanoi while European film crews recorded and tens of thousands of Vietnamese civilians watched from bleachers. That was the plan, at least.

But instead of a peaceful spectacle, the two-mile prisoner parade descended into a violent riot as the Vietnamese civilians charged down from the sidelines to beat the POWs to bloody pulps.

"A man came running up from the side, gave me a soccer-like kick in the groin and I went down in a heap. There was so much yelling it sounded like Notre Dame scoring a touchdown at South Bend. It lasted about 45 minutes," Galanti told the ex-POW nonprofit AXPOW. Even though there was much disagreement back home and abroad as to the injustice of the Vietnam War, all voices came together to disparage the barbaric treatment of American POWs brought to light by the Hanoi March.

The Vietnamese were desperate to turn the POWs into anti-war propaganda, thus souring Americans on the fight in Southeast Asia. At one point they tried to force Galanti to appear in a video, but he refused to be their propaganda slave. Extending both middle fingers to the camera, Galanti ruined their image of the docile POW. The image ended up on the cover of *Newsweek* — his fingers politely airbrushed out of the photo. Back then, newspapers and magazines were much more squeamish than today, not to mention the deception led his nephew back home to believe that his uncle had lost both his middle fingers in the war.

Over the coming months and years, the brotherhood that unites all American armed forces would be the foundation for everyone's continued survival in their journeys through hell. They weren't fighting and surviving for LBJ or the Democrats or the Republicans; they were surviving for and because of one another.

Through all the torture and the attempts to broadcast Americans admitting wrongdoing, their credo was BACKUS. B: no bowing; A: stay off the air; C: admit no crimes; K: don't kiss the enemy goodbye with a statement; US: unity over self.

"Unity over self" was his connection to the other POWs, a crucial lifeline that would help him survive the more than 2,432 days he'd spend as a prisoner in Vietnam. But even the darkest years end in daybreak eventually. The sun rose for Paul Galanti on February 12, 1973, when he was finally released from his chains and allowed to return home. In the end, he had spent nearly seven years in 10 different prison camps. His first meal as a free man: a 16-ounce steak and a half-gallon of vanilla ice cream. He told the *Richmond Times-Dispatch* that he'd had to prove to a Navy dietitian that he was strong enough to handle the bombshell of calories by doing 25 handstand push-ups. He pounded out 25 handstand push-ups, then feasted like a king.

Years later, the credits were rolling for an air force documentary that involved Paul Galanti. Feet shuffled around as people got out of their seats to leave, when a producer walked up to Galanti and asked, "What three things did you learn?"

Paul Galanti had far more than three things he'd learned after years of captivity, but he tossed ideas around in his head to give a quick response to this waiting producer.

"I wasn't as tough as I thought I was," was the first answer,

"No matter how tough I had it, somebody had it tougher," was the second.

And finally, after wracking his brain for a third answer, he said, "There's no such thing as a bad day when there's a doorknob on the inside of the door." Those words and their

Life magazine photo of Lt. Paul Galanti in Vietnamese prison cell.
(*Richmond Times Dispatch*, October 3, 2004)

everlasting wisdom are etched into stone at the Virginia War Memorial, where they will stand for eternity.

"Despite all efforts to break the POWs, we remained as unified as it was possible to be under the circumstances. Our excellent leadership under Col. Robbie Risner, USAF, and Cdr. Jim Stockdale held us together under these difficult circumstances, and we came out, most of us, better men than when we went in," Paul Galanti said later of his time spent imprisoned. "It makes me appreciate everything that we have. I didn't do that before. Most people don't understand why I'm so happy all the time, and I am. What's not to be happy about? I didn't wake up ... in a god-awful cell."

Paul Galanti went on to become one of the Navy's top recruiters, a successful businessman, and Director of the Virginia Department of Veterans' Services. Phyllis Galanti would continue to be a champion for prisoners in the Soviet Union and the US hostages in Tehran.

Lt. Col. Ernest Childers (left) with General Jacob Devers shortly after receiving the Medal of Honor. (Office of War Information)

Lieutenant Colonel Ernest Childers

US ARMY

Medal of Honor

February 1, 1918–March 17, 2005 (87 years)

Ernest Childers learned how to survive from the Great Depression, how to be disciplined from his modest country schooling, and how to fight with a warrior's spirit from generations of Native Americans before him. Childers himself would likely never want the attention of a biography — he was as humble a man as you could find — but often it is those who are least willing to shout out their glories who deserve it most.

It was the summer of 1943, and although the US Army had sharpened their teeth with their hard-won successes in North Africa, all three of the Axis powers remained atop their thrones of skulls. But one of these powers, Benito Mussolini's fascist Italy, was cracked and shaken from the years of brutal warfare. The Allies smelled blood in the water and sought to deal a death blow to the dictator's waning power before Italian strength could be regained.

This bloody theater would see both Allied and German forces occupying the Italian "boot," turning the once-great nation into one of World War II's most brutal arenas of battle. And it's against this bloody backdrop that 2nd Lt. Ernest "Red Eagle" Childers of the 45th Infantry Division would fight side by side with thousands of others to rid Italy of the German menace once and for all.

Ernest Childers was born in 1918 in Broken Arrow, Oklahoma, to a family of Muskogee Creek Native Americans. As told in an April 16, 1944, article for the *Daily Oklahoman*, his older half-brother Walter practically raised him in lieu of his father's constant travels to Washington as the tribe's lawyer.

Growing up through the Great Depression was a tough storm to weather for the whole family; Ernest received his first gun as an 8-year-old boy, not as a gift, but as a responsibility. He would be the one to feed his family in the dark times when dust roiled up over the Great Plains and millions found themselves without work.

In a 1994 interview with the same paper, Childers told the story of being given a single, precious .22-caliber bullet every day; he was tasked with turning that little piece of metal into a meal. Shouldering that kind of burden from a young age made Ernest a fine shot, as well as a humble, dependable man. He wasn't interested in the life of the city-dwellers in nearby Tulsa; he was much more motivated by upholding his family's farming traditions than joining the ranks in the factories.

After graduating from the country school, this all changed when his brother Walter took him behind the barn and told him he would be going to college. Ernest was dumbfounded, always seeing his future in tilled earth rather than written papers.

But Ernest was nothing if not diligent, and his family's wishes were ultimately his own. He graduated from Chilocco Indian School, having amassed skills in mechanics and boxing and took the pledge of the National Guard along with many of his friends. It wasn't long before he removed his private patch and stitched on that of a sergeant. His division, the 45th "Thunderbird" Division, would be one of only 18 called into action early in World War II.

That iconic symbol of the Thunderbird was a Native American symbol of good luck and magic. It heralded the 45th's legacy as one that would stand proud of its many Native American soldiers.

On June 8, 1943, the 45th set off to enter the battle for Europe, and after a short layover in Algeria, they landed in Sicily. There, 180,000 US troops were pitted against 230,000 entrenched Italians and Germans on the southernmost Italian island. The 45th would spearhead the amphibious assault. They hit the beach, braving the ocean swells before running right into Italian pillboxes and German tanks. With astounding coordination between the 82nd Airborne Division and the 2nd Armored Division, the 45th was able to expel the German infantry while surviving the German tanks, pushing forward the US force's eastern flank.

It was slow going for two weeks as the Thunderbirds pressed onward through the mountainous interior of the island, ridding the area of Italian resistance. The Italians were steadily losing morale — with hindsight we know that it would be a short time before they would negotiate their surrender — but that just meant that the infamously war-savvy Germans would take over the defense. Once the 45th arrived at Motta Hill, they clashed against Italian and Germans making their last stand; for four days they fought against opponents who, under German Field Marshal Albert Kesselring, were able to make clever use of the terrain and force their American foes to fight for every inch.

Operation Avalanche would be the next engagement for the 45th Thunderbirds, and it would be on those harrowing battlefields near Salerno where Ernest Childers would rise to heroism or die trying.

It was September 22, 1943, and rain blanketed the once-beautiful landscape, now twisted and torn by battle. Childers and his company marched forward toward the enemy. The Germans had determined it best to retreat to more defensible positions, but the US was not letting a moment go to waste, closely following their retreat with guns in hand.

As reported by *Warfare History Network*'s William F. Floyd, Childers was moving steadily forward when he plunged into a scar in the earth created by the devastating artillery shells that now dotted so much of Europe. His foot now fractured,

Childers had begun moving toward an aid station to get treatment for his injury, when right at that moment a German mortar round fell like a meteor right next to the station, killing the doctor and any chance of relief. Fate had spoken harshly. Childers returned to his company, stalwart even through the pain, and readied himself for the coming onslaught.

The macabre chorus of several German machine guns are second only to German tanks in the fear they inspire in the men who hear them, and suddenly that chorus rose to an operatic volume as German automatic fire rained down upon Childers and his company from houses on a hilltop. They had hit a wall of death, and no victory would be won while those guns continued their barrage. Childers took account of the men around him, selected the eight he considered best for the job, and set out to create a deathly silence where there was currently deafening gunfire.

The rough terrain gave no easy path to their targets, but Childers and his men climbed upward all the same. Eventually, they came to a large cornfield — dangerously open grounds in war — and Childers gave the order for his men to take cover behind a nearby stone wall and unleash as much covering fire as they could while he advanced alone. Several shots rang out; German snipers were taking turns at the approaching Childers, but to no avail. Having blown their chance, Childers took this opportunity by the horns, raised his rifle, and blasted back at the house with resounding gunfire. Now two fewer Germans stood against him.

Childers killed the remaining Germans inside the house, leaving the machine gun to rest in utter silence. He then noiselessly crawled around the second house, his shrewd senses telling him that marching in with a full contingent on alert would be suicide. Instead, he used a brilliant trick: Childers had no grenades, but he did have rocks. And it was rocks he tossed into the building, hoping that the sound of "grenades" hitting the floor would inspire enough terror that the Germans wouldn't stick around to uncover the illusion.

It worked, and out ran two Germans, fleeing from the not-explosives. Childers put one down himself, while the other was finished off by one of his brothers across the field. The second machine gun position was no more.

As Childers kept moving up the hill, he ran face-to-face into a German mortar observer. Childers, as the best soldiers do, had counted his rounds. The German aimed his weapon straight at Childers; Childers pointed right back at him with an ammo-less rifle, perspiration pouring off of him.

"The German must have been watching the action, because he came out toward me. I was on my knees training my 30-caliber carbine on him," said Childers as reported by *Warfare History Network.* "I was yelling to one of my men, 'Take him prisoner!' My sergeant yelled back, 'Shoot the bastard.' I yelled, 'I can't! I'm out of ammunition.'" Childers was not a gambling man at heart, but he'd just scored the best bluff of his life. The German dropped his weapon, defeated by an empty gun. That mortar observer was the only surviving German prisoner that day.

For his stalwart dedication to his men and country in destroying those two machine-gun nests and allowing his company to continue forward, he was awarded with the Medal of Honor. Ernest Childers was the first Native American to be endowed with the nation's highest honor since the 1890s.

Childers would go on to fight with the Thunderbirds in Anzio, Italy, where he was wounded a second time, and again returned to serve his country in Korea and Vietnam. Ernest Childers retired both as a lieutenant colonel and a hero; his hometown will forever feature a nine-foot statue honoring the brave Native American who only ever wanted to work the land yet ended up a leader of men.

"The exceptional leadership, initiative, calmness under fire and conspicuous gallantry displayed by Childers were an inspiration to his men," his Medal of Honor citation stated. But beyond that, even the legendary Gen. George S. Patton saw within the 45th Thunderbirds a group of men with few equals. When the fighting in the Sicilian campaign wore down, Patton said of the Thunderbirds, "Your division is one of the best, if not the best division in the history of American arms."

Yolander Childers (left) with sculptor Sandra Van Zandt and work memorializing Lt. Col. Ernest Childers. (Jim Beck for *Tulsa World*, September 26, 2009)

40

Major Richard "Dick" Ira Bong

US AIR FORCE

Medal of Honor
Distinguished Service Cross
Silver Star (2)
Distinguished Flying Cross (7)
Air Medal (15)

September 24, 1920–August 6, 1945 (24 years)

Known as the "Ace of Aces" for his rank as the top American flying ace during World War II, Major Richard Ira Bong is credited with downing a record of 40 enemy aircraft over the course of his career as a fighter pilot.

The twin-piston engines of the Lockheed P-38 Lightning hummed their pleasant tune as ace pilot Tommy McGuire cruised the Southwest Pacific, looking for bogies to shoot at. The skies were disappointingly clear; it looked to McGuire like the Japanese had taken their toys and gone home today, which was a damn shame since McGuire was still eight confirmed kills behind that towheaded Swedish kid Dick Bong. Just when he was about to call it quits, he and his squadron spotted a couple enemy pilots flying above the treetops near Panubulon Island.

"They were on my side and I figured maybe Dick hadn't seen them so I barely whispered over the radio to my wingman to follow me and I dive to take one of the Nips," McGuire told Gen. George C. Kenney in Kenney's book *Dick Bong: Ace of Aces*. McGuire unleashed a salvo from his eight .50 caliber machine guns, and the fighter dove into the ground. McGuire had pulled around to land a knockout against the remaining enemy just in time to watch it combust into smoking scrap metal. And there's Dick Bong, pulling up alongside McGuire, playfully wiggling his wings and sheepishly grinning at him in his way that was just impossible to hate. McGuire had gone up to a stellar thirty-one confirmed kills, but Bong hadn't let up, now at thirty-nine.

"I'm still eight behind," McGuire said to Gen. Kenney, wishing he could be angrier at the affable Bong. "I'll bet when this war is over, they'll call me Eight Behind McGuire." Bong, on the other hand, would end his stint in the Pacific with the highest air-to-air kill count in American history, surprising the hell out of everyone that the kindhearted Swede from the Midwest had grown up to become the Ace of Aces.

The seeds for the great life of Richard Ira Bong would be sown on a small family farm in Superior, Wisconsin. While helping run the farm on a hot summer day, Bong would often look up to the sky as he caught the familiar sound of aircraft soaring overhead. These weren't just any aircraft — they were carrying mail destined for President Calvin Coolidge's summer White House in Superior. Keeping the farm machinery running smoothly was a full-time job, but as he worked, he dreamt of flying the boundless sky. Bong would reach the clouds eventually but watching those silver beauties cut through the stratosphere and obsessing over his model airplane collection would have to do for now.

And so Bong began to acquire all the ingredients — contemplating the airplanes flying overhead, his obsession over the makes and models of the modern airplane, and the mechanical expertise he gained by working on farm equipment — to make himself a damn fine pilot. Nobody could have guessed that the farm boy from sleepy Superior would become the "Ace of Aces," the greatest pilot to command the skies in World War II, whose legendary antics could be ripped right out of *Top Gun*.

The year was 1941 and Bong was a promising student at Superior State Teachers College, but it was his inherent genius in the sky that really caught the eyes of everyone around him. For the past couple years, he had been enrolled in the Civilian

Pilot Training Program, taking private lessons every chance he got. But his time in the cockpit was what clearly marked his path forward: he was bound for great heights far from the stuffy interior of a classroom. On May 29, 1941, he made the decision to leave college life behind and enlist in the Army Air Corps program, where he ended up with Barry Goldwater (later a US senator and the 1964 Republican party nominee for US president) as his flight instructor. Once commissioned a second lieutenant and awarded his pilot wings, Bong had his first dance with the love of his life, the Lockheed P-38 Lightning.

The P-38 Lightning was the workhorse for the ace pilots of the war. From dogfights in Europe to long-range escort missions in the Pacific, and from the Attack on Pearl Harbor to Victory over Japan Day, America never went anywhere in WWII without the Lightning. Franz Stigler, a Luftwaffe ace who flew Bf 109s against the P-38 in North Africa, said of the Lightning, "One cardinal rule we never forgot was to avoid fighting the P-38 head on. That was suicide."

Bong got into his Lightning and never looked back — it was love at first sight, and he wasn't taking it slow. Bong's first achievement came early. In June 1942, still in training, Bong "buzzed" a house in San Anselmo, flying low enough that the newlywed pilot inside immediately took it to his superiors. When Gen. George C. Kenney finally sat Bong down to give him a reprimand, the list of Bong and his P-38's exploits had grown: in addition to buzzing the house of an airman, he had also loop-de-looped around the Golden Gate Bridge, flown low down Market Street in San Francisco, as well as the disgraceful deed of blowing a woman's clothes off her clothesline. Bong's exuberance and talent for flying was not lost on Gen. Kenney, even if his way of expressing himself was reckless. "If you didn't want to fly down Market Street, I wouldn't have you in my Air Force, but you are not to do it anymore and I mean what I say," Kenney told him. Later, the legendary general would write, "We needed kids like this lad."

To the day of his death, Bong denied flying under the Golden Gate Bridge, but (most) of his superiors didn't find his laugh-worthy denial funny, and he was still grounded while the rest of his group went without him to England in July of 1942. After a short but likely painful wait stuck on the ground, he was then transferred to the 78th Fighter Group, bound for the Pacific Theater. By November 1942, Bong was transferred to "The Flying Knights," veteran fighter pilots who flew the P-40 Warhawk and gained their knighthood from their famous aerial defense of Darwin, Australia, between March and August of 1942. Now, though, the Knights were slated as one of two units in the 5th Air Force for conversion from P-40 Warhawk to the P-38 Lightning. Bong, a rising star in the group of new pilots arriving at the Pacific Theater and a prodigy with the new twin engine fighter, was tasked with helping these veterans make the shift.

One day, the greatest American pilot of WWI, Eddie Rickenbacker, came by to chat with the youngbloods, both to raise their morale and to allow them to glean insights into the mind of an ace pilot.

"Eddie," Gen. Kenney recalled saying in *Dick Bong: Ace of Aces*, "I'm going to give a case of scotch to the first one to beat your old record." And thus the race of the aces began. The top flyers of the Pacific Theater, Medal of Honor recipient Neel Kearby, Thomas Lynch, Tommy McGuire, and others, now had a score to keep in this most dangerous of games. Bong, however, was playing his own game.

"He didn't seem to worry about anyone else's score," Gen. Kenney remarked. "He just was not in a race."

It was now November 1942, and Bong and his squadron were waiting for the delivery of more precious P-38s. The tension wouldn't last long as a new order came down: Bong and other pilots would be temporarily reassigned to fly missions and gain some real combat experience with a fighter squadron based in New Guinea. Bong took full advantage of this learning experience, and in his first brush with live combat, he managed to claim victory after shooting down a Mitsubishi A6M "Zero" and a Nakajima Ki-43 "Oscar" during the Battle of Buna-Gona. Before, Bong had been a great pilot, but that day he'd become a legendary fighter pilot, and for his bravery and skill he was awarded the Silver Star.

His piloting ability now recognized, Bong rejoined the Flying Knights in the 9th Fighter Squadron, now fully equipped with operational P-38 Lightnings. In April 1943, Bong was promoted to first lieutenant, but the rank wouldn't stick for long. On July 26 he blew four Japanese fighters out of the skies of New Guinea, a quartet that earned him the Distinguished Service Cross. That August, he was promoted to captain.

Just two days later Bong and nine other fighters got tangled up with fifteen Japanese, Bong bursting down one of them. During the heated brawl, one of the Allied P-38s lost one of its engines and was being hunted by a Japanese airplane. Bong quickly worked out his solution to the scenario. First, he zoomed in close to make himself the juicer target. Then, he feathered his engine so that he appeared to have a crippled bird. After that, he pulled every aeronautical acrobat technique he had on one engine while the wounded P-38 escaped intact. With his diversion complete, Bong gave the juice back to his other engine and left the dumbfounded Japanese pilot in the dust.

Rebounding back to the airstrip, Bong realized his brakes were shot and he had a punctured tire. As Gen. Kenney recalled in *Dick Bong: Ace of Aces,* after a risky landing in a ditch at the end of the runway, everyone gathered around to assess the damage. The P-38 looked crumpled, as if a hundred hammers had pummeled it all over; there were at least fifty bullet holes peppering the wings and fuselage; and both primary fuel tanks were punctured. The only negativity that Bong felt was the fate of his beautiful plane.

"Boy, I'll bet that guy wondered what kept that P-38 flying and he sure must have been mad when he saw that I had foxed him into thinking I had only one engine," he joked.

His rapid promotions were welcome, but they didn't hold a candle to what would happen to Dick Bong that fall. While on leave in the United States, Bong met Marjorie Vattendahl at a teachers' college homecoming event, and they fell in love. When he returned to the Southwest Pacific in January 1944, he celebrated his new sweetheart by naming his P-38 "Marge," sticking his favorite photo of her on the nose of the aircraft. The following April, Captain Bong downed two Japanese aircraft, bringing his total to 27 and surpassing Eddie Rickenbacker's American record of 26 credited victories in World War I. It wasn't long afterward that he was promoted to major by Gen. Kenney and dispatched to the United States to see Gen. "Hap" Arnold, who gave him a leave of absence to promote the purchase of bonds to folks back home.

Bong returned to New Guinea in September of 1944 and was assigned to the V Fighter Command staff as an advanced gunnery instructor. He was given permission to go on missions but not to seek combat. Losing a good pilot happened all too often, especially thrill seekers like Bong — and his superiors leashed him for his own good. Their trepidation was well warranted: all other pilots who had competed in the race of the aces — the friendly competition between the Pacific pilots to see who would beat the World War I record of twenty-six aerial victories — would end up dead.

Yet despite his orders to stay out of combat, and after spending more time in the Philippines, he had increased his air-to-air victories to an all-time American record of 40 — always claiming the kills were in "self-defense" to assuage the fears of his superiors who wanted their top pilot to return home safely. Finally, Gen. Kenney couldn't keep Bong in harm's way any longer. He got him out of the war — permanently.

"The reason I am sending him home is that he is so popular with the personnel of the Fifth Air Force and so many of them have begun to worry about the possibility of his being shot down that I can no longer take the chance at the loss of morale ..." Kenney wrote at the end of Bong's career.

When the legendary Gen. Douglas MacArthur personally awarded Bong his Medal of Honor, he temporarily went off the script, creating an awed silence among all who watched. Gen. Kenney recalled MacArthur's praise with pride that dripped off the page in *Dick Bong: Ace of Aces*:

"Maj. Richard Ira Bong, who has ruled the air from New Guinea to the Philippines, I now induct you into the society of the bravest of the brave, the wearers of the Congressional Medal of Honor of the United States." Bong would leave the Pacific Theater with 40 confirmed kills, the highest record of any American pilot in history, and likely, the future. But Bong's incredible humility likely stripped him of many kills, as he was so gracious with giving them to others that it caused an uproar among his mates.

"General, you've got to do something about Bong," one confused pilot complained to Gen. Kenney. "He's giving away Nips (Japanese) ... This business today is not the only time he's given away Nips either. Every wingman he's ever had will tell you the same thing." Bong would be known among all who met him as having a far bigger heart than kill count. He even refused to shoot up the Japanese who were parachuting down after he knocked them out of the sky, admitting that he thought they had it bad enough.

Just what made this maverick such a good pilot? After all, Bong considered his own gunnery accuracy to be poor. The answer is surprising: Bong compensated for his less-than-stellar shooting skills by getting as close to his targets as possible. In some cases, he even flew through the burning debris of exploding enemy aircraft, and once he collided with his target, which was claimed a "probable" victory. After everything, perhaps it's not so surprising that Gen. Kenney had seen something in him. The man who did loop-de-loops around the Golden Gate Bridge and blew ladies' clothes off

their lines ended up the greatest American pilot of all time. It took guts to fly down Market Street, and those same guts are what let him go head-to-head against other more accurate pilots and win.

Unfortunately, the curse afflicting the Pacific Theater aces followed Bong all the way home. While flying as a test pilot for the Lockheed P-80 Shooting Star jet fighter, the plane's primary fuel pump malfunctioned, and Bong died in the crash. The premature mortality of America's kindhearted Ace of Aces shared the front page with the bombing of Hiroshima. Bong's legacy lives on through the Richard Bong State Recreation area in the Midwest, as well as a bust commissioned by the Wisconsin State Historical Society.

Bong's Medal of Honor citation, awarded to him in December of 1944, mentions that he flew some of his combat missions despite his status as an instructor. Along with the ultimate tragedy of his story, we can only hope he still smiles in the afterlife at the thought that even his transgressions became legendary.

Maj. Richard Bong in a P-38.
(US Federal Government)

Michael Thorton. (*Asbury Park Press*, November 2, 2009)

Lieutenant Michael E. Thornton

US NAVY

Medal of Honor
Silver Star
Bronze Star (3)
Purple Heart (2)

Born March 23, 1949

When Michael Thornton was attacked by dozens of enemies, he met them head-on. When his friend and fellow SEAL Thomas Norris got shot in the head, he carried him on his back. Thornton's story serves as an iconic view into the values and valor of the Navy SEALS and shall never be forgotten.

Michael Thorton's path was clear to him from the beginning. In an interview with the American Veterans Center in 2021, he recalled being swept up into a tidal wave of inspiration when he watched *The Fighting Sullivan Brothers* as a young boy. The "frogmen" and their willingness to live and die for one another wove tightly together with his father's teachings. His father only had a sixth-grade education, but he taught his children well about the unbreakable bonds of family. The bonds also shared by military men spoke to Thornton. Even beyond that, his father and uncles' legacies of serving in WWII stood as a monument for him to look up to.

In school, despite working hard, he was considered "dumb" because of his extreme dyslexia. Society had not yet figured out the condition, and simply categorized anyone with the affliction as a weak link. Many doors were closed to him, especially for employment. For Thorton it was only a matter of when, not if, he would enlist.

When Thornton was told he had to wait for his eighteenth birthday to become what he knew he was born to be, he didn't get discouraged. He enlisted under the 120-day program as a 17-year-old, went through Underwater Demolition Recruit Training after high school, and became one of only 12 graduated Navy SEALs out of a class of 129.

October 31, 1972. It's Halloween and Michael Thornton is on the other side of the world from the costumed crowds and smiling faces of his home in South Carolina — he's on his fourth tour of duty in Vietnam, once again, one man among only 12 US soldiers left in America's dissolving presence in Southeast Asia. These elite few would serve as the only immediate recourse for downed US airmen, and they were the eyes and ears that carefully watched and took note of the North Vietnamese's inevitable progress into South Vietnam.

On this particular day, five men — three South Vietnamese commandos and two Navy SEALs, Tom Norris and Michael Thornton — were on a reconnaissance mission, collecting intel on hostile activity at the Cua Viet River Base. Under the cover of dusk, a rubber boat was quietly loosed from a Vietnamese junk, paddles lapping the water and propelling the floating silhouettes toward the darkened sands of the beach. About a mile from land, the men slipped into the murky liquid and made the rest of their journey below the dull water's surface.

They crept inland, weaving between the enemy encampments that dotted the jungle with potential danger. After hours of difficult work, the sun threatened its arrival over the horizon; their armor of protective darkness would soon disintegrate. Worse still, no identifiable landmarks stuck up out of the earth; in the fading blackness it dawned on the men that they had gone deeper north than planned — they were in the heart of hostility, North Vietnam.

As Thornton and Norris recounted in their interview with the Academy of Achievement on May 5, 2001, the mission began to fly off the rails as they headed back to the beach. A North Vietnamese soldier crested the top of a dune while another rounded the bend of the beach, both of them armed and patrolling right toward them. From their cover they had time to work out a plan, but the South Vietnamese officer was already springing into action, barking orders to his two commandos to capture the enemies for interrogation. The South Vietnamese enlisted men jumped up and approached the enemies.

"Stop, put your hands up and come here!" one of the South Vietnamese shouted across the beach. The enemies whipped out their AK-47s and started to rapidly close the distance. Thornton noticed one hostile coming over the dune: He readied his weapon and cold-cocked him in the face, dropping him silently to the sand. At the same moment, one of the South Vietnamese commandos opened fire on the second patrol, but the man dropped into cover just in time, the bullets sinking uselessly into the side of the dune. The enemy patrol disappeared into the depths of the jungle, every footstep taking him closer to a nearby village which would mean disaster and certain death for the SEALs.

Thornton wasn't going to let that happen. As Thomas Norris observed the unfolding situation from a vantage point, he witnessed Thornton chasing the escaping soldier into the jungle. The sounds of gunshots cracked through the air as Thornton nailed the fleeing patrol. But Norris's hopes of an end to the problem are dashed when he spots Thornton again, sprinting out of the jungle at top speed with around fifty angry NVA troops chasing after him.

Everyone was sweating bullets, but the group kept their cool and set up a position to hold off the encroaching flood of enemies. Norris got on the radio and made contact with a nearby destroyer-class ship capable of raining some hell down on the NVA. But the young officer on the other end of the line wasn't used to giving gunfire support to troops on land, and although Norris calmly gave him the proper coordinates and the best type of ammunition to use, they were getting nowhere fast.

As recounted in the Academy of Achievement interview,

while Norris was busy with the radio, Thornton wielded his years of experience as a SEAL. He took stock of their current manpower and went into action, placing one of the South Vietnamese soldiers at their rear to watch the dune behind them and another at their flank to keep an eye on the beach. Thornton himself took the forward position where the enemy force was concentrating.

Thornton was a phantom of death on the battlefield. When an enemy raised their head up over the dune to fire, he'd nail them and roll to another position before another could pinpoint his position. Seventeen enemy soldiers were killed this way, while the NVA had no idea if they were facing four enemies or fourteen.

"They never had a target to shoot at. So I kept picking my targets, I'd knock them off, I'd move to another target." Still, the enemy crept closer, so close that they started lobbing grenades back and forth like it was baseball practice. One grenade plopped in the sand next to Thornton — he grabbed hold of it and tossed it back, counting the seconds of the fuse: "1,000, 2,000, 3,000, 4,000 ...." The same grenade sailed back to Thornton moments later "... 5,000, 6,000 ..." and he pitched it back. "8,000, 9,000 ..." and the same grenade lands next to Thornton again. It went off. Pain as hot as fire seared Thornton's back as seven shards of shrapnel dug into his flesh. Norris yelled for Thornton, unsure if he was dead or alive, but Thornton held his tongue as three enemies rushed his position.

Thornton blasted one — his body fell into the bloody sand at Thornton's side, and the two other soldiers retreated. Then, all grew quiet; the offensive stalled. Taking advantage of the moment, Thornton crawled to where Norris could see him.

"Tommy — " he said, "Yeah, I'm okay."

After a lot of back and forth over the radio, the officer on the destroyer asked Norris, "Well, how long can you last?"

"They asked how long can we hold out?" Norris yelled over

to Thornton. Thornton's eyes focused on a growing mass of shapes moving across the nearby lagoon.

"Have you seen what's over there?" Thornton said, pointing across the way. Seventy-five NVA — Thornton had counted — were coming at them from the north and south, bringing a storm of bullets. The five men were caught right in the center of it.

Norris's time on the radio was running out — he could only communicate in short bursts as the enemies poured over them, some of them getting so close they had to be fended off in hand-to-hand combat. The destroyer Norris had talked to was readying itself offshore, preparing to give fire support ... but before it could help, NVA shore batteries blasted the ship with rockets, taking it offline. Another destroyer attempted to move within range, but the rocket barrage kept them away. A forward air control aircraft, able to coordinate with the naval forces to lay down gunfire on the enemy would have helped, but this air support never materialized.

Desperate, Norris made a call to the Vietnamese junk boats that he knew had at least one mortar on board. Unfortunately, the only way they could get in range was by moving directly into the destroyer's firing line; the destroyers canceled that order.

None of these support failures would be known to the Thornton or Norris until long after the horrific experience ended. As the enemy force of 75 had ballooned into a monstrous 150, all the two SEALs could do was wonder when support would arrive.

"These guys, how come they're not firing and I'm not getting any gunfire support?" Thornton thought at the time. The gunfight had reached a fever pitch; Thornton had bodies strewn all around him. Norris made the decision to get the hell out.

"Fire for effect," Norris told the battleship Newport News. "Blow this place away. We're extracting." Norris recalled in the

Academy of Achievement interview that he was laying down covering fire for the team as they extracted when a group of 15 or 20 enemies came into view. Norris took account of the force and saw a target ripe for high explosives; he changed his rifle out for a LAW rocket launcher and took aim — he'd land a payload right into the center ... and that's when a bullet tore straight through his head.

Thornton hadn't seen it. He'd leapfrogged back to the covering sand dune — Norris had chosen it because it gave them 400 yards of open beach, a veritable killing field the enemies would be forced to cross. Deng, the radioman, rushed up to Thornton, bullet holes covering his radio and shrapnel covering his back.

"Mike, Da Wei's dead! Da Wei's dead!" he shouted, speaking of Norris.

"Are you sure?"

"Yeah."

Dead or alive, Thornton had to see his comrade for himself, so he took hold of his gun, sprang up, and sprinted back to the position where he'd last seen Norris. Sure enough, there was his friend, lying on his side, the side of his head blown out — completely vaporized. His friend was dead, but he'd be damned if he was going to let his body waste away in North Vietnam. Thornton grabbed Norris, but enemies jumped him before he could make a retreat. Thornton cracked one, two, three ... several shots, killing the men who were all over him. More appeared and took aim. Thornton knew he couldn't take on the whole NVA by himself, so he tossed Norris over his shoulder and booked it in the other direction.

Thornton had no idea about the orders Norris had given the *Newport News*. The battleship was indeed "firing for effect," and that awesome firepower was about to come down right on top of Thornton's head. The first round hit the dunes and launched Thornton 20 feet into the air, Norris getting tossed away like a ragdoll. The second round had the good fortune of blasting a chunk out of the earth to the south, the concussive force hitting the enemy and taking the heat off of Thornton for a few key moments. Thornton returned to Norris's crumpled body, and as he's picking him up, he hears a voice.

"Mike, buddy." With half his head hanging out of his skull, Norris was still hanging on to a single strand of life.

Thornton hoisted Norris up onto his shoulders once again and made a run for it. Back to the sand dune near the beach, the South Vietnamese officer had already started to swim out into the water, but the two other soldiers — hand-picked by Thornton — had stayed put as ordered and were laying down covering fire.

Thornton made the 400-yard dash miraculously unharmed; he laid Norris down, turned, and opened fire.

"Mike, what do we do?" the South Vietnamese soldiers asked.

"We swim for it," Thornton said. "When I say 'go' we go."

The Vietnamese allies agreed and released covering fire, allowing Thornton to get his downed friend into a fireman's carry on his shoulders. Thornton was running dry on rounds, so he picked up Norris's AK-47 and web gear, still with plenty of ammunition. Locked and loaded, there was nothing left to do but make their escape.

"Ready, go." Sand flew underfoot as the three men made a mad dash for the water. Bullets were flying as they reached the South China Sea; Thornton stumbled and fell, Norris rolling off his back.

"Gosh, if they didn't kill him, I'm going to kill him dropping him all these times," Thornton remembered thinking.

Thornton picked Norris back up and stuck him beneath one of his tree trunk–like arms, but once they hit the water Norris started moving so he moved him to his front and swam into the surf. Just then, one of the young Vietnamese men loyal to Thornton, Kwan, came flying by, pushed back inland by the tide. He'd been shot through the buttocks and would never make it to safety on his own. Thornton grabbed him and hauled him onto his shoulders.

"God, don't let it hit me now," Thornton recalled thinking as the bullets rained down. One man carrying two others through the surf: if even one round found its mark, three lives would snuff out.

At last the bullets slowed, then stopped. Through sheer force of will and strength of body Thornton had made it out of the range of fire. In the distance, he could see their life-line, the *Newport News* — except it was turning around. Was it going to leave them stranded in the water? "Where in the hell are they going?" The problem was that the forward observer hadn't spotted them; as far as anyone knew, they were all dead.

Treading water, Thornton tried to get his life jacket over Norris's head.

"What if you get shot through your life jacket?" Norris said.

"Tommy, if you get shot through the chest you're dead anyway. Who cares about your damn life jacket."

Norris accepted the help. Then, with nothing better to do, Thornton took two 4x4 medical patches, stuffed one in Norris' head and wrapped the other around his skull.

"Do we have everybody? Do we have everybody?" Norris kept asking Thornton.

"Yeah, we've got everybody. We've got everybody." Thornton replied.

Norris couldn't actually see much of anything from his position on Thornton's back, so he pushed himself off to make a count.

"Mike probably thought, 'What's this nut doing?'" Norris recalled. He never gave up looking out for his team even with half his head missing.

Hours passed. The stars faded, the sun rose. They treaded water. How long could they last? Then, in the distance, Thornton spotted a friendly Vietnamese junk and he's struck by an idea: He aims his AK-47 into the sky and holds down the trigger. The junk turns and makes its way toward them.

In the interview with the Academy of Achievement, Thornton remembers carrying Norris down into the operating room of the *Newport News*, unwilling to let his brother die even as Thornton's own blood pooled around his feet.

"He can't make it." The doctor said as Thornton set him onto the operating table, "Mike, there's no way he's going to make it." But he did make it. The cleansing properties of the salt water, the warming rays of the sun, and Thornton's own body heat kept Norris from going into deep shock. He would have to go through three years of rehabilitation, but because of his friend and fellow SEAL, Norris would return home to his country and his family.

"... Once I was wounded, obviously it changed my whole lifestyle and existence. ... I spent from 1972 to 1975 in surgeries." Norris was certain that what kept him alive was his DDT SEAL training; it had cultivated the desire to survive against all odds.

"I don't know how you made it ... but you just wouldn't give up," the doctor told Norris after he had beaten the odds.

But what drove Thornton to do what he did? What fuels such reckless self-sacrifice for the benefit of his companions?

"... The camaraderie and the love that you feel for each other — because I know if that had been me on that beach that Tommy would have done the same thing for me," Thornton recalled. "And that's what type of commitment you have to have in each other, and belief you have to have in each other, to do something like that."

Thornton also had this to say: "I'll always have the memories of guys I lost over there. And I've lost friends since the war, but I'll always have the memories. The riches are great, but riches aren't everything, because when you go you can only take your memories and your word and your honor to the grave with you."

Private Allen "Mouse" Owen

US MARINES

October 4, 1943–September 9, 1981 (37 years)

Allen "Mouse" Owen was a 4'11" powerhouse who astounded everyone he met. First a Marine, then an airborne firefighter, Owen was a man who loved life — especially when his adrenaline was pumping and he was jumping out of airplanes.

"How *tall* are you, boy?" the drill instructor snarled out of his grimace, the living embodiment of the hardcore, humiliator-in-chief Marine D.I. as made famous in the movies. Pvt. Allen Owen was a full 4'11" of unadulterated confidence, never flinching an inch. He responded to the instructor: "Sir, I'm six foot two and 200 pounds and the meanest man in the state!"

Nobody outside of Missouri or the Marines would've ever known who Allen Owen was — until that day on May 6, 1966, when *LIFE* magazine published those words in their profile of the shortest Marine to ever serve. A bright, extroverted 22-year-old, Owen never let his short stature put anything out of reach. He had grown up in a household where nobody stood much taller than five feet, but his father made sure all his children went out into the world with their heads held high. In fact, according to Paul Fattig in his book *The Mouse That Soared: Tales of the Siskiyou Smokejumpers*, Allen's brothers Larry and Lane both went into the Marine Corps and Air Force, respectively.

Allen Owen was never supposed to become a Marine. Many laughed in his face at his insistence that he could be just as good a soldier as any other. Not only that, but he faced lofty legal hurdles to joining the armed forces. Five-feet-two-inches was the ironclad cutoff for men joining the Marines at the time — with a Marine Corps commandant's "OK" it could be snipped down to 5 feet. Owen still didn't make the grade, and that just made him fight harder. According to a story by Pat Harper on Jefferson Public Radio, Owen wrote his congressman, sending him a resume that outlined how a college-educated, tough-as-nails wrestler wanted to serve his country and could pull his own weight despite being an inch off the mark.

And Owen did pull his own weight — literally. He was accepted into the Marines and was soon running up and down mountains in advanced infantry training all while carrying around more than his body weight — all 112 pounds of it — in gear.

"He's a mass of muscle and strong as an ox," the recruiting officer said in the *LIFE* magazine article.

"This little fellow doesn't ask for anything special; sometimes we have to slow him down," an astounded company commander stated.

At the time, Owen was the shortest Marine to ever put on the combat fatigues and would go on to break the record for the shortest airborne firefighter — or "Smokejumper" — that ever was. Owen was humble enough to know he'd never be a star basketball player but was a pioneer for little people in every other respect.

It wasn't just his stature that garnered Owen the nickname "Mouse." Marine tradition at the time — always seeking to belittle young men in an effort to test their mettle — required the shortest man in the platoon to be the errand-boy for the drill instructors: they got the degrading title "House Mouse." The name would stick with him for the rest of his life, but far from being a distasteful denigration, everyone who knew him would come to say it with pride. Even his superiors couldn't deny the bravery, strength, and knowledge of the intrepid Mouse. Owen graduated as "honor man" in his platoon according to *The Mouse That Soared*, no small feat for any Marine recruit.

Continuing to raise eyebrows everywhere he went, and with a college education to boot, he was put on the fast track to become a respected officer in the armed forces, but behind the scenes and at a desk. Owen wasn't having any of it — he wanted to walk side by side with the everyman on the battlefield as an enlisted soldier. He desired to see the world and make it a better place, and he'd do it just like everyone else, with no special accommodations or exemptions.

"He was also an adrenaline junkie who wanted to go where the action was," his brother Larry recalled. On January 11, 1966, it was officially written into the records: Allen "Mouse" Owen was a Marine, and he would start his four years in the Corps by getting shipped off to Vietnam. He would spend a few days shy of three years in the chaos of Vietnam, earning the rank of sergeant and the Vietnamese Cross of Gallantry Medal with Bronze Star for his valorous actions in combat with the enemy.

It was Owen's 14th patrol in Vietnam, and his team was on a mission deep in the labyrinthian jungles of the Quang Nam province, the sounds of the helicopter chopping the air fading into the distance, when suddenly the wilderness came alive with tremendous enemy gunfire. From his diary entry recorded in the pages of *The Mouse That Soared*, Owen and his team would be playing a dangerous game of cat-and-mouse, skillfully evading the larger hostile force for three excruciatingly long days.

They couldn't escape their dogged attackers forever; the recon unit was eventually caught in a potentially lethal encirclement — enemy Vietnamese troops surrounding them on three sides and firing inward at the Americans. The trees and brush provided a thick wall that denied Owen and his team from achieving significant visual contact with the hidden enemies — instead they relied on the sounds of guns firing upon them to gauge their positions. "We knew that we were surrounded, and as soon as we moved, they would close in and try and wipe us out," he wrote in his war-time diary.

Owen saw the situation violently turning from bad to worse, and he advised getting choppers down there fast to pull them out while they were still alive. The incredibly tall jungle canopy, however, hung maliciously over them, making withdrawal into the skies a herculean task. For this extraction, they'd need a jungle penetrator: a conical metal contraption that burst through the forest canopy, and upon hitting the ground, fold three metal prongs out to form simple seats.

"The pilot hovered over us for 15 minutes despite the fact he was receiving ground fire from 360 degrees," Owen wrote in his diary. He would later go on to recommend medals for those pilots, but in that moment, disaster came for them in the form of miscommunication, one of the most dangerous forces working against soldiers since ancient times. The pilot had not known that the three Marines were loaded up to the brim with over a hundred pounds of equipment — both the strength of the "penetrators" metal bars and the Marines' ability to hold on would be tested to their absolute limits.

"We didn't realize our predicament until we got to the 'hell hole' in the floor of the chopper and they said they couldn't get us in. It wouldn't have been bad except that the lieutenant was just barely hanging on and couldn't last much longer even though Pete and I were trying to hold him on."

The pilot tried to touch down to safely let the Marines off, but as their altitude dropped to 800 feet, mass weapons' fire crackled from every direction, and they had to push forward or get shot out of the sky. Owen's iron grip on the penetrator was faltering. "It finally occurred to me that if we didn't land soon, we would all die."

They almost made it. They were one minute from the safety of a sandbar, their altitude dropping to 500, 400, 300 feet ... when Lt. Slater could hold on for no longer. He slipped from the metal bar and tumbled to the earth.

"To the day I die I will never forget the look on his face or the sight of him falling and hitting the ground," Owen wrote. The moment he and the other Marine jumped out of the helicopter, they ran to reach Slater. It was clear their brother-in-arms was dead.

This was not the first nor the last brush with death Owen would contend with. Lt. Col. Herb De Groft, a man who had served with Owen as a corporal but became an officer by the time he left the armed forces, recounted one particularly dangerous mission in the pages of *The Mouse That Soared*.

They were on an operation to retrieve the body of an Army spotter plane pilot who was downed in January of 1967. Twenty Marines' lives were taken in the ensuing firefight, but they got the pilot's body back, and killed a hell of a lot of Viet Cong in the process. Despite the horrific loss of life — and the grueling day-in-day-out of not knowing who was going to live to see the next sunrise — Owen was grateful for the life-altering experiences his time in Vietnam provided.

"I would not trade this past three years for anything because I learned a great deal about other people, about myself, about life. I really don't think a person can truly appreciate life unless he's been near death!" he wrote with tremendous wisdom for a young man in his twenties. And beyond that, it gave him the opportunity to find what would become the next love of his life: jumping from airplanes.

"The greatest 35 days I've spent in the Marine Corps: Airborne," he wrote, his joy practically leaping off the page. Owen would go on to become a Smokejumper, a specially trained firefighter who drops from the sky to do battle with deep-wilderness wildfires. Beyond just providing initial firefighting support, Smokejumpers would also sometimes jump into burning wildlands with enough food, water, and firefighting tools to make them self-sufficient firefighting machines for up to 48 hours.

Owen's experience in the Marines was the perfect preamble to the plane-jumping, 110-lbs-of-gear-carrying Smokejumpers. And that match made in heaven was no accident: in 1940, then-Maj. William C. Lee of the US Army observed the antics of the precursor to the Smokejumpers and based on what he saw, went on to create the 101st Airborne Division.

Owen's greatness couldn't just be captured by his time with the Marines or the Smokejumpers, though. He was a man who brought joy to everyone he ever met.

"He was a terrific fellow Marine who you knew you could depend on, all the way to the gates of hell and back," De Groft, a fellow Marine, said of his friend. "He was a Marine's Marine: small in stature but mighty in every other human respect." His infectious smile could melt his worst enemies; everywhere you find stories of Allen "Mouse" Owen, you find he left a mark of happiness on those around him.

At one point he helped track down a lost Boy Scout troop, and upon finding them, made a request for a care package of hot dogs, ice cream, and marshmallows. As reported by Pat Harper on Jefferson Radio in 2016, this led to an annual training jump onto a local Bible camp to deliver ice cream. On Fourth of July, he would fly from the sky dressed as Superman to deliver goodies to delighted children.

"Everyone who worked with him was inspired," fellow smokejumper Troop Edmonds said of Owen. In the book *Wind Loggers*, Dorcey Alan Wingo remembers Owen saving his soaked posterior from nearly drowning. Owen strode up and cheerfully dragged him out of the water, never letting up on the witty, upbeat banter.

"Say, Wingo," Owen said. "That was your first engine-out landing here at Gobi, wasn't it?" On September 9, 1981, Allen "Mouse" Owen jumped out of a

(Springfield History Museum)

plane as a Smokejumper in Alaska and made a high-impact collision with another parachute. Owen lost his life that day, but he died doing what he loved, and nothing can take away all the lives he touched and people he inspired.

"He stood head and shoulders above those physically taller because of the character and leadership qualities he exhibited as a Marine NCO as well as a stellar man," De Groft said of the 4'11" American hero. As of 2020, the height requirement for the Marines is 4-feet-8 inches, and it was trailblazers like Allen "Mouse" Owen and his bravery that made that change possible.

Colonel Lewis Lee "Red" Millet

NATIONAL GUARD
ARMY AIR CORPS
CANADIAN ARMY
US ARMY

Medal of Honor
Distinguished Service Cross
Silver Star
Legion of Merit (3)
Bronze Star (3)
Purple Heart (4)
Air Medal (2)

December 15, 1920–November 14, 2009 (88 years)

Col. Lewis Lee Millet's patriotism shone so bright he deserted the army — not to escape war, but to begin fighting sooner. When he learned that the Chinese believed Americans feared hand-to-hand combat, he showed them the error of their ways: Millet would lead the last major bayonet charge in modern military history, trampling his enemies under his feet while doing it.

Lewis Lee Millet put on his National Guard uniform on Memorial Day, 1940, before he headed into high school. He was vice president of the senior class and a National Guard soldier of two years, and he had been invited to make a speech. Millet's family had lived through 10 years of the Great Depression in a garage on their farm, but these days there was a different crisis that plagued his thoughts.

"Adolf Hitler had overrun Europe, and I warned my classmates that we would soon be in a war," Millet told *Military History* magazine in February 2002. "I told them that it was better to go prepared." He let his actions speak for himself, joining the Army Air Corps at Lowry Field after graduation, where he learned how to use machine guns.

But even as Germany burst into Poland, powerful isolationist currents moved through an America where many were wary of yet another world war. President Roosevelt acknowledged that a peace broken anywhere is a threat to peace everywhere, and yet a proclamation of neutrality was given.

Millet could not live in a world where he was "neutral" to the Nazis; Canada had entered the war in September 1939, and he decided that if he couldn't fight under American banners, he would desert to their northern neighbor instead.

During Vietnam people ran to Canada to escape the war — Millet ran to Canada to join it. He and a man who had been discharged from the Marines on bad conduct hitchhiked north and joined the Royal Regiment of Canadian Artillery. Instead of firing artillery, however, they were sent to a top-secret facility to learn how to use radar.

"I have to laugh now when I think about it. Two Americans, one a deserter from the US Army and the other with a bad conduct discharge from the Marine Corps, selected for top-secret training," he told *Military History.* In a twist of fate, by the time he had reached England, America had entered the war, so Millet transferred to the Army and set off to Africa with the 1st Armored Division.

Operation Torch was underway, and after landing near Oran in Algeria, his division went on to wrest Tunis from the Germans. Gas was running low, however, and they only had enough to send their division piecemeal into hostile territory. It was a disaster. Millet recalled the 37mm cannon of their Lee tanks bouncing off the German armor without the Nazis even noticing; of the 20 tanks that attacked the Germans, 20 were reduced to scrap metal. "It was a good indoctrination in how good we weren't."

In the chaos of combat, a halftrack vehicle loaded with ammunition went up in a blaze, threatening to blow itself and all the men around it to kingdom come. Instead of watching,

Millet jumped into the driver's seat, sped away, and rolled out just before it blew. The white phosphorus and red shells made for a spectacular explosion, and Pvt. Millet earned a Silver Star and a promotion.

The 1st Armored Division went to Stuka Valley to rest and re-equip, but the valley was anything but peaceful. It had earned its name from the endless bombardment by German airplanes (*Sturzkampfflugzeug* is the German word for dive bomber), and all their time there was spent in foxholes scattered across the cratered landscape. Despite the constant bombardments, they were able to regroup and drive to Kasserine Pass to take part in the critical counterattack.

It was here where Millet's machine-gun training at Lowry Field paid dividends. A German Me-109 fighter was strafing down the road; Millet aimed the .50-caliber machine guns mounted on his halftrack and shot the pilot right through the windshield with flawless precision. The plane dove into the dirt and Millet was promoted to corporal. His record of excellence would come to serve him well in Italy. Then, after a year of combat, the Army disciplined him for his desertion from the National Guard.

"'Sgt. Millet, yesterday you were court-martialed for desertion. You were found guilty, fined $52 and sentenced to 30 days' hard labor,'" Millet recalled Lt. George Crick telling him in his interview with *Military History*. He sent a flurry of letters, cursing the officers every which way he knew how, and before long he was standing in front of his battery commander. He'd find out the War Department had ordered three times that he be court-martialed, and they finally did it to curtail the compounding repercussions. After a few weeks they turned cheek and promoted him to second lieutenant. "I must be the only regular Army colonel who has ever been court-martialed and convicted of desertion," Millet said.

He continued the fight in Italy, working with the 36th Division and even the British 1st Special Service Force. When World War II drew to a close, he returned to Maine, starting college along with so many other veterans. But the peace was short lived; before he could finish his degree, North Korean tanks rolled into South Korea. Millet flung himself back into battle again.

After earning three "E Flags" for excellence as an artillery officer in a severely undersupplied artillery division, Millet was wounded in the Battle of Ch'ongch'on River. Unable to walk but unwilling to sit around, he joined the fearless pilot Capt. James Lawrence in an observation plane. From their perch in the clouds, they witnessed a South African fighter crash land into a frozen rice paddy behind enemy lines. Capt. Lawrence swooped into place right next to the downed pilot and Millet, seeing no other acceptable option, gave the wounded South African his seat on the plane. Lawrence flew and dropped the pilot off, then soared back to Millet just as a Chinese patrol caught wind of the stranded American. Lawrence swept him up and flew off amid a blaze of gunfire.

Once recovered from his injuries, Millet became commander of E Company in the 27th Infantry Regiment — taking over from the deceased Medal of Honor recipient Reginald Desiderio — and immediately instituted several changes. First, he placed two Browning Automatic Rifles (BARs) in the hands of each squad. Then he loaded each man with up to six grenades, an increase from the standard two. Finally, he introduced bayonet training to the men under his command.

"We had acquired some Chinese documents stating that Americans were afraid of hand-to-hand fighting and cold steel. When I read that, I thought, 'I'll show you, you sons of bitches!' So I had every rifleman in the company fix his bayonet to his rifle and leave it fixed, 24 hours a day."

It would not be long before those sharpened bayonets would see their first taste of melee combat. The first bayonet charge would earn him the Distinguished Service Cross. The second charge would go down in history and was so successful that it would christen the ground it took place on with a new name.

Millet led E Company cautiously up the road that straddled Hill 180 on February 7, 1951, with the objective of locating the enemy. G Company was meant to cover their left flank, but they lagged behind; Millet had kept his 3rd Platoon in reserve, moving them to protect the left to avoid encirclement. It was the 3rd Platoon that discovered the Chinese and North Koreans had taken their position on Hill 180.

Millet sprinted to the tanks, ordering them to start firing their machine guns at the top of the hill and not to stop until the men had neared the top. He then raced to organize his platoons into a line near the base of the hill.

"Then I went in front of the platoon in the rice paddy and yelled, 'Follow me!'" The men ran across a frozen rice paddy and began their ascent, bayonets fixed and faced forward. Millet was halfway up when he whipped around and saw the line of men had gone ragged.

"'C'mon you sons of bitches and fight!'" he yelled, as he turned to lead the last major bayonet charge in modern military history. Chinese hand grenades started flying and would continue to rain down for the rest of the battle. Bullets washed across the hill. One explosion caught Millet in its radius, sending shrapnel shooting into his shins — it didn't slow the charge for a second. Millet blitzed right into an anti-tank rifle crew; he bayoneted all three of them while screaming bloody murder and overflowing with adrenaline. He tossed grenades and wielded his bayonet and the butt of his rifle in vicious hand-to-hand combat, all the while shouting encouragement to the men he led. The momentum of the charge swept up the hill all the way to the crest, where the enemy's formation shattered into disarray.

Casualties amounted to strikingly few among Company E while those who faced them were scattered to the wind: Almost half of the enemy was found to have been killed by bayonets.

They had won the day and changed the very character of the hill they'd conquered. US troops would rename Hill 180 to "Bayonet Hill." For his shining leadership and the over-whelming victory, Millet was awarded the Medal of Honor, though he was quick to share the honor among the hundred men that followed him into the fires that day.

"So this as much belongs to the men of my unit as it does to me. ... I'm alive today because I had damn, damn good men!" Millet said in his interview with the Library of Congress Veterans History Project. His warrior soul would cause him to lead three different bayonet assaults in Korea, and twice they would prove so wildly successful he'd receive awards for them.

"And then they ordered me not to do it anymore, cause they were afraid I'd get killed — probably would have." Later that year, President Harry Truman would present Millet his Medal of Honor. Even then, Millet would continue to serve in the military through another war, the Vietnam War. He would complete Ranger school in 1958, and his tactical talent so impressed Maj. Gen. William Westmoreland that he'd lead a school for small unit leaders and set up three more. Millet retired from the military in 1973 at the rank of colonel, having fought in three wars, all of which he volunteered for.

"I believe in freedom, I believe deeply in it ... because I believed as a free man, that it was my duty to help those under the attack of tyranny. Just as simple as that," he told *Military History*.

Millet would go on to champion the return of US prisoners of war from Vietnam and then work as a deputy sheriff in Tennessee before settling in the San Jacinto Mountains resort village of Idyllwild, California. Col. Lewis Millet passed away in 2009, but his legacy remains. His bottomless bravery will stand for eternity at the US Army Infantry Museum at Fort Benning, Georgia, where a life-size diorama depicts the unbreakable Millet leading the charge, preparing to bayonet a North Korean enemy soldier.

Sergeant First Class Modesto Cartagena de Jesús

US ARMY

Distinguished Service Cross
Silver Star
Legion of Merit
Bronze Star (2)
Purple Heart

July 21, 1921–March 2, 2010 (88 years)

Army Sgt. 1st Class Modesto Cartagena de Jesús is for many the most decorated Hispanic soldier of the Korean War. Cartagena earned almost every medal of valor including a Purple Heart, the Silver Star, the Distinguished Service Cross, the Legion of Merit, and two Bronze Stars.

Mired in the swampy rice paddies below Hill 206 near Yonchon, Korea, the Chinese had Modesto Cartagena's men right where they wanted them, claiming a small victory with intense, direct fire. This was the Korean War, the date April 19, 1951, and today Modesto Cartagena would earn his nickname, "The One Man Army."

Most heroes have behind them a humble beginning, and Cartagena was no different. "The One Man Army" was born Modesto Cartagena de Jesús in a small town named Cayey, a mountainous region in central Puerto Rico, in 1921. His life began amid the crisis of the Great Depression and times were hard for his family. And then came the Second World War.

Cartagena was among the first to join in the Army when the war broke out. He enlisted in San Juan and was immediately assigned to the now-famous 65th Infantry Regiment. This was an all-Hispanic unit, and the discrimination from

Cartagena at a Korean War memorial service in 2000.

the rest of the Army was strong. They came to be known as the Borinqueneers ("*Boricua*" being slang for someone from the island) and were all Puerto Rican men with the exception of the officer staff. Segregated and demeaned by the rest of the Army — they were called a "rum and Coca-Cola outfit" — the soldiers nonetheless received great praise from their commanding officer in the Korean War. Brig. Gen. William Harris called them "the best damn soldiers in that war."

Cartagena first served in the Caribbean during World War II, guarding military infrastructure, and was then sent over to Germany as a part of the Allied occupation. When the Borinqueneers returned to Puerto Rico, Cartagena was discharged. But it wasn't long before the Korean War reared its head. Cartagena reenlisted and entered with the rank of sergeant, assigned to Company C, 65th Infantry Regiment, 3rd Infantry Division.

The men of the 65th were trailblazers, part of the first group of infantrymen to arrive on the battlefield. When China entered the war in November of 1950, the intensity of the conflict grew molten hot even as the weather turned freezing, and the 65th was involved in numerous brutal fights against the Chinese People's Liberation Army. The cold ushered in dark times for the Puerto Rican fighters who lacked warm clothing during the harsh, frostbitten winters. The Borinqueneers were true survivors, and together they could get through anything.

But as winter turned to spring, the 65th Infantry found themselves trapped in the middle of the legendary battle on the rice paddies below Hill 206. As Cartagena and his men began crawling slowly toward the enemy's rear left flank, the maneuver turned deadly, and almost immediately Pfc. Antonio Colon Flores was killed and 11 more men wounded. Cartagena heard a soldier call out to him.

"He had been wounded by two rounds to his thigh. I dragged myself to him, applied morphine, and filled out an evacuation card," Cartagena recalled years later. And then his rifle broke into two pieces from enemy fire. He took the wounded man's weapon, ammunition, and grenades and continued to make his way uphill, alone.

"When others would not dare go to missions, I would go," Cartagena said with pride in a video interview on *borinqueneers.com*. Finally, Cartagena reached the top of the hill. There, a lone warrior, he encountered 80 to 100 Chinese soldiers hidden in mortar nests, wielding mortars, machine guns, and automatic weapons. He managed to reach the first mortar nest and silence it with a hand grenade. Then came the second, and a third, upon which he hosed automatic fire before finishing it off with explosives.

"And that's how I destroyed three positions with machine guns, mortars, and five automatic weapons," Cartagena said. "When the Chinese discovered my position, they threw so many grenades that three landed on me. One landed on my back, another in between my legs, and the third on my right side. The last one wounded me. The bone was sticking out from my arm. I lost a lot of blood, but luckily I didn't faint." He fought, wounded with an open fracture, for three more hours.

"The Chinese would hurl their grenades at me, and I would catch them in the air and quickly throw them through the air opening in the Chinese trenches. ... They would take cover and I would advance my position." After taking out the emplacements, he was thrown to the ground twice by exploding grenades. He continued to get up and continue the fight each time.

As the dust settled, Cartagena then found himself in sole possession of the hill. The Chinese had met their match in this one wildly brave soldier and withdrew in defeat. Cartagena had killed 33 Chinese soldiers in machine gun and automatic weapon emplacements and 15 more in other strategic positions along the slope. While the battle was done, however, the work certainly was not. He ordered two squads to help dig out a tank and two more to search out and retrieve the fallen soldiers. Only after all of this was finalized did he allow himself to return to a first-aid station for medical attention.

Cartagena was sent to Taegu in a helicopter, then to Japan to the 128th Station Hospital where he remained hospitalized for two months.

"Sgt. Cartagena's actions prevented much heavier casualties within my platoon and I feel that his courage and superior leadership and own initiative were decisive factors for the accomplishment of the mission of the unit," said 1st Lt. Reinaldo Deliz Santiago.

His actions on that hill near Yonchon cemented his legendary status as the Borinqueneers' "One Man Army." Cartagena was awarded the Distinguished Service Cross for "extreme gallantry and risk of life in actual combat with an armed enemy force." When the war ended, he then went on to spend 20 more years in the Army, retiring in 1971 with the rank of sergeant first class. Even after retirement, he continued to be an active member at the 65th Infantry Headquarters in Puerto Rico.

When his family learned of his actions that day, they took it upon themselves to request to Congress that he be awarded the Medal of Honor. They received support from the Republican Veterans Committee, but unfortunately, this wasn't enough. Cartagena's supporters argue that the segregation of the army coupled with the checkered English of his fellow soldiers when filling out the forms for the application resulted in the awarding of the nation's second highest decoration, the Distinguished Service Cross.

Years later, on the very day that Puerto Rico commemorated the 93rd anniversary of American citizenship, Modesto Cartagena died in his home in Guayama. He suffered a severe heart attack after years of battling stomach cancer and Alzheimer's. He was buried with military honors in the Puerto

Rico National Cemetery in Bayamón, and Secretary of State Kenneth McClintock attended the funeral. McClintock delivered to Cartagena's family a personal letter from Governor Luis Fortuño that said that while Cartagena was being buried with a Distinguished Service Cross, "in our hearts we're sending him off with the Medal of Honor he deserves."

Company C of 65th Infantry Regiment. (www.army.mil)

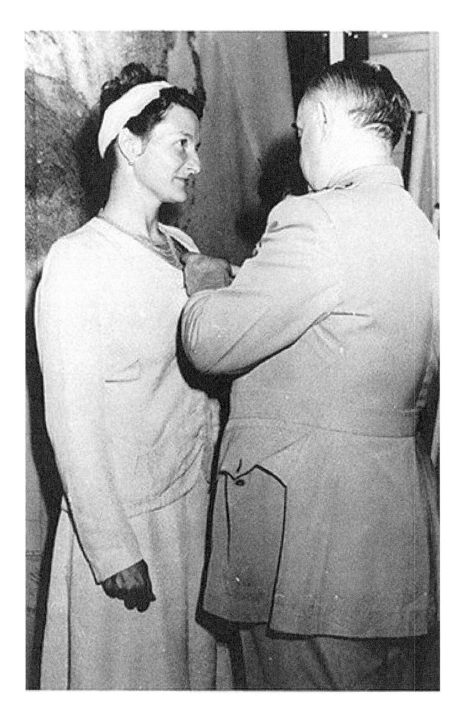

Virginia Hall receives the Distinguished Service Cross in 1945 from OSS director General Donovan. (CIA Official Website)

Virginia Hall

SOET
OSS
CIA
US DEPARTMENT OF STATE

April 6, 1906–July 8, 1982

"The most dangerous of all Allied spies." — The Gestapo

Virginia Hall once wore live snakes as bracelets to school. Her mother was horrified but she'd soon find out there was nothing she could do: Her daughter was immutable. You could say this young woman was born upright with her fists out. Her legacy would paint the picture of a woman both daring and ingenious, who would retire from the war as one of the Allies' greatest intelligence assets.

Born in Baltimore to a well-to-do family, she would spend the rest of her life in a cold war with her mother, who wanted her to marry a rich man and settle down. But Virginia's destiny was not that of a housewife; she had other plans and yearned for adventure. Even grievous injury would prove no obstacle to her great dreams. After a hunting accident where she shot herself dead in the foot while climbing over a fence, she was undeterred and instead found ways around this disability.

After her university years at Radcliffe College, Barnard College, and then Colombia University where she studied French, German, Italian, and economics, she went off to Europe to finish her education. She spent many months trying to fulfill her dream to become a diplomat at the United States Foreign Service. She aced all the tests, surprising everyone by getting 100 percent in her oral diplomat exam, only to be rejected over and over again. She was eventually told that there was a policy against disabled people. This was, however, perfectly untrue: There were various male diplomats with prosthetic legs.

Hall decided that if she couldn't be a diplomat and work for the Americans, she would go to France and offer her services there. The French said yes, and for a time she drove an ambulance, delivering medicine to the 10 million people fleeing Hitler's tanks.

But after six weeks, in August of 1940, she abandoned France for Britain and offered her services this time to the British Army. On the journey to Britain, at a railway station, she was approached by George Bellows, an undercover British agent. He noticed her "force of personality" and struck up a conversation. Almost at once, he realized that a personality like Hall's doesn't come along often and gave her the phone number of a friend that he said she should call once she reached London. This man was no ordinary friend; he was a senior official of the Special Operations Executive (SOE), the British espionage agency. She went to dinner with this "friend" and was recruited right then and there. And so it was that Virginia Hall became a spy and the mastermind behind one of the most daring rescues of the war.

It began one morning in the spring of 1942, at the Grand Nouvel Hotel in Lyon, France, when Hall met Gaby Bloch. Hall was immediately impressed by the small French woman, the wife of former French deputy Jean Pierre-Bloch, one of the few parliamentarians to oppose the Munich Agreement. He and 11 others — they were known as the Clan Cameron — had been arrested on treason charges and sent to Périgueux, a prison in southwest France. Freezing and damp, with barely any water and only an oily sludge once a day for food, Lt. Jumeau described it as "degrading and humiliating to the last degree."

The Camerons were "star agents," with expertise ranging from wireless transmitting, weapons, and sabotage. It was of paramount importance to prevent them from being executed — or worse, handed over to Hitler as trophy prisoners. The

SOE was eager for an escape, but the Camerons had lost faith in their efforts.

This wouldn't be Virginia's first prison break, and the Camerons had already heard about the woman with piercing eyes and a limping leg from Gerry Morel, a French agent in service with the SOE. Morel's successful escape, he reported, was mostly due to the ingenuity of Virginia Hall. And that brings us back to the smokey cafe in Lyon where these two shrewd and unimaginably brave women were seated facing each other. Gaby Bloch explained the efforts she had put in lobbying ministers in Vichy and complained that no one was listening to the small distraught Jewish woman. Hall understood both the woman's frustration and the magnitude of the problem.

Hall got to work. She devised a plan and told SOE leadership that she was going to give the project a go. Finding little support, she then appealed to Adm. William D. Leahy, the American Ambassador to France. Hall argued that the Camerons were "symbolically important prisoners," although she couldn't reveal they were also secret agents facing trial and most likely execution — that was classified.

Perhaps Leahy was concerned about bad press if he ignored her pleas, but whatever the reason, Leahy agreed to look into it. That original plan went awry, however, when it was announced that the prisoners were transferring from the prison to an internment camp in Mauzac.

This was good news. Mauzac was in the countryside, the conditions were better, and the men would be living in a hut. At the same time, the transfer brought up a few cons: Hall was well known in those parts, the prison was armed to the teeth with cruel guards, it was surrounded by two barbed-wire fences, and further encircled by watchtowers. This is where Gaby Bloch came in: Hall supplied her with a load of bribe money and taught her techniques on how to recruit guards to help relay messages.

Jose Sevilla was the first recruited guard: In exchange for

being taken to London to join the Free French, he would make sure that Watchtower Five (the tower nearest to the men's hut) would remain unmanned at night and he smuggled as many messages as he could to the Camerons.

But even with his help, Hall needed a more reliable way to communicate with them and get them supplies. She armed Bloch with money to buy black-market groceries, and with her convincing act of devastated and distressed wife, Gaby got them jam with a file at the bottom of the jar, some laundry with wire cutters hidden inside, hollowed-out books with a screwdriver and hammer, lots of tins of sardines chosen for the very useful reusable metal, and maybe, most importantly, bread. For their part, every night the Camerons had "choir practice," singing as loudly as they could to drown out the noises of hammering — they were making a mold for a key.

This was still not enough though. There was a desperate need for clearer communication. Hall found an old French priest, a veteran of WWI who had lost both his legs, and under the guise of bringing pastoral visits to the prisoners the priest brought them paint to "spruce up their hut." When this hut makeover was finished, he asked to be taken inside to see how it turned out. Alone with the men, he lifted his cassock: The French priest had smuggled in a transmitter disguised as a piano! Now there was a direct line in and out of the prison — London was gobsmacked at this feat of subterfuge.

With the escape plans now almost complete, the men tested the makeshift key they had made from the bread mold, but to their utter horror, it didn't work. The choir began again while a new key was hammered into existence. This time they got it right, which was a saving grace as their limited time was rapidly dwindling. They needed to get out during the new moon, the only time it was dark enough to not get caught.

On July 15, the men waited anxiously for the all-clear sign: if they were good to go, an old lady would pass by the camp; if the plan was called off, an old man would walk by. Thankfully, at the given time, a little old lady inconspicuously walked by.

The men went to work stuffing rags under the blankets to make them look as if they were all asleep. The watchtower was clear, and the lock worked this time. Once opened, they immediately hung a painted sackcloth, made to look like a door, and sped through the wire using an old carpet. At that moment, a guard showed up. They froze in place. Then, the guard whispered: "Well don't make so much noise." And so with that, the men made the rest of the journey under the barbed wire. It took exactly 12 minutes: a minute a man.

Once they were out, Hall had arranged a safe house stocked with groceries, clothes, and beds for the first and most crucial hours of the escape, and then transportation to get them all back to London.

She had done it — she had gotten 12 of the most important spies out of a so-called impenetrable internment camp and back to safety. She officially became an SOE legend. The historian M.R.D. Foot wrote that this jailbreak was "one of the war's most useful operations of its kind." Hitler was furious.

After the Mauzac escape, Hall continued her work as one of the most important Allied spies of World War II. She blew up bridges and tunnels, she swindled and schemed, and she killed when necessary. At one point, escaping the Nazis, she crossed the Pyrenees in the dead of winter with barely any food or proper clothes — all on foot while her prosthetic leg gushed blood.

After the war was over, Hall went back home to Baltimore where she was awarded the Distinguished Service Cross by none other than the famous "Wild" Bill Donovan. Instead of marrying into a life of luxury as her mother had wished, she became one of the CIA's first female intelligence agents.

Robert F. Kennedy once said, "It is from numberless diverse acts of courage and belief that human history is shaped.

Each time a man stands up for an ideal, or acts to improve the lot of others, or strikes out against injustice, he sends forth a tiny ripple of hope ..." Virginia Hall's many acts of courage were absolutely essential to defeating the Nazis, and we all owe our freedom today to the courage of people like the "Limping Lady."

Les Marguerites Fleuriront ce Soir (the daisies will bloom at night) by Jeffrey W. Bass; oil on canvas; 2006; donated by Richard J. Guggenhime.

Lieutenant Colonel William J. Donovan in uniform, September 6, 1918. (War Department. Army War College. Historical Section. World War I Branch. ca. 1918-ca. 1948 -)

Major General William Joseph Donovan

NEW YORK NATIONAL GUARD
US ARMY
US ARMY RESERVE

Medal of Honor
Distinguished Service Cross
Distinguished Service Medal (2)
Purple Heart (3)

January 1, 1883–February 8, 1959 (76 years)

A lawyer, soldier, and diplomat, the only American to have earned all four of the most prestigious awards: the Medal of Honor, the Distinguished Service Cross, the Distinguished Service Medal, and the National Security Medal. The OSS and the CIA, the monumental institutions which he founded, are all he needs as his introduction. "Wild Bill" is a legend the likes of which will not be born again.

The orders had come down to Maj. William Donovan and the other regimental officers of the 165th Infantry, 42nd Division: under the cover of darkness provided by the night of July 27, 1918, four infantry regiments would make a surprise attack at Ourcq Valley, not loudly with gunfire but silently with bayonets. There was a sickening feeling among the officers as they contemplated their orders, for the reconnaissance they'd done during the night revealed dozens of German machine gun nests waiting hungrily for such an attack. Still, this priceless intelligence did not shift their orders. Donovan, knowing full well the madness of the attack they were undertaking, gritted his teeth and prepared himself and his men to win the day.

The human cost of their attack was breathtaking; the relentless *pop-pop-pop* of German machine guns chewed into

Donovan's First Battalion from three sides as they pushed forward. According to *Father Duffy's Story*, a published diary of Canadian American Francis Patrick Duffy, who was himself a part of the 69th Regiment of "Fighting Irish," the Germans who were captured during the relentless three-day engagement came to see the Americans and their suicidal push as "crazy."

Donovan was never happy unless he was in the thick of it; almost always in an exposed position, inspecting and advancing his men and delivering his messages personally. The song of death sung by rifles, machine guns, and artillery never stopped, and Donovan's men — his friends — dropped by the dozen around him.

First his close friend and adjutant Oliver Ames would die right next to Donovan, a sniper's bullet whizzing past the major's head straight into the head of Ames. Donovan took a bullet in the hand when he instinctively reached out to grab his friend. Next, Joyce Kilmer, the much-loved poet of the regiment, jumped in to take Ames's place. Kilmer too found an untimely death that day at the hands of a German marksman. Mess cook John Kayes would not leave Donovan's side, and he met his end pumped full of machine gun fire. Donovan would come to be known as a magnet for death, yet the soulful young men beside him agreed that battle for a worthy cause under the leadership of Maj. Donovan was worth the likely death sentence. Donovan himself would also be grazed across the thigh and have the heel of his boot shot off. Later, shrapnel from a shell that should've meant his death miraculously managed to only damage his respirator. "Wild Bill is a son-of-a-*****, but he's a game one," Father Duffy heard one soldier say.

After a week of watching those around him be violently pulled from this life on into the next, a week of following orders and pushing forward regardless of the casualties, they finally had achieved the objective. They had pushed the Germans back 18 kilometers. Afterward, Donovan and his battalion could say they "had gone the farthest and stayed the longest." The cost was grave: more than half of the brave men of the 165th Regiment had become casualties. Donovan's First Battalion saw 600 men killed or wounded.

For his valor, Donovan had earned the Distinguished Service Cross and was promoted to lieutenant colonel. This had been, in so many ways, the defining moment of William "Wild Bill" Donovan's life. And yet, Donovan saw in the battle of Ourcq Valley a defeat as much as a victory.

As Donovan thought of his men throwing themselves headfirst into the cogs of war, he would contemplate how things could be different. Military intelligence — in this case, the local reconnaissance before the battle — had clearly warned of the sacrifice required by command's plan of action, but that intelligence had gone unheeded. Donovan saw how the rigid army structure had failed to meet the moment with the necessary flexibility, and he wondered how he, if he had been in charge, would have met the challenge with more success and less needless death.

Donovan had an unshakable obedience to the chain of command and always demanded the same from his men. But it's in the failures of that rigid obedience that the flames of the OSS and the CIA would be kindled. He would create an organization that liberated its operatives to use local knowledge and experience to make decisions on the best courses of action. His vision would only grow grander alongside his rank and status; the lessons burned into him from the failures of command witnessed in World War I would rise from the ashes and seed the era of modern military intelligence. But that achievement merely brushes the surface of one of the most distinguished men in the history of the United States government.

Donovan was born in Buffalo, New York, on New Year's Day in the year 1883. His parents were both first generation Irish immigrants but came from starkly different backgrounds. His mother, Anna Letitia "Tish" Lennon was from a wealthy, propertied family. His father, Timothy P. Donovan, worked as the superintendent of a Buffalo railroad yard, and then for a time as the secretary for a cemetery. "From Anna's side of the family came style and etiquette and the dreams of poets," Donovan's biographer, Douglas Waller, wrote. "From Tim came toughness and duty and honor to country and clan." They were a happy, rowdy family and William was the eldest of six children.

Donovan earned his Bachelor of Arts in 1905, after which he spent two years at Columbia Law School. This was a crucial time in his life; he was brushing shoulders with diverse, important people and intellectually expanding his mind by the day. Donovan caught the eye of Harlan Stone, an attorney and jurist who served as an associate justice, then as chief justice of the United States Supreme Court as well as Attorney General under President Calvin Coolidge. Stone was "impressed by a kid from a rough Irish neighborhood, who asked and answered questions in such a thoughtful, measured tone."

In 1909 he joined the prestigious law firm of Love & Keating, a move that opened many doors for Donovan. Suddenly he had access to important business contacts, and he was admitted to coveted clubs, like the Greater Buffalo Club and the Saturn Club, where millionaires sipped lemonade and cocktails and hatched lucrative deals.

After two years at Love & Keating, he decided he wanted to be his own boss. He had the contacts and the confidence now to branch out on his own. So he and Bradley Goodyear, a former classmate from Columbia, opened their own firm. They specialized in civil cases, and one time even settled a disagreement between neighbors about the death of a dog. These were good years for Donovan: his firm was successful and he was gaining confidence and contacts by the day.

Three years later, the firm merged and became Goodyear & O'Brien. This was in part because Donovan's interests had expanded. In the spring of 1912, a group of young business-men and professionals (many from the Buffalo social clubs) organized the formation of their own Army National Guard or Troop I. The group originally began as a "camping club for well-to-do city boys" but soon turned into a serious operation. After four years of organizing, the group had a hundred caval-rymen with more in training.

In the summer of 1916, his unit was sent to serve on the US-Mexico border during the United States government's campaign against the Mexican revolutionary Francisco "Pancho" Villa. Donovan's biographer wrote that the Mexican Expedition was "miserable ... with temperatures soaring past 100 degrees during the day and Gulf storms turning their chigger-infested camp into a muddy swamp ... they ended up battling the elements more than the Mexicans." It wasn't all for nothing though; he was promoted to major during the ex-pedition, one more rung up the ladder.

Troop I returned home in March 1917 and Donovan im-mediately joined the famous 69th Regiment that could trace its history to the Revolutionary War. The regiment was made up of more than 3,000 of New York's "finest Irish sons." Don-ovan was recruited to head the regiment's 1st Battalion, and in the fall of 1917, the 69th traveled to Camp Mills on Long Island to begin combat training for the war in Europe. The 69th became the 165th Regiment and joined the 42nd Divi-sion or the "Rainbow Division," with Douglas MacArthur as the chief of staff.

On August 3, 1917, Donovan's wife, Ruth, gave birth to a baby girl, Patricia. She was baptized at Camp Mills and des-ignated "the Daughter of the Regiment." But the war was waiting and so the next month, in October, he and his battal-ion embarked on the long trip across the Atlantic. His wife and daughter went back to Buffalo. Donovan "did not expect to come back alive."

William Donovan was an extremely prepared man — hard-working, a distinguished lawyer, and an accomplished soldier. But no amount of training can prepare a man for what war will actually feel and look like.

In France he sustained a shrapnel wound in one leg almost immediately and was nearly blinded by gas. After the Germans blasted heavy *minenwerfer* mortars at his regiment at Rouge Bouquet, burying his men under many tons of earth, Donovan participated in their rescue while under heavy fire. When he was told that the French wanted to award him the *Croix de Guerre*, he outright refused it. He thought it was a great insult that the Jewish sergeant who had been at his side during the entire rescue operation was not being offered the same honor. Once the French government corrected the affront, Donovan accepted the recognition.

Donovan continued to train his troops relentlessly. He would run them on a three-mile course through ice-cold streams, over barbed-wire walls, and up and down hills. Some of the men would finish gasping for air and begging for mercy. "What the hell's the matter with you guys?" he would yell. "I haven't lost my breath." One of the troopers shouted out, "But hell, we aren't as wild as you are, Bill." And from that day on, he was known as "Wild Bill" Donovan.

Then, on May 27, 1918, came the Third Battle of the Aisne or the Aisne-Marne campaign. Part of the German spring offensive, a massive bombardment (*Feuerwalze*) — over 4,000 artillery pieces — directed at the American and Allied forces. The Germans were dead set on capturing the Chemin des Dames Ridge before the American Expeditionary Forces arrived, and the day turned devastatingly bloody.

Hundreds of men in his regiment perished. They were either killed, severely wounded, or missing, plus Donovan lost every single one of his company commanders. Despite the heavy casualties, he told his wife, Ruth, that "he was thrilled by the danger of combat."

Five months later, Donovan was now Lt. Col. Donovan and the commanding officer of the 165th Regiment. On October 14–15, 1918, he and his regiment were part of a fierce battle near Landres-et-Saint-Georges, France. It is during this fight that William Donovan showed the world his true colors.

It was customary for men going into battle to remove or cover up any insignia of rank because of the easy target it made for snipers. But half of Donovan's regiment was made up of new recruits, so he decided to wear his Sunday best. He got "decked out in his finest hoping that these young replacements, sure to panic under intense fire, saw him clearly and followed his orders in the fog of battle that would unfold that day." According to the article *Spymaster General* by Evan Thomas, he told his men: "They can't hit me and they won't hit you!"

But men *were* hit, and in large numbers. The troops were suffering serious casualties and the enemy was strong and organized. This absolutely was not going to stop "Wild Bill" however, not by a long shot. He kept right on going, "moving among his men in exposed positions, reorganizing decimated platoons, and accompanying them forward in attacks." He suffered a bullet right through the knee but refused to be evacuated and instead continued to direct his men through the intense fire until his unit was in a less exposed position. For his extraordinary actions and unsurpassed bravery, he was awarded the Medal of Honor, albeit not until 1923.

Following the Armistice on November 11, 1918, he remained in Europe as part of the occupation, only returning to New York five months later. There were rumors floating around about making him a candidate for governor of New York, but he rejected the idea: he was a lawyer and he intended to resume his law career.

But spending time with his family was first and foremost. He took his wife, Ruth, on a vacation. They traveled to Japan,

China, and Korea where he and Ruth attended many elegant parties at the American embassies and where diplomats would slip Donovan business and intelligence information. These were essential trips, as they were slowly harnessing his ideas about the powers of covert operations and intelligence gathering. He was sowing the seeds of his future career. Back at his law firm, he often traveled to Europe and Asia to gather intelligence on the growing threat of international communism and negotiated business deals on behalf of J.P. Morgan. Donovan was establishing himself as a major player in the international world and at the same time he was sharpening his skills as an overseas intelligence gatherer.

In 1922 he became the US Attorney for Buffalo and western New York; he would work here for four years and became known as a "vigorous crime fighter" and an impassioned prosecutor who never let anything slide. Going after bootleggers, profiteers, opium dealers, and strikers made him very popular, at first. But when he went after his own club, the Saturn Club, for illegal liquor sales, the well-heeled of Buffalo were ready to run him out of town.

There was one group that was happy though — the working class Buffalonians. They cheered the operation as a confirmation that equal justice should be for all, not just the ones that couldn't pay their way out. Nonetheless, Donovan's political career in Buffalo was over. A newspaper reported that "the city's underworld was as glad to see him go as high society."

Politics may have been out, but Donovan's life in law enforcement was far from over. One year later, in 1924, President Calvin Coolidge named Harlan Stone Attorney General and Donovan as his assistant in the department's criminal division. When Stone was later appointed to the Supreme Court, Donovan began running the Department of Justice's antitrust division and often served as the de facto Attorney General in the absence of John Garibaldi Sargent, Stone's predecessor.

In 1929 he resigned from the Department of Justice and moved to New York City to open a new law firm: Donovan, Leisure, Newton & Irvine. Just a few months later, Wall Street crashed. It was the most devastating stock market loss in United States history, ruining millions. Not Donovan. He made a success out of the Great Crash, handling the bankruptcies, mergers, and acquisitions that were consequences of the economic disaster. In 10 years, his firm was making over $800,000 a year (or about $14 million today) with over 40 associates on staff.

But Donovan was not a man that did one thing at a time. He argued big cases and made big business deals but he was also traveling the world. He met with Benito Mussolini, established connections (and enemies) in Nazi Germany, publicly assailed Hitler and Stalin, and worked hard to protect his Jewish clients from the Nazis. Donovan made it known that he thought a second major European war was on the horizon. His experience abroad and his pragmatism caught the eye of President Franklin D. Roosevelt. Although Donovan and Roosevelt held vastly different views on domestic policy, they were very similar in personality and Roosevelt came to value Donovan's judgment.

World War II officially erupted on September 1, 1939, after Germany and the USSR invaded Poland. When Roosevelt began churning the wheels of war, Secretary of the Navy Frank Knox urged him to give Donovan important intelligence assignments. So, in 1940 and 1941 he traveled as an informal emissary to Britain, where he was asked to gauge Britain's ability to withstand the Germans. After all, Hitler had declared Britain the main enemy and Poland's obliteration was a "necessary prelude."

Donovan met with Winston Churchill and the directors of the British intelligence agencies who were in charge of the British War effort. According to the article by Evan Thomas,

Churchill was very taken with Donovan. They shared war stories together and at one point recited in unison the poem "The Cavalier's Song" by William Motherwell. *"Then mounte! then mounte, brave gallants all, And don your helmes amaine; Deathe's couriers, fame and honor, call Us to the field againe."* Churchill ordered that Donovan be given unlimited access to all classified information, and Donovan assured him that he would urge Roosevelt to give Churchill the aid he had requested.

Back in the US, Donovan did just what he said he would and asked Roosevelt to send aid and weapons. Roosevelt wanted to oblige but he needed to find a way to get around the congressional ban on selling armaments to the United Kingdom. He asked Donovan to work his magic.

As an unofficial envoy for both countries, Donovan began to learn more and more of British tactics and strategies. He also traveled to investigate the conditions of the US naval defenses in the Pacific and visited several countries along the Mediterranean and Middle East to advocate for punishing Germany for its crimes. (Hitler once called Donovan "utterly unworthy," which undoubtedly made him proud.) Walter Lippmann, a political columnist, wrote at the time that Donovan's findings about the actual strength of Britain's fighting capability "almost single handedly overcame the unmitigated defeatism which was paralyzing Washington."

Douglas Waller once said that he was sure Donovan could not have started his spy agency "without the British, who provided intelligence, trainers, organizational charts and advice," all with the idea of making OSS an adjunct to British intelligence. But Donovan wanted to mount his own operation. Roosevelt came through and on July of 1941, he named Donovan Coordinator of Information (COI). At the time, there was no real centralized intelligence gathering department, but with this new job, he could begin to lay down the groundwork for one. He got to work fast, securing the agency a headquarters and a boss, Allen Dulles. They worked out of Room

3603 at the Rockefeller Center, right above the location of the operations of MI6.

Evan Thomas described the beginnings of the OSS as "informal" and "freewheeling," and criticism of the agency during the war was unceasing. But the unit persevered, and Donovan became more influential than ever. He set up spy schools, sabotage schools, front companies, arranged secret collaborations with the Vatican and international corporations, supervised the making of new espionage-friendly guns, cameras, and bombs, and recruited a skilled and diverse workforce. He hired intellectuals, artists, ex-criminals, women (at the time unheard of), poets, scientists, and famous people like John Ford, Eve Curie, Julia Child, and Carl Jung. There were so many celebrities in the agency that the joke was that OSS really stood for "Oh So Social." Then, in 1942, Roosevelt took the agency to the next level: he changed the name to Office of Strategic Services (OSS) and transferred its command to the Joint Chiefs of Staff. Donovan was supportive and said, "I want the OSS to recruit young men of disciplined daring who are calculatingly reckless."

Under Donovan's leadership, the OSS did eventually conduct successful espionage and sabotage missions in Europe and Asia; however, due to his rocky relationship with J. Edgar Hoover, he was kept firmly out of South America. Not only that but the OSS was blocked from entering the Philippines by General Douglas MacArthur, the commander of the Southwest Pacific Theater.

Donovan spent a considerable time in the Balkans. He met with anti-Nazi Germans to try and broker a peace deal to move forward with the occupation by the Western Allies, the establishment of a democratic Germany, and to cut the Soviets out for good. In China, he received permission for he and his men to carry out espionage activities. He also inspected OSS operations in Burma and met with Vyacheslav Molotov, a Russian and future Soviet politician and diplomat in Moscow to arrange for cooperation between the OSS and the People's Commissariat for Internal Affairs (NKVD). All in all, the OSS was most effective in the Balkans, China, Burma, and France, and it was all because of "Wild Bill" Donovan.

As Donovan made the OSS more and more powerful, turf wars started to heat up and his relationship with the British became strained. Not only did they have diametrically opposed styles and temperaments — the British accused the OSS of playing "cowboys and red Indians" — but both sides had very different outlooks on what the post-war order would look like.

For example, after a trip to India, Donovan filed a report on the "grinding poverty" of Britain's Colonial rule and concluded that it "stands in the way of any immediate economic development." Adm. Louis Mountbatten, top commander for Southeast Asia, India, and China, was of the opinion that Donovan was the typical red-blooded American man who was too loud and didn't follow orders. He, and most of the British establishment, of course, also wanted to keep the empire that had made them so rich and powerful. To Donovan, it was all a waste, an "impediment to democracy and economic development." Mountbatten was the least of his troubles, however.

Stewart Menzies, chief of MI6, absolutely could not stand Donovan and his OSS. He outright forbade the OSS to operate in the United Kingdom or to have any dealings with allied governments in exile in London. But Donovan had pull and Menzies finally relented. By May 1944, Donovan had about 11,000 American and foreign agents all around the world. He even had a network of Catholic priests across Europe who engaged in espionage on his behalf without the Pope's knowledge.

But the London station was the most impressive with 2,900 men and women working around the clock. There were tailors for specialized clothing, a photoengraving plant to print fake identifications and documents, and a special mill that supplied paper with watermarks that matched up exactly to continental Europe's. The OSS even began to make their own songs.

> *The brass doesn't know F all, the rest are snafu too,*
> *It takes a damned magician to know just what to do,*
> *An order here, an order there, it's anybody's guess.*
> *You can too be a fubar if you join the OSS.* [1]

Donovan enjoyed these little ditties. After all, he was the spymaster general and loved that his baby had come into its own and even had the tunes to show it.

Donovan also loved combat, and he made sure he got his fair share. On D-Day, June 6, 1944, he was part of the landing on Utah Beach. Of course, he had been strictly forbidden from participating because of his rank and his secrets, but Donovan couldn't have cared less — no one was going to talk him out of an adventure.

While going ashore, Donovan and his commander of covert operations in Europe, Col. David K. E. Bruce, were shot at by a German plane. "Falling on top of Donovan, Bruce inadvertently cut his boss in the throat with the edge of his steel helmet," wrote Evan Thomas. Donovan "bled profusely," but "sauntered inland" despite the blood spurting everywhere. Donovan was in his element.

Back in Washington, Donovan reported directly to Roosevelt on what he had observed in Normandy. "The success of the invasion showed that German naval and air forces were definitely no longer 'Big League' and that something has died in the German machine."

During the last year of the war, Donovan spent most of his time at Claridge's in London, where he had a command center that took up an entire floor of the five-star hotel. His days were

---

1 "Snafu" means "situation normal, all fucked up." "Fubar" is an acronym for "fucked up beyond all repair."

made up of handling intelligence. One of the most important and consequential initiatives he coordinated at that time was sending out teams of Allied nationals to identify Gestapo officers who had tortured them and were trying to get away with it by blending into the crowd.

The Germans surrendered to the Allies on May 7, 1945. The bombings on Hiroshima and Nagasaki came in August and then in September the Instrument of Surrender was signed in Tokyo, marking the end of World War II, the deadliest war in history ... but that is a story for another time.

In November, the Nuremberg Trials opened, and the Allies began trying Nazi Germany leadership for war crimes and the invasion of sovereign countries. It was Donovan's idea to hold the trials — he had been lobbying Roosevelt to arrange the prosecutions starting in October 1943. Donovan brought in 172 OSS officers to help the prosecution's team. They interviewed Auschwitz survivors, tracked down SS and Gestapo documents, and uncovered other sources of evidence. Donovan also released OSS funds to pay for the prosecution effort and chief US counsel Robert Jackson, a Supreme Court Justice, called him a "godsend" because the OSS had proven "vital for the prosecution team."

So important was the OSS to Jackson that he lobbied in person to Truman to let Donovan continue with his plans to set up a permanent intelligence agency. But his efforts were in vain. Donovan had made too many enemies in Washington and on September 20, 1945, the OSS was dissolved by the president. That next January, Truman presented Donovan with the Distinguished Service Medal and the spymaster returned to his life at the law practice. He attempted to write a history of American intelligence (he never finished it) and ran an unsuccessful campaign for the US Senate — but all he really wanted was a new intelligence agency.

Later that year, he got his wish, or a half-wish at least. Truman approved a "watered-down interdepartmental" Central Intelligence Group. Donovan was not impressed, calling it a "debating society," and Truman soon realized he was right. The Cold War was intensifying, and Truman recognized the extreme need for strong intelligence abroad. So, in February 1947, Truman asked Congress to approve a Central Intelligence Agency, and in private, Donovan lobbied for the passing of the National Security Act of 1947 to enable the creation of what is now known as the CIA.

Donovan wanted to head the CIA, and he had many supporters, but the president gave the job to Adm. Roscoe Hillenkoetter. Donovan begrudgingly accepted the appointment as head of a committee studying the country's fire departments, but all the while he was working behind the scenes. He recommended that Hillenkoetter hire Dulles and other OSS veterans, suggested the need for various covert operations, and shared with him the many contacts he had made over the years. Truman was furious at Donovan for working behind his back and called him an "intrusive meddler."

Donovan campaigned for Eisenhower in the 1952 presidential election and after his victory, Donovan thought for sure he would be named head of the CIA. Eisenhower appointed Allen Dulles instead. Eisenhower offered Donovan the position of Ambassador to France, but Donovan refused. The following year, he did accept the position of Ambassador to Thailand but only because the country was an important Cold War front. While there, he frequently traveled to Vietnam, which to him was clearly vulnerable to a Communist takeover. One source said he "was deeply involved in setting up CIA operations in Vietnam and throughout Southeast Asia." The Thai government gave him "glowing reviews," but he decided to resign in August 1954.

Donovan returned to the US and resumed his law practice and registered as a lobbyist for the Thai government. President Eisenhower appointed him chairman of the People to People Foundation, and he also worked with the International Rescue Committee, co-founded American Friends of Vietnam and raised money for Hungarian refugees.

He had begun experiencing symptoms of dementia and was hospitalized in 1957. Shortly before Donovan passed, he was visited by Eisenhower, who later told a friend that Donovan was "the last hero." Donovan died at the age of 76 from complications stemming from vascular dementia. The CIA cable says it all: "The man more responsible than any other for the existence of the Central Intelligence Agency has passed away."

General John J. Pershing decorates Brigadier General Douglas MacArthur with the Distinguished Service Cross in 1918. Major General Charles T. Menoher reads the citation as Colonel George E. Leach and Lieutenant |Colonel William J. Donovan (second from right) await their turn. (U.S. National Archives and Records Administration)

Gunnery Sergeant John Basilone

US ARMY
US MARINE CORPS

Medal of Honor
Navy Cross
Purple Heart

November 4, 1916–February 19, 1945 (28 years)

The only Marine to earn both the Medal of Honor and the Navy Cross in World War II. A hero of the battles at Guadalcanal and Iwo Jima, John Basilone held the line against wave after wave of Japanese forces.

"'Sarge, the Japs are coming,'" John Basilone heard over the phone, as recorded by Bruce Doorly in his *Raritan's Hero*. Basilone heard explosions and gunfire sounding off as the voice spoke to him with terror in his voice. "'Thousands of them, my God! They just keep coming, Sarge, they just keep coming.'" Then, silence — the phone went dead. Basilone and the 7th Marines, 1st Marine Division, were posted on the Solomon Islands — an alien environment and as miserable a field of battle as one could imagine, and worse yet, legions of fearless Japanese were headed for their position. In the coming moments Americans would face the Japanese in man-to-man combat for the first time, and John Basilone would be there to prove through sweat and blood that American troops could hand Imperial Japan their first land defeat by westerners in a half-century.

America would be floored by the stories that trickled back of the handsome, young Basilone and his exploits in the Pacific Theatre. But just how did this 25-year-old from the east coast compete with, and ultimately beat, the battle-hardened Japanese? His story began in Buffalo, New York, where he was born into a big, tight-knit Italian American family, the sixth of 10 children. Soon after they moved to Raritan Town, New Jersey, where he attended the Saint Bernard Parochial School. However, the confines of school bored him; he was much more interested in living his life in the wider world than being penned in a classroom. So, before his first semester at high school and at the tender age of 15, he decided to drop out. He worked as a golf caddy for a brief while before deciding to enlist in the Army in 1934, one year after the beginning of the Nazi crimes against the Jewish people, crimes that would further fuel the flames of World War II.

He was first assigned to the 16th Infantry, after which he was discharged. He waited a day, then reenlisted and joined the 31st Infantry. The 31st Infantry was originally formed in 1916 and was always a unique unit in that it spent the majority of its time on non-American soil; this would only serve to further tantalize Basilone's taste for adventure. But, after three years in Manila, he was released from active duty — to his disappointment. He returned home and began working as a truck driver for a few years, yet dreams of Manila always seemed to come back to him. He decided his best plan of action for getting there was to join the Marines.

He did exactly that, becoming a Marine in 1940. After two years served at various posts in the eastern US and Guantanamo Bay, Cuba, he and nearly 20,000 Marines set off to the Solomon Islands — needless to say, the bizarre landscape would be a rude awakening to many of the Marines. World War II veteran and author Robert Leckie, in his book *Challenge for the Pacific,* quoted a local "coast watcher," Martin Clemens, describing the Guadalcanal as such: "She was a poisonous morass. Crocodiles hid in her creeks or patrolled her turgid backwaters. Her jungles were alive with slithering, crawling, scuttling things; with giant lizards that barked like dogs, with huge, red furry spiders, with centipedes and leeches and scorpions, with rats and bats and fiddler crabs and one big species of land-crab which moved through the bush with all the stealth of a steamroller."

The Marines — including Basilone and his 7th Marines, 1st Marine Division — would not have to wait long for fighting to break out in the hostile jungles of Guadalcanal. American forces attempted to probe their Japanese counterparts, but what started as a "probe" soon became a three-day brawl that would leave sixty Marines dead and a hundred wounded. That was nothing compared to the brutal Battle for Henderson Field, the knock-down, drag-out fight that would see Basilone make history with his battlefield heroics.

It was October 24, 1942, and the malevolent terrain and weather seemed aligned against them. But that was merely a preamble: two military giants of roughly similar force were about to clash on the Guadalcanal, and whoever scored a victory here would gain a leading position in the war. The battle would be fought on land, sea, and air; everything hung in the balance, and the weight of the moment was not lost on John Basilone.

A thousand Marines were stretched thin along a mile and a half, overwhelmed and under threat of being overtaken. To say they were all exhausted would be an understatement; many of the men were suffering from malaria, but there was to be no rest or recourse. At midnight, hundreds of screaming troops from the fearsome Sendai Division hurled grenades and rained machine gun and mortar fire on Basilone's unit. They threw themselves over the barbed-wire fence protecting the field and formed human bridges so that their fellow soldiers could easily cross. Before the war, an ignorant America had seen Japan as a quaint island nation on the other side of the world. As the Japanese attacked on this October day without fear or mercy, a truer image came to life: this was a nation of timeless martial tradition, a nation that had humiliated the much vaster Russian and Chinese empires. They were proving their superiority in the art of war.

With the incredible wave of warriors launched at them, war cries of "Blood for the Emperor!" cutting through the pouring rain, Basilone realized it was up to him to raise up morale and keep his men fighting and firing.

"Basilone was everywhere at once, clearing jams, calming nervous gunners, replacing parts and repositioning guns ... he became the glue that bound Company C together," recalled Eric Hammel in his article "October on Guadalcanal." The barbed wire having already failed, Basilone told his men to let the enemy get within fifty yards before unleashing hell upon them.

"The noise was terrific and I could see the Japs jumping as they were smacked by our bullets," *Raritan's Hero* quoted Basilone saying. "One thing you've got to give the Japanese, they were not afraid to die, and believe me, they did." That first charge would only be the tip of the iceberg: Basilone was in charge of two sections of machine guns and his unit fought for two days straight in torrential rain and bottomless mud until only Basilone and two other men were left alive. The three men had to keep fighting. The battle was still raging and the Japanese had cut off their supply lines, their ammunition quickly draining to nothing. Basilone needed to figure out a way to get more ammo, or they'd all die.

What he did next would win him the military's highest award for extraordinary valor. Basilone fought fiercely without rest, food, or water until he had penetrated hostile ground. He was able to resupply the heavy machine gunners with desperately needed materials, then sent an extra gun into position and maintained a nonstop, brutal fire against the incoming enemy troops. Since their conception, machine gunners have always had a special place in the military: they are focused warriors wielding an impossibly destructive weapon, exceptional at both killing en masse and at being killed themselves. Basilone exemplified this portrait of the machine gunner, restoring and taking over another machine gun which he used to sustain the defensive line until support arrived.

The restocked supplies didn't take long to run out again. Basilone's equipment was whittled down to only a pistol and a machete. At this point most men would try to retreat — not Basilone. He used all he had and held off the Japanese forces, "thereby contributing in large measure to the virtual annihilation of a Japanese regiment" as his Medal of Honor citation states.

In the end, reduced to his bare feet and exhausted to the core, Basilone finally earned a moment of respite. His line had held. The battlefield was strewn with appalling numbers of casualties, particularly for the attackers, with at least 38 Japanese dead confined to Basilone. Basilone's men credited him with inspiring them and restoring in them the will to keep fighting.

In his speech at the Medal of Honor ceremony, he said, "Only part of this medal belongs to me. ... Pieces of it belong to the boys who are still on Guadalcanal." He returned to the United States in 1943 and his arrival was highly publicized; he was returning home a hero. Raritan Town held a parade in his honor that drew a crowd of thousands of people, including politicians, celebrities, and the national media. The parade even made national news in *LIFE* magazine and *Fox Movietone News*.

Basilone participated in war bond tours for a time, traveling around the country raising money for the war effort. But like many military men, "normal life" made him uneasy, and he began to feel out of place. He requested to return to the front lines, but the Marine Corps denied his request, telling him he wasn't ready — he needed more time at home. They offered him a commission. He turned it down. They offered him an assignment as an instructor; he turned that down too. He wanted to return to the operating forces. "I ain't no officer, and I ain't no museum piece," Basilone said. "I belong back with my outfit."

His request was eventually approved, and he went to Camp Pendleton in California for training, a seemingly ordinary event that would greatly change his life. While stationed at Camp Pendleton he met the love of his life and future wife, Lena Mae Riggi, who was a sergeant in the Marine Corps Women's Reserve. They were married soon after, on July 10, 1944, in Oceanside, California, and had their honeymoon at an onion farm close to Portland, Oregon.

His training ended, he was assigned to C Company, 1st Battalion, 27th Marine Regiment, 5th Marine Division. Then came the invasion of Iwo Jima on February 19, 1945.

The Japanese had been preparing for this battle for months. James Bradley described in *Flags of Our Fathers* that they had "the most ingenious fortress in the history of warfare ... Kuribayashi transformed Iwo Jima into the equivalent of one huge blockhouse." The Japanese had built a city underground that could house 20,000 Japanese soldiers, all prepared to die.

Employing ingenious mining engineers, the Japanese had constructed a system of caves, tunnels, underground meeting rooms, and various communication centers. The subterranean city had multiple levels, some that reached a depth of 75 feet. So sophisticated were the tunnels that there was even electricity in some areas — the rest used fuel lamps. The entrances of the tunnels were armed with a multitude of well-hidden blockhouses reinforced with steel and concrete; knowing where to fire at them proved extremely difficult.

On the morning of the attack, the bombardment was so heavy that the island blurred under a cloud of grey, obscuring the view. On the shore, the Japanese concentrated all their fire on the disembarking Marines, mowing down the American troops with ease. Basilone was serving as machine gun section leader on Red Beach II when his unit's position became untenable. He began to cautiously make his way around the flank of the Japanese positions until he found himself on top of one of their blockhouses and began to rain a fury of grenades and demolitions on them, single-handedly wiping out an entire garrison and its strong point.

He moved on to the next challenge. He fought himself through to Airfield Number 1 to get to the aid of a Marine tank trapped in a Japanese minefield and under extreme mortar and artillery fire. He got behind the wheel of the tank and carefully guided the heavy machine to safety. This was to be his last heroic act: as he was guiding the tank across the airfield, mortar shrapnel hit him and several other men who were killed instantly.

Basilone held on as long as he could. The explosion had ripped through his insides and his intestines were exposed. Waiting for a medic, he held his hands over the enormous wound as blood gushed out. The doctor told him that his only chance of survival was to get him to a hospital ship. Unfortunately, there were no more ships coming in or going out at that time; it was a chaos of ships, wreckage, and an ocean of bodies. The medic gave Basilone a shot of morphine to ease the pain. He held on to life for about 30 more minutes. A machine gunner to his final moments, his reported last words, printed in the *New York Times*, were "All right, you guys, let's go on in there and set up these guns for firing."

The Americans were victorious in the end, but the brutal and chaotic battle came with a terrible price. The Navy Department Library states that "the 36-day assault resulted in more than 26,000 American casualties, including 6,800 dead."

Basilone's death was in no way in vain however — not by a long shot. Many of the men recalled that his death renewed the Marines motivation to keep on going. His actions helped his fellow Marines get off the landing beach and penetrate the enemy defensive lines during the most deadly stages of the invasion. For his exceptional bravery he was posthumously awarded the Navy Cross.

His citation summarizes justly his actions of that fateful day: "Stouthearted and indomitable, Gunnery Sgt. Basilone, by his intrepid initiative, outstanding skill, and valiant spirit of self-sacrifice in the face of the fanatic opposition, contributed materially to the advance of his company during the early critical period of the assault, and his unwavering devotion to duty throughout the bitter conflict was an inspiration to his comrades."

He was buried at Arlington National Cemetery in Virginia. His widow, Lena Basilone, never remarried. She died at the age of 86 and was buried still wearing her wedding ring.

John Basilone receiving the Medal of Honor in 1943. (US Marine Corps)

Staff Sergeant Clifford Chester Sims

US ARMY

Medal of Honor
Purple Heart

June 18, 1942–February 21, 1968 (25 years old)

War makes many kinds of heroes out of men. One of the most treasured and tragic are those that, having everything to go back home to, willingly give up their life to save their fellow soldiers. No questions asked, no second thoughts. This is the story of Clifford Chester Sims.

Born Clifford Pittman in Port St. Joe, a city in the Florida panhandle, Clifford Sims was orphaned early in life and sent to live with his stepfather's relatives. He came to find out, however, that his was one mouth too many for them to handle. So, not wanting to be a burden, he left in the middle of the night and went to live in an abandoned school bus in Panama City, Florida. This would be where he slept and scrounged for whatever food he could find. Years later, as destiny would have it, he would spend his honeymoon with the girl of his dreams in a hotel not far from that same school bus.

"At the time, at a nearby school, they would deliver the morning's milk and donuts at the rear where the kitchen was, while the school wasn't open yet," Sims's widow, Mary Sims-Parker, told the *Tennessean* in an interview. "He would go there and get some milk and donuts. That's how he ate." Sims fully survived off the kindness of strangers during those times. He would go into stores where shopkeepers would turn a blind eye while he took what he needed to survive. And despite all the hardship, Clifford still made it to school as much as possible. A sixth-grade teacher let him come to class, no matter what. "Whenever you can, come to school, I don't care if you're late or if you're clean, you come on to school and stay as long as you can, whenever you can."

At the age of 13 he was adopted by a loving couple — James and Irene Sims. And so it was that Clifford Pittman became Clifford Sims. With his new name, he went to George Washington High School where he fell madly in love with a young woman named Mary. Shortly after graduating, in September of 1961, Sims joined the Army. On Christmas Day of that same year, he and Mary were wed, and they had a quiet honeymoon in a hotel to celebrate before he went off to become a soldier.

He completed his basic training in Fort Jackson, South Carolina, and Airborne School at Fort Benning, Georgia. He was then sent to the 82nd Airborne Division at Fort Bragg in North Carolina. In August of 1967, Sims moved to Fort Campbell, Kentucky, and this is where he became a part of the infamous combat unit the Delta Raiders. The Raiders were known, and still are, for their extraordinary spirit. Much of this had to do with the unorthodox way this group was formed and trained. This was a combat unit organized from many different specialties (even cooks), and after eight weeks of training they were sent to fight in the deadly Tet Offensive. The intensive training and camaraderie turned the young men into a tight-knit unit that was more than willing to fight and die for one another.

The Raiders were composed of three battalions, and on February 21, 1968, all three were on a search and destroy mission outside of the city of Hue in central Vietnam. Sims, now serving as squad leader with Company D, was given a mission: attack a fortified enemy position deep in hostile jungle.

Sims was leading his squad through the danger-drenched jungle when heavy fire erupted around them. He positioned his squad within the wood line and proceeded to marshal a devastating attack against the Viet Cong, which had pinned down the 1st Platoon and was doing everything in their power to overrun it.

Sims radiated leadership, and that day his adept management was what allowed the 1st Platoon to unfurl themselves from the grip of enemy fire, giving them back the freedom of movement to rejoin the fight. With that achieved, Sims moved his squad to a position where they could provide cover for the company command group as well as reconnect with the 3rd Platoon, now under heavy enemy pressure.

Suddenly, he saw something that made his stomach sink. A brick structure stocked full of ammunition was on fire, and this explosive hazard threatened to vaporize everyone in the vicinity. Sims took immediate action to get his squad out of Dodge. He succeeded, saving his men yet again.

The squad then cautiously continued through the dense woods. With Sims leading the way, they approached a bunker. Knowing the dangers that could lie within, he took it upon himself to make sure it was safe and empty. As he moved inside, his heart stopped cold. He had heard what he had come to know as the unmistakable noise of a booby trap being triggered right in front of him. Sims screamed a warning to his men, and then unhesitatingly launched himself onto the device as it exploded, his body taking the full and deadly impact of the vicious blast. He was killed instantly. He had protected his men at the cost of his own life.

1st Lt. Cleo Hogan was in command of the Raiders and wrote the main eyewitness account of Sims's actions on that fateful day. "Realizing that he was so close," Hogan wrote, "and that the lives of his men were in extreme danger, [Sims] violently yelled, 'Get back! Get back!' and then threw himself on the device, equal to twice the force of a fragmentation grenade ... Sims saved the lives of at least three of his squad and two of the company headquarters by absorbing the shock of the blast himself." Each and every man of the 2nd Squad owes his life to Staff Sergeant Clifford C. Sims. He was 25 years old and newly married — a bright future stretched in front of him — but he still made the ultimate sacrifice.

"It is because of Americans like him that we enjoy the liberties that we do today," said Rear Adm. LeRoy Collins Jr., US Navy Reserve. Sims was buried in the Barrancas National Cemetery in Pensacola, Florida.

Decades later, Mary's daughter found a website of the former Raiders. Mary connected with former platoon sergeant, George Parker, who knew Sims well and deeply admired him. Mary and Parker hit it off right away and ended up getting married. George Parker had won a Silver Star during the war and Mary hung the citation on the wall of their home right next to Sims's Medal of Honor citation. "I've got heroes around here," she said.

Mary Parker examines the remains of the flower she wore when she received the Medal of Honor on behalf of her first husband, Sgt. Clifford Sims. (Philip Grey for *The Leaf Chronicle*, February 15, 2015)

Dieter Dengler with his mother, 1966. (*Redwood City Tribune*, September 14, 1966)

Lieutenant Dieter Dengler

US AIR FORCE
US NAVY

Navy Cross
Distinguished Flying Cross
Bronze Star
Purple Heart
Air Medal
Navy Unit Commendation
Prisoner of War Medal

May 22, 1938–February 7, 2001 (62 years)

Dieter Dengler is a survivor, an author, and a pilot. Having lived through torture most people could never imagine, Dengler's legendary escape from Viet Cong imprisonment stands as a monolithic testament to the power of mankind's resilience, even in our darkest hours.

World War II had struck Europe like a hurricane of death, and even after the war had ended, incalculable scars remained. The small town of Wildberg, nestled in Germany's Black Forest region, bore many of these scars: craters in the streets, bullet holes in the buildings, and broken families. Dieter Dengler had never known his father, who had been drafted into the army in 1939 and killed on the Eastern Front during the disastrous (for the Axis) winter of 1943–44. The extreme poverty was a constant pressure, but though the war had made their family smaller, their familial bonds grew stronger in spite of the hardship. Dieter, his mother, and brothers would look after each other with a passion that only a struggling family can muster.

The Dengler boys would go into bombed-out buildings to strip the walls of wallpaper and bring it back home to boil for the meager nutrients in the wheat-based wallpaper paste. When the small Moroccan community who lived in the area slaughtered sheep for meals, Dieter would sneak over to scrounge the discarded scraps for dinner. Even with the suffocating poverty that surrounded him, Dieter Dengler was not a boy without dreams: there was always the dream of flying. During World War II, he'd witnessed an Allied fighter plane blasting its guns as it buzzed past a window young Dieter was peeping out of. That was the moment Dengler knew he would one day become a pilot.

After seeing an advertisement in an American magazine urging young men to become pilots, he salvaged and sold scrap metal until he'd earned enough to make the trip across the Atlantic. It took years of work to finally step into the cockpit: peeling potatoes, working as a mechanist and gunsmith, going to college, but he finally achieved the dream. In 1965, his squadron joined the carrier USS *Ranger*, and in December they set sail for the coast of Vietnam.

It was February 1, 1966, and four aircraft tore through smoke-filled skies above a landscape of burning fields. Running into low-visibility smoke this far behind enemy lines was a bad omen, and thunderstorms had already forced Dengler — now lieutenant, junior grade — and the other pilots to divert to their secondary target: a two-and-a-half-hour flight deep into hostile territory. Their duty today was to complete an air interdiction mission, the bread and butter of virtually every air force that ever was. Air interdiction involves using tactical bombing and strafing to delay, disrupt, or hinder the enemy's ability to engage friendly forces, often by destroying supplies or the ability to resupply.

The target — a truck convoy on a road intersection west of Mu Gia Pass, Laos — was just now coming into focus from Dengler's cockpit. But, as the convoy came into view, all pilots lost sight of one another, swallowed up in the low visibility of the ashes springing from burning fields below. There was no turning back now. The target was disappearing underneath his plane. Dengler — as comfortable in his Douglas A-1 Skyraider as in any car — rolled the airplane over on its back so that the ground appeared above him in the cockpit. As he rolled around to keep his eyes on the prize, an explosive rocked his aircraft — hard.

"Just as I was inverted there was a large explosion off my right side, half my wing was gone. I remember the brightness of it was like lightning striking," Dengler recalled in his interview for Werner Herzog's 1997 documentary *Little Dieter Needs to Fly*. The Skyraider — rugged as it was — didn't take the hit gracefully and started its violent tumble toward certain doom. Dengler flashed into action, dropping his external fuel tanks to reduce drag and weight, increasing his maneuverability. Pumped full of adrenaline and with his brain working overtime, his eyes quickly found a place to belly his airplane in the valley and avoid a deadly impact with a tree. But the storm hadn't yet passed — far from it.

"But then more explosions went off over my right wing — *boom boom boom* — I decided maybe I can fly this airplane and glide it over this ridge but there was a lot of trees like I said." An enormous tree appeared right in front of him, but just before he hit it, he pulled the plane to the right as fast as he could. An impact rocked his left wing, snapping a thick tree in half. "Then the entire tail — the rudder, the horizontal stabilizer — everything just tumbled by."

Going 300 miles per hour and watching your vehicle disintegrate around you would be the breaking point for most people. Dengler didn't have time to break — he had to survive. As the ground pulled closer by the millisecond, the glass around his cockpit grew cracks as if in slow motion, before the immense physical forces at work tore it off like it was a flimsy baseball cap. The airplane started to cartwheel. Then, darkness.

Afterward, when his squadron realized that he had been downed, they remained confident that he would be rescued. Time would eventually prove them right, but only after Dengler had made an unthinkable odyssey through the darkest places of human experience.

The last thing Dengler remembered from the crash was the airplane starting to cartwheel. "Then I must've passed out. Maybe a minute later I was back, I was laying maybe a hundred feet from the airplane, dust was still in the air, it was very quiet." For a man that was just shaken, stirred, and tossed a hundred feet, Dengler remained remarkably clear-minded. Taking his survival radio in his hand, he smashed it into scrap and stashed away most of his other survival equipment to keep hostile search parties from finding it. For a pilot trying to hit a target, the mountains, jungle, and narrow river valleys of Laos weren't ideal; for a crashed pilot trying to hide out until rescue, they were perfect.

For two days, Dengler managed to survive under the cover of the thick jungle canopy. But while Dieter Dengler is a hero down to his core, he was also only a man, and after two days the inevitable happened: He made a mistake. "I did the unforgivable," Dengler stated matter-of-factly in his interview on *Little Dieter Needs to Fly*. "I crossed a small clearing."

After coming out of the thick jungle, likely sleep-deprived and hungry to keep moving toward safety, Dengler came to a small trail. He did his due diligence, looking both ways for any signs of enemy movement, and seeing nothing he made a break for the other side.

"Stop," came a voice, speaking in Laotian. Dengler turned to his right to see two sets of eyes and two gun barrels greeting him. Dengler's arms shot in the air in surrender and immediately six other men rushed him, stripping and disarming him on the spot.

"And then we started to run." The rest of the day was spent running. Every so often Dengler would collapse, partly from exhaustion but also from a wound on his left leg sustained in the crash. After collapsing, the Laotians would massage his leg, give him some water, then force him up again to continue the marathon. As the day ended, they reached a thick canopy where no American airplanes would be able to spot them. Now, grabbing each of Dengler's limbs, they would rope and stake him to the ground until he was completely immobile and spread-eagled on the hard earth. That would be the sleeping arrangement Dengler would get used to in the days to come.

During this period, Dengler would fall asleep to dreams of trying to fly back to his home in Germany, only to find all the planes completely smashed. He waited desperately for them to be fixed by some miraculous force, but they never were, and these dreams — these nightmares — would crush the hope out of him while he slept. "... I was glad when I finally woke up, bitten by mosquitos." Unfortunately for Dieter Dengler, the worst was yet to come.

Upon waking up, Dengler would have extreme difficulty seeing out of his swollen, bloody face; at night, the mosquitos had been all too happy to gorge themselves on the undefended veins of this imprisoned man and they'd left his face in such poor shape he was nearly blind. This cycle of walking, getting staked to the ground and getting eaten alive by mosquitos continued for days before Dengler was given a moment to retaliate; but that moment finally came.

Subtly placed in the tobacco pouch of one of his captors, the glint of a survival mirror caught Dengler's eye. He waited until darkness to hatch the first step of his plan. While the group traveled at night, the men would switch their walking procedure, linking up with one another — Dengler included — to make sure he couldn't get away. This method of travel put Dengler pressed right up against the man with the survival mirror. His plan succeeded, and before getting staked down for a few hours of "sleep," Dengler would have a mirror to his name and a sliver of hope to keep him going.

It was freezing that night in the lofty mountains of Laos, and the cold fingers of the night air were gripped tightly around Dengler. This particular evening, he and his captors had the pleasure of staying in a small hut. Dengler was staked down and naked in the usual way; on his left and right were two armed guards sleeping close enough that any movement Dengler made would most likely wake them. Even though it was the frigid cold that had awoken Dengler, he took the chance he was given; now would be his best shot to escape. Dengler freed himself starting at his feet and working his way up; kicking his legs upward several times, he loosened his bindings before he carefully undid the ropes constricting his arms.

The bindings were loose — loose enough to make an escape. He rocked himself off the sleeping platform, his feet nearly feeling the touch of the ground below.... Roosters, pigs, dogs — what sounded like a whole barn full of animals — chose that moment to come to life. Terror came over him and he jerked back into the position next to the guards, living on a prayer that his undone ties wouldn't be noticed by the guards. Not only did they fail to notice, but the uproar caused by the animals didn't cause the snoring guards to so much as twitch. Dengler rocked himself back to a standing position— this time without triggering the alarm roosters — and escaped into the darkness of the jungle and the sweet arms of freedom.

Towering over the landscape and bathed in moonlight was a mountain Dengler had seen often while walking. He had decided it would make the perfect location to signal for help. What he didn't realize was that it was a karst mountain: crevice-filled, viciously sharp monsters of rock that don't take kindly to being climbed. After finally reaching the peak, Dengler spent a day signaling for rescue — none came. The only thing that did come was the blasting heat of the sun, an unwelcome companion even after so many cold nights. With no planes in sight and delirium starting to kick in, Dengler descended from the mountain, giving up on rescue and instead focusing on survival. And to survive, he would need water. His guards knew that too.

As soon as he began to drink from a nearby spring the guards pounced on him, and his brief stint at freedom was cut short. After his escape attempt, the real torture began. "I had escaped from them, [and] they wanted to get even." His captors hung him upside down by his ankles, placing a nest of ants over his face until the pain of the biting swarm made Dengler lose consciousness. During nights, he was suspended in a freezing well such that falling asleep might drown him.

On one occasion he was dragged by a water buffalo through a village — to the entertainment of his guards — as they encouraged the animal onward with a whip. Eventually, Pathet Lao officials tried to make Dengler sign a document condemning the US, and after he made it clear that would never happen, he was tortured by inserting tiny wedges of bamboo under his fingernails and into the wounds on his body which grew and festered. "They were always thinking of something new to do to me," Dengler recounted.

After weeks of soul-crushing torture, Dengler was handed over to the Vietnamese. As Dengler was marched through a village, a man stole Dengler's engagement ring off his finger. After he made the guards aware of the theft, they found the culprit, chopped off his finger with a machete and handed the ring back to Dengler. "I realized right there and then that you don't fool around with the Viet Cong," he said.

After a period of travel, Dengler arrived at a prison camp near the village of Par Kung where he met six other imprisoned POWs. Three of the prisoners — Phisit, Prasit Promsuwan and Prasit Thanee — were Thai civilians, taken by the Viet Cong for their involvement with Air America, an organization owned by the CIA. One Chinese man, To, was there as well, and two other Americans, Eugene DeBruin and Duane Martin.

Dengler had hoped to see other pilots; what he found were victims. The first prisoner he saw was carrying his intestines in his hands. Another had no teeth and was in so much pain that he begged them to knock him out with a rock. All of them had been languishing in prison for two years.

"I realized that was how I would look in six months. I had to escape."

The day Dengler entered the prison camp was the day his escape plan started to take shape in his mind, and it began with the other prisoners. In no uncertain terms, he told them that he was going to escape, and he invited them to escape together. Their response: wait until the monsoon season. A short time after Dengler arrived, all the prisoners were moved to a different camp at Hoi Het, ten miles away. It was then that a heated argument erupted among the prisoners with Dengler, Prasit, and Martin making the case for escape and the other prisoners, particularly Phisit, initially opposing them.

Food — or lack of it — turned up the heat and desperation in the prison camp even further. Given just a single handful of rice to share between them, a deep hunger began to take hold. Resentment simmered to a boil. Sometimes, after the guards hunted deer, the prisoners would receive the grass pulled out of the animal's stomach as a meal. For "treats," they would occasionally catch an unsuspecting snake that hung around the latrine, or they'd skewer rats with pieces of sharpened bamboo. At night the men would be handcuffed and shackled together to wooden foot blocks. Chronic dysentery was the norm, and they were made to lie in their excrement until morning.

The discussions and arguments among the prisoners came to an abrupt end several months later. While the guards thought they were alone, one of the Thai prisoners caught them speaking about a plan they'd been cooking up. You see, it wasn't just the POWs who were starving: the guards were starving too, and this backwater assignment looking after shit-covered prisoners was starting to look like a bad deal. What the Thai prisoner overheard was a murder. Why not murder their captives and make it look like they'd tried to escape? This revelation convinced the previously begrudging men to quickly make up their minds. The date was set; they would escape or die trying.

The escape plan went like this: Dengler, Martin, and De-Bruin would go outside when the guards were eating, seize their weaponry and pass it back down to the others. After that, they'd take over the camp by force and signal the C-130 Hercules that they knew made nightly flights over the vicinity. "There were two minutes and twenty seconds in the day when I could strike." And that was all the time Dengler would have to release the rest of the prisoners from their handcuffs.

It was June 29, 1966, and for the guards, it was a day like any other. But while they were enjoying their meal, the prisoners slipped out of their restraints and stole the guards' weapons. Having been so powerless for so long, getting their hands on M1 rifles, Chinese automatic rifles, an American carbine, and an early version of the AK-47 automatic rifle must have felt exhilarating.

For his part, Dengler took the AK-47. Shackles on the ground and gun in hand, Dengler went outside first, followed by Martin. They crept to the guard hut to seize a remaining M1, but as they did the guards noticed the breakout and made a mad rush toward Dengler. Shots rang out and three bodies hit the floor. None of them Dengler. Another guard reached for his rifle; Phisit stopped him with gunfire of his own.

Two guards fled the scene, at least one of them wounded, presumably to get backup. From there, the seven prisoners split up into three groups to make them tougher to catch. Unfortunately, their plan hit a road bump. DeBruin was meant to go with Dengler and Martin, but To, the Chinese man, had a piping hot fever and couldn't keep up. Because of this, DeBruin stayed with To while Dengler and Martin went on ahead. They headed toward the banks of the Mekong River with the hopes it would sweep them out of Thailand.

But it was out of the frying pan and into the fire. Quickly the mens' feet resembled mangled stumps more than anything else, brutalized from the trek through dense jungle. They happened across the sole of an old tennis shoe which they cherished dearly, strapping it to one foot for a brief moment of respite before handing it over to the other man. With a single sole and a dream of freedom they were able to persevere to a fast-flowing river. "It was the highway to freedom," said Dengler. "We knew it would flow into the Mekong River, which would take us over the border into Thailand and to safety."

After fashioning a makeshift raft, they piled on, held tight, and prayed for dear life. The vicious rapids constantly made threats upon their lives, and the nights spent tied to a tree amid constant, torrential water made for poor sleep. When the sun peeked over the horizon, they would be greeted by mud and hundreds of leeches.

Time passed, and the Mekong never materialized. The awful realization dawned on them that the river had spun them in a circle. While they had managed to pass by a few villages undetected, the incessant, pounding rain was beating them into submission and they decided to find shelter in an abandoned settlement. Starvation was knocking on their door now; time was running out.

That night, they tried to create a fire signal, but their energy reserves were exhausted and the task of starting a fire with nothing but bamboo demanded a strength that had been strangled out of them. But Dengler, always resourceful, found a carbine cartridge that had been thrown out, used the powder to enhance the tinder and from that, created fire. Using torches, they went about signaling an SOS, and to their dumbfounded amazement their cry for help was answered: a C-130 Hercules airplane managed to spot them, dropping flares and circling overhead. Dengler and Martin went to sleep with high hopes. But they woke up to fog, drizzle, and absolutely no rescue in sight.

Starvation, malaria, and dashed hopes ate away at Martin in particular. Desperation began to overshadow commonsense survival. They would approach a nearby village to steal food, said Martin. And even though Dengler thought the plan was too dangerous, Martin wasn't going to budge, so they both went together to try and get their hands on something — anything — to eat. On their approach they spotted a little boy playing with a dog. The boy saw them too.

"American!" the boy called out, running into the village. Within seconds a villager appeared before them. Weak and skeletal, they knelt down in submission, hoping to get any scraps of food they could, even if it meant begging.

The first swing of the villager's machete struck Martin in the leg. The man swung a second time, taking off his head. Dengler scrambled onto his feet and lunged for the man, who turned and ran into the village for help.

"I reached for the rubber sole from his foot, grabbed it and ran. From that moment on, all my motions became mechanical. I couldn't care less if I lived or died." This tragedy, following months of torture, sank Dengler into the darkest state of his life. More zombie than human, Dengler drifted between hallucinations and reality, between life and death. "I was just crawling along," he said. "Then I had a vision: these enormous doors opened up. Lots of horses came galloping out. They were not driven by death, but by angels. Death didn't want me."

Dengler continued to avoid the search parties on the hunt for him, returning to the abandoned village where they had signaled the C-130. That night another C-130 flew overhead, and Dengler was going to make damn sure they didn't miss him this time. He set the entire village ablaze and the crew of the airplane threw down flares in response. Another morning came; no rescue materialized. At this point Dengler was willing to try anything. Finding a parachute hanging on a bush, he decided that would be the signal that worked where fire had failed. The day was July 20, 1966, 23 days after escaping from the POW camp. It was a day Dengler would never forget.

Eugene Deatrick, the pilot of the lead plane in a Skyraider

squadron, was flying up the river when he spotted a white flash while turning at the river's bend. Coming back around to investigate, he saw a man waving something white. Deatrick was told there were no known downed pilots in the area, but he persisted. The man of course was Dieter Dengler, and a plane had finally come to rescue him, proving his nightmares of broken planes false. He had wished for a miracle to happen, and after fighting and suffering day-in and day-out, that miracle had finally come true.

"If God put me on the earth for one reason," Deatrick said in *Hero Found: The Greatest POW Escape of the Vietnam War*, "it was to find Dieter over there in the jungle." As it happened, Deatrick had been pushed off schedule when he spotted Dengler. Had he been on schedule, the world may never have gotten to know the legendary story of the German American who just wanted to fly and ended up in hell.

The night Dengler was brought back to the Navy, he was tormented by night terrors. After much struggling, his friends put him to sleep in the cockpit of an airplane, surrounded by pillows. "It was the only place I felt safe," he said in *Little Dieter Needs to Fly*. Dengler's lifelong fascination with airplanes and aviation continued for the remainder of his life, and he continued to fly nearly until his death in February 2001.

Eugene Deatrick and Dieter Dengler, NAS Miramar, 1968. (US Navy)

Michael A. Monsoor. (*Hawaii Tribune Herald*, November 15, 2009)

Master-at-Arms Petty Officer Second Class Michael A. Monsoor

US NAVY

Medal of Honor
Silver Star
Bronze Star
Purple Heart

April 5, 1981–September 29, 2006 (25 years)

Michael Monsoor conquered his asthma to join the Navy SEALs. After 11 operations, where he routinely took it upon himself to become the center of the enemy's attention, he made the ultimate sacrifice for his fellow soldiers in a final act of heroism that will never be forgotten.

Petty Officer Monsoor held his machine gun steadily in his hands; he was part of an elite three-man team of Navy SEALs who were providing security to the Iraqi Army Brigade on May 9, 2006. The SEALs were working as a tactical overwatch element, a small military unit supporting another friendly unit — usually from a vantage point — providing firepower and intelligence to those they protect. But this was the dangerous part; it was time to extract. The men made their way toward the extraction point, hoping that the insurgent forces in the area wouldn't jump them. It didn't work out that way — the nearby allied Iraqi troops came under deadly-effective fire from automatic weapons. One SEAL soldier, doing his best to protect his allies, took a bullet and was badly wounded.

Immediately, Monsoor catapulted into the action, putting himself in the sights of heavy enemy weaponry and hosing down enemy positions with a barrage of bullets. The insurgents reeled back from the suppressive fire, and Monsoor fought with tooth and claw to reach his downed brother-in-arms in the hostile terrain of the Arabian Peninsula. One hand tightly gripped his machine gun and continued to spray hot lead at those who sought to kill him, and the other held onto the wounded SEAL.

Against all odds, Monsoor was able to keep the heads of the terrorist forces down for fear of their lives while another man rushed in to provide desperate medical attention to the damaged leg of their brother. Triage complete, Monsoor loaded his companion into the back of the extraction vehicle, turned around, and jumped back into the ensuing firefight. Monsoor's heroism did not go unnoticed, earning him a Silver Star, but even beyond that, everyone who witnessed this man's unshakable dedication to his fellow soldiers that day knew he was destined for a lifetime of great deeds on the field of battle.

Michael Monsoor was born in Long Beach, California, in 1981, and those who knew him from school may have doubted his dreams of joining the armed forces ... but Monsoor never doubted himself. Asthma afflicted Monsoor as a child, inflaming his lungs and knocking him out of consideration for high-impact sports, let alone serving the pursuit of American freedom overseas. But Monsoor's father had been a Marine, and he would fight fate till the end to achieve his dreams of becoming a warrior as his father had been.

From a young age, Monsoor never let his asthma get in his way. In friendly competition with his siblings, he raced across his family's swimming pool, back and forth, time after time, until he'd strengthened his lungs to the point where he'd conquered his asthma.

Monsoor was described as a "quiet professional" by those who knew him, and that kind of hard-eyed determination allowed him to go on to complete basic training and graduate with Class 250 from Basic Underwater Demolition/SEAL training as a top performer. After completing numerous advanced SEAL training courses, from California to Alaska, he had achieved what before had only been a dream: he was assigned to the prestigious Delta Platoon, SEAL Team 3.

During his first five months, he was deployed with legendary SEALs Jocko Willink and Chris Kyle, often taking the lead position to protect the platoon from frontal assaults in the withering 100-plus-degree Iraqi heat.

It was on September 26, 2006, that Michael Monsoor would prove once again that he would stop at nothing to protect those around him — even at the cost of his own life. Operation Iraqi Freedom was underway, and Monsoor joined the more than 60,000 boots on the ground to overwhelm Saddam Hussein's regime. He was part of a combined SEAL and Iraqi overwatch element, and today they were in the thick of enemy-controlled territory in Ar Ramadi, Iraq. From the rooftops of the city, the early morning sun beat down on them as their keen eyes were able to spot insurgents long before they spotted them. Suddenly, a coordinated attack began, a gathering storm of hostile forces showing up in the area.

Shots rang out — allied snipers thwarted the first attack and instead, two insurgent bodies dropped to the ground. Those bullets might as well have hit a wasps' nest, though, as suddenly rocket-propelled grenades and small-arms fire began flying at them with hot vengeance. The enemy activity only continued to grow in strength, the SEALs vigilant over the amassing threat. But the nightmare scenario struck amid the chaos — Monsoor felt something bounce off his chest. It was a grenade. It fell to the ground, all its devastating potential just moments away from going off.

Monsoor knew exactly what had happened. He had every chance to jump out of the lethal blast radius. There were no guarantees, however, that his teammates, his brothers, would escape with their limbs or lives. Nobody can claim to know exactly what calculations Monsoor made in that moment, but we do know the outcome: Monsoor made the ultimate sacrifice. He threw himself on top of the grenade, absorbing the explosion and all its terrible consequences. He traded his life for the lives of at least two others.

In July 2008, Michael Monsoor's coffin moved from hearse

to grave along two lines of mournful Navy SEALs. Every single SEAL removed the gold Trident from their own uniform and stuck it to the surface of the coffin. Monsoor had reached his eternal resting place and his coffin was adorned from top to bottom with gold — with the eternal sigils of his brothers' love and respect. President George W. Bush attended the ceremony and was deeply moved by this awe-inspiring show of solidarity. "... When it was all over, the simple wooden coffin had become a gold-plated memorial to a hero who will never be forgotten."

At the time of his death, Michael Monsoor had fought in 11 different military operations, often exposing himself to dire threats at the risk of his life, many times acting with uncanny tactical awareness, and always serving his country and his men with a zealous dedication.

Michael Monsoor lives on in the hearts and minds of the Navy SEALs and continues to serve his country in spirit. At present, a Navy Destroyer, a SEAL training facility, a Naval Sea Cadet Corps, and the stadium at the high school he attended have all been named after the man who gave everything to protect those around him.

Monsoor (far right) during Navy SEAL training, 2004. (www.navy.mil)

Clockwise from top left: Sgt. La David Johnson, Staff Sergeant Dustin Wright, Staff Sergeant Bryan Black , Staff Sergeant Jeremiah Johnson (US Army)

Staff Sergeant Brian Black
Sergeant La David Johnson
Sergeant Justin Wright
Sergeant First Class Jeremiah Johnson

US ARMY

Four brave soldiers unjustly disgraced. Four devastated families. A high-level investigation that lasted years. This is a story of tragedy and triumph. This is the story of ODA 3212.

On October 6, 2017, the prime-time headline splashed all over screens across America was a horrific military tragedy:

ISIS KILLS 4 US SOLDIERS,
ONE POSSIBLY TAKEN ALIVE

The names of the dead scrolled by: Sgt. Justin Wright, Sgt. 1st Class Jeremiah Johnson, S.Sgt. Brian Black, and Sgt. La David Johnson. Berets donned the heads of the four young men killed by ISIS in Niger, Africa.

The men's parents had already received the news: "On behalf of a grateful nation, we regret to inform you that your son has been killed in action." Though only one sentence, those words live forever in the memories of mothers and fathers, husbands and wives, sons and daughters. For the families of ODA 3212, the news was even worse than usual — something wasn't quite right about the official narrative of their sons' deaths. The stories were not adding up.

"They tell me that he was in a rapid gunfight, and that the sergeant's whereabouts are unknown," Myeshia Johnson said in an interview for *ABC News*' documentary *3212 Un-Redacted*. Someone had told Myeshia, wife of La David Johnson, that her husband was still alive, while yet another source confirmed his death. A whirlwind of emotions swept her life into chaos as she tried to figure out whether to grieve or to hope. "After that I couldn't eat, I couldn't sleep. I'm just sitting here wondering about where's my husband? Then they call and say that they have an American soldier and they're willing to do a trade for him. ... Every little thing they tell me I'm going 'Could this be my husband, could this be my husband?'"

But there were no soldiers to trade. The false information had been given to her as part of an unconfirmed report, a mistake that cost Myeshia Johnson and Sgt. La David Johnson's mother horrific loss of sleep, and sanity. And this first chink in the armor around the official narrative would only serve as an introduction in the struggle to figure out the truth of what happened to these four from ODA 3212.

"If I could go back and figure out who gave them that first report, I'd f****** choke the shit out of them," said Mark Mitchell, former Asst. Secretary of Defense, who served 28 years in active duty as an Army Special Forces officer. He had strong words in the documentary interview about the disaster. "It's egregious that someone would share that unconfirmed report with them, and unconscionable that the family would be given conflicting statements."

Shortly after, Gen. Thomas Waldhauser gave a press conference in which he implied that the men died due to inadequate training. Subsequent interviews would paint a picture of the soldiers going off script, hunting down a high-level ISIS sub-commander on their own without proper support. The idea that an entire team of trained, non-commissioned officers would go rogue didn't sit right with anyone who knew the men personally, and especially not with soldiers and veterans who had a good idea of how troops in an incredibly dangerous insurgent-controlled area would act.

"What exactly went wrong? Why did these four men lose their lives? And no one would give us an answer," Ray Gannon, stepfather of Sgt. 1st Class Jeremiah Johnson said to *ABC News*.

The war on terror had taken the lives of these young sons

of America — that much was certain. But as a cloud of questions surrounded the tragedy, the families found themselves asking: *What really happened?*

On August 28, 2017, the sun blasted relentlessly down upon the scrublands of the Republic of Niger, skies completely clear of any clouds that could provide the slightest protection.

ODA 3212 (the codename for the unit), the elite 12-man operation made up of Green Berets, met with villagers of Tongo Tongo as they stocked up on food and water for the allied Nigerian forces. Staying stocked up on supplies is the difference between life and death in Niger, a country that's inhospitable even to the hardiest survivors. The Sahara covers more than 80 percent of the country's landmass, and desertification advances steadily toward the population centers clustered in the south and west.

ABC's investigation uncovered that ODA 3212's mission parameters had changed drastically. They should have been heading back to base, but for reasons unknown at the time, they were issued orders to turn around and head back north — driving through the night and into the next day. As it turned out, the last-minute orders were to support the CIA and another Special Operations Group in the capture of an ISIS subcommander. Due to bad weather, that team never showed up, and by the time ODA 3212 arrived on scene, the target was gone anyway.

But why the hell were they so far out in the Sahara? It certainly wasn't because they'd gone "Rambo," as Gen. Waldhauser alleged. Capt. Perozeni made it clear to his superiors twice that he was deeply uncomfortable with the shifting parameters. How, in the middle of a routine mission, were they given the task of working with undercover CIA operatives? They were not prepared for that kind of confrontation. They were going in too deep and Perozeni knew it.

Once again, new orders: the ODA 3212 would return to base. Tongo Tongo was a necessary resupply, but it was taking far too long.

The delay caused in the village was no accident — intelligence officials who spoke with *ABC News* said that the village elders were deliberately stalling the team to allow ISIS the precious time they needed to get in position.

As the convoy rolled out of the village, they were immediately ambushed. The official story in 2018 was that they were outnumbered three-to-one. The reality that *ABC News* uncovered was that they were facing an insurmountable force 10 times their size.

Bullets from small arms flooded over ODA 3212 with the Americans and Nigerians returning fire as best they could. Perozeni, La David Johnson, and others managed to make it out of this first deadly confrontation in their vehicles, but in the chaos Jeremiah Johnson, Black, and Wright had been cut off and left behind.

Although able to get some distance, Perozeni and La David Johnson became pinned down by massive firepower and were unable to regroup with their compatriots. According to *ABC News*, the enemy could be seen riding in on motorcycles and pickups with weapons mounted to their frames. Using a sniper rifle, M240 machine gun, and an M4 carbine, La David Johnson used his superior American training to suppress seemingly endless ISIS attackers.

Capt. Perozeni accelerated, and *ABC News* was told that La David Johnson was seen jumping into the next vehicle. As Perozeni stepped on the gas, a bullet pierced his side and Bartels, the driver, was hit in the elbow.

As the situation deteriorated, La David Johnson was forced from his vehicle. Seeing a chance of escape, he, along with two Nigerian soldiers, rushed 900 meters to find cover. Both Nigerians were struck down. Using a tree to block as many bullets as he could, La David Johnson fired back with a vengeance at the encroaching ISIS combatants. Eventually, the overwhelming gunfire took his life.

The three soldiers that had been separated from the team — Jeremiah Johnson, Black, and Wright — fought back with everything they had. Their vehicle provided as good a piece of cover as they could ask for in this doomsday scenario, but one of the hundreds of rounds shot from ISIS weapons finally caught a target. Black went down. Wright and Johnson pulled the soldier's body behind cover even as an unbelievable volume of gunfire poured over them. Johnson reached down to his friend, checking his vitals, calling out his name. Realizing they didn't have a radio connection to the rest of their team, the two soldiers decided to stay with Black instead of retreating on foot.

The helmet camera Jeremiah Johnson wore was key to much of these detailed insights — footage first captured by ISIS and later recovered by the French.

"Where is everybody?" Johnson calls out to Wright in the midst of the crazed Saharan battlefield.

Later, Johnson says he's "been shot seven times" but was somehow still standing. Forced to abandon the cover of the vehicle by the encroaching enemy, the two made a run for it. The hundred ISIS combatants pinned them down again, dooming the brave soldiers to stand their ground and fight to the death. Johnson fell and Wright rushed back, firing his weapon to the very last moments of his life.

As the whole unit teetered on the brink of annihilation, American helicopter pilots, aware of the situation, were chomping at the bit to jump in the pilot seats and fly to save their compatriots. For some reason, command denied their desires. But at the darkest moment, a jet plane did fly low over the scene, a threat to the mass of ISIS forces. Frightened at the possibility of death from the sky, the terrorists fled and scattered into the sunset. The French had arrived, and French helicopters soon swooped in to rescue the surviving men from the bloody desert sand.

Back at the American base, the pilots who had volunteered to help and were denied were furious, alleged company commander Maj. Alan Van Saun in the *ABC News* documentary. Van Saun was not present during the operation as his wife was giving birth. Nonetheless, Van Saun received a General Officer Memorandum of Reprimand, effectively ending his career, citing his failure to ensure that the soldiers of ODA 3212 "were adequately trained prior to conducting combined operations with the Nigerien partner force." "My words to him were, 'Sir, just so we're straight here, just so I understand, so we're on the same page: You're essentially ending my career over something that I was not part of, nor did I have authority over. ODA 3212 was trained and certified and validated by Lt. Col. Painter and Col. Moses.'"

"[Van Saun] was a scapegoat to protect higher officers from being punished," retired Gen. Donald Bolduc and former commander of Special Operations Command-Africa said.

"They gave him a reprimand," Myeshia, La David's wife said. "For what? ... His daughter was born the same day my husband died, and I'm pretty sure that eats him up every day."

In addition, Capt. Perozeni, who twice objected to the new orders, received two career-ending letters of reprimand. "And I think that's probably the biggest injustice," Arnold Wright, father of Justin Wright and an Army veteran himself, said. "... I walked around pissed off for a year and my anger was directed toward somebody that was completely innocent of what they told me he did."

"It's clear that if he had been listened to, my son, and Jeremiah, La David, and Justin would be here today," Black's father said to *ABC News*. Perozeni's reprimands were later rescinded, and he was instead awarded the Army Commendation Medal. While in so many ways the disaster in Niger is a story of injustice, it is also a story of untold hero-

Bryan Black and Jeremiah Johnson alongside their unarmored SUV. (U.S. Army Special Forces)

ism and an unfairly disgraced band of brothers finally getting the recognition they deserve.

"I know what it took to take him down," Wright's brother, Will — a soldier himself who has since reenlisted — said of his brother. "It makes me want to strap on my boots and go back. It does. I have no problem with how he went ... He fought more than 10 men could fight, until his dying breath. He did it for love. He did it for the man standing next to him."

Due to the incredible reporting done by *ABC News*, not only was the story set straight, but it also brought all the families together in closure. In many ways, they are one family now, just as their sons had been before them.

Master Sergeant John F. Baker, Jr.

US ARMY

Medal of Honor
Silver Star
Legion of Merit
Bronze Star
Purple Heart
Order of St. Maurice (Primicerius)

October 30, 1945–January 20, 2012 (66 years)

John F. Baker Jr. could have been an Olympic athlete, but this 5'2" American hero was destined for the Army and the Medal of Honor instead. Within a few short months of his first tour in Vietnam, all those around him would see him for what he truly was: a larger-than-life figure who would stop at nothing to save his fellow man.

As a high school student in Moline, Illinois, John F. Baker Jr. had an incredible life of professional athleticism laid out before him; he'd been training for two years to be an Olympic gymnast and the sky seemed the limit. But upon reaching his senior year, he realized he had very little interest in a safe and fancy college life. Instead, the worldly experience and adventure the military offered called out to him. He had one big hurdle to leap over though — his own God-given height.

"I always wanted to be a Marine," he said in a 2008 interview for the Pritzker Military Museum & Library in Chicago. Baker's 5-foot-2-inch frame just wasn't what they were looking for. "They said, 'No, you're an inch too short.'"

That setback didn't stop Baker for long, however, and he joined the Army shortly thereafter. Basic training in Fort Polk cemented the importance of teamwork and brotherhood for

Baker, and his time in airborne school showed him that the Army would provide him experiences nothing else could.

"The first time I ever rode in a plane I had to jump out," Baker reminisced with a smile in his interview with the Library of Congress Veterans History Project. In August of 1966 he shipped out to Vietnam, landing in the sweltering, suffocating heat of Saigon. Even though the infernal temperatures made everyone feel a little weak, there was no time spent sitting around. During his first month with the 25th Infantry Division, he was already spending weeks at a time out in the wild, engaging with hostile forces. Not only that, but in addition to his duties as part of a machine-gun team, he had one of the most harrowing jobs one could imagine in Vietnam: tunnel rat.

The tunnels that the Viet Cong dug over the years are like nothing else found in the world. They were a complex of halls and chambers underlying much of the country ranging from squad-size — six feet deep and no more than 100 feet long — to battalion-size, which could stretch on seemingly forever and reach 50 feet beneath the earth with four different compartmentalized levels.

Early on it was thought that they were primarily foxholes for the Viet Cong to hide in, and Operation Crimp was developed to demolish the supposedly simple squats using explosives at the entrances to trap the enemy. Only after an Australian specialist engineering troop led by Alexander "Sandy" MacGregor explored the under-labyrinth did the full extent of the problem come to light. There were communication centers, supply routes, hospitals, food and weapons caches, as well as living quarters for countless Viet Cong. These were no mere foxholes: a vast underworld lay unnoticed right beneath them.

And that's where "tunnel rats" like Baker came in. Armed with a pistol, a knife, a flashlight, and some string, Baker and his tunnel-rat brethren would move through this nightmare world an inch at a time, attempting to map the tunnels, disarm booby traps, and kill the enemy.

The layout of the web of tunnels alone was enough to drive one mad. "... sometimes they'd take turns and go back up, and back down, and back up. It's really a scary place," Baker said in his interview with the Veterans History Project. The traps and monstrous creatures within are straight out of a horror movie, with "... snake pits and spider pits, bamboo pits, scorpion pits ..." and lots and lots of rats.

American soldiers called it the "Black Echo" because of the unparalleled claustrophobia and at times paralyzing fear they would feel while attempting to travel safely through the mazes.

Baker deserves the title of hero just for braving the depths of these tunnels but, in only his third month of action in Vietnam, an even more harrowing mission would fall in his lap. He would rise to face this new challenge with all his might and receive the Medal of Honor for his valor in stealing victory out of the jaws of defeat.

It was November of 1966, and the day before another company had been trapped by an overwhelming force of Viet Cong in the jungles near the Cambodian border. Baker and 257 other soldiers in the 25th Infantry Division were tasked with rescuing the survivors.

The area they were in was all dense jungle awash in a sea of bamboo and sugarcane thickets. Baker described it as being so thick that the canopy completely devoured the sun, and upon stepping into it, day would turn into night. As their company commenced the rescue, their point man removed his heavy gear and crawled forward to get a lay of the land. Bullets shredded him, killing him instantly.

Baker went in to take his place, slowly crawling forward. What he saw was a host of concrete bunkers with guns pointing right at them. All hell broke loose. More than 3,000 hardcore Viet Cong fighters had been hiding in the trees, bushes, and bunkers, and the air went thick with bullets.

"They started firing from the left, right, behind us. We were trapped ourselves and the only way we could get out was fight our way out. ... Our men were getting killed right and left."

"Come on, G.I., come and get us," Baker heard the Viet Cong taunt. The company commander Robert Foley and Pvt. Baker — one man 6'7", the other 5'2" — teamed up and made their battle plans. Foley took the right side, Baker took the left. Baker answered the call of duty with an iron will, knocking out two of the enemy bunkers.

"When you see your buddies get killed you automatically ... lose your mind, and you do what you're trained to do to survive.... Especially when you see someone's head get blown off right in front of you, you have that certain moment, that certain burst of energy, to get in there and take care of the situation," Baker said in his interview with the Veterans History Project.

However, in the process of dealing that blow to the enemy, one of his comrades was mortally wounded. Baker made his way to the soldier and spotted an immediate threat: four enemy snipers were training their sights on his position. But they had met their match; Baker blew them all away, dragged his brother-in-arms' body back to safety, and sped back to the front, leading more assaults against the entrenched enemies and killing numerous Viet Cong. Baker and another man joined together, targeting two more hardened bunkers. This time, though, the Viet Cong were more vigilant, firing upon them with a vengeance and then striking with a devastating explosive grenade. The force blew Baker off his feet, but the enemy had made a terrible mistake — they had only put shrapnel in his arms and legs but had failed to kill Pvt. Baker.

"You don't know where you get the energy to do it. It's really hard to explain. You have that moment in life, no matter who you are ... if you see someone hurt, you need to go in there, and you need to get them out." Rising up like a revenant, Baker single-handedly laid waste to another bunker, but looking around afterward, he noticed that the man he'd been working with was wounded. Baker seized the machine gun of his wounded comrade and charged directly through the stormfront of hot lead, delivering swift and final justice upon yet another bunker. With not a moment to spare, he returned to his fallen comrade and brought him to safety. After replenishing his dwindling ammunition, he rushed back to the forefront to continue this brutal brawl with nothing but a gun and his indomitable fighting spirit.

Finally, the order came down: the forward element was to withdraw. In his interview with the Pritzker Military Museum & Library he recounted that he was "shaking like a leaf" thinking of the casualties in his company. "... My uniform was solid blood" from his comrades' wounds.

In the ensuing retreat, Baker took the opportunity to carry another wounded man back to the rear. When he saw yet another downed soldier, he went to save him too, but a vicious attack from snipers stopped him dead in his tracks. They only halted him for a moment; Baker steeled himself, raced beyond the line of friendly troops and silenced the snipers for good. After evacuating the other soldier, he returned to cover the deployment of the unit. His gun was dry — exhausted of all ammunition — but to him that just meant he was done shooting, not done fighting. In the time he was without ammo, he decided his best course of action was to rush ahead and drag two more men back to safety.

When all was said and done, Baker had dealt unbelievable damage to enemy forces and had personally carried eight wounded men to safety. Through the calamity, Baker had been told three times to evacuate, and eight times he went out to do what he deemed was the right thing to do. When he had officers telling him to stop, to retreat, he just couldn't. What makes someone charge into certain death against the orders given to him?

"Because you got your buddies in there, gettin' killed," he said in his interview with the Veterans History Project. "You've got that instinct, you want to get your friends and buddies out of that situation, and the only way to do that is to go back in.

... Our other platoon was caught in there, in the center of it, our job was to go get them out of there. And the only way to do that was to break through their lines." Baker recalled being floored when President Lyndon B. Johnson called him to congratulate him on receiving the Medal of Honor. But it also must be said that Medals of Honor don't fall from the sky; it had come from his fellow soldiers — the friends with whom he'd served with on the battlefield — who had recommended that he receive it. In that way, Baker shared in the joy of the honor with his extended military family.

For the Medal of Honor ceremony, Baker and Foley, opposite in height but both towering giants of courage, stood by one another to receive their awards. In addition to reading their Medal of Honor citations, President Lyndon B. Johnson spoke the following lines in honor of those two men, and indeed, all those who fight for their country.

The battlefield is the scarred and the lonely landscape of man's greatest failure. But is a place where heroes walk. Today we come here to the East Room of the White House to honor two soldiers, two soldiers who — in the same battle and at the same time — met the surpassing tests of their lives with acts of courage far beyond the call of duty. Captain Foley and Sergeant Baker fought in the same company. Now, together, they join the noblest company of them all. They fought because their Nation believed that only by honoring its commitments, and only by denying aggression its conquest, could the conditions of peace be created in Southeast Asia and the world.

Baker was a career man, and didn't retire from the military until 1989 after serving for more than two decades. Afterward, he transferred to a job working as a computer analyst at a Veterans Hospital in South Carolina. In addition to serving as the Vice-President of the Congressional Medal of Honor Society, he also served as a member on the Nation's Monuments and Cemeteries Committee. In 2008, the I-280 Bridge was renamed the Sergeant John F. Baker Jr. Bridge in his honor. On January 20, 2012, complications with his heart took his life at age 66, but M.Sgt. John F. Baker will forever remain in the hearts of his family, his comrades, and his country.

President Lyndon Johnson presents Sgt. John F. Baker, Jr. with the Medal of Honor. Capt. Robert F. Foley (left) also received the honor. (*The Salt Lake Tribune*, May 2, 1968)

Major Gregory "Pappy" Boyington during World War II.

Colonel Gregory "Pappy" Boyington

US MARINE CORPS
REPUBLIC OF CHINA AIR FORCE

Medal of Honor
Navy Cross
Purple Heart

December 4, 1912–January 11, 1988 (75 years)

Gregory "Pappy" Boyington was a Sioux-Irish American and the inspiration behind the 1970s TV show Baa Baa Black Sheep. A larger-than-life figure, Boyington was even better at shooting down planes than he was at drinking, and he could drink better than anyone. Boyington has one of the highest airborne kill counts in history.

The first time Gregory "Pappy" Boyington ever went airborne, he was only two years old. Waddling over to an open window on the second floor of the family home in beautiful Coeur d'Alene, Idaho, he tumbled out and down the precipice, landing headfirst in his mother's flower bed and knocking himself unconscious.

Far from searing a sense of vertigo into his young brain, Boyington came away from the encounter with a taste for aeronautics that couldn't be sated by anything existing at ground level. Climbing to the tops of trees, jumping out of windows, and tightrope walking the beams of the town's 100-foot-tall grain tower ... feeling the rush of the wind on his face, the sky above and danger below was what Boyington lived for. Once, he fell from such a height and knocked his eye out of its socket, scaring his mother half to death.

"How I ever survived all these things I got mixed up into — my poor mother never will know. ... [A]pparently I have been blessed with nine lives," Boyington was quoted as saying in the biography *Black Sheep: The Life of Pappy Boyington*. While some might deride young Boyington's antics as early markers of insanity, his childhood addiction to death-defying stunts made him fit right in with pilots of the era.

While landings and takeoffs give some passengers panic attacks, the reality is that the modern airplane is so safe it makes its grounded counterpart — the automobile — look like a coffin on wheels. But in its infancy, aviation was seen as the purview of madmen and daredevils. Planes were flimsy death traps, completely at the mercy of the weather and prone to malfunction; pilots, especially those who flew in wartime, did not step into the cockpit to work a cozy job and retire peacefully. They flew because — like Boyington — they were compelled to sweep across the skies and through the clouds, danger be damned.

"Everybody expected to be killed," said one Army pilot in *Hap: The Story of the U.S. Air Force and the Man Who Built It.* "Good Lord, I don't know of anybody who didn't figure he'd be killed before he got through." Boyington might've been a tad too crazy for most jobs, but he proved to be *perfectly* crazy to rule the skies as one of the best pilots of World War II.

After attending Lincoln High School, where he was re-membered as a tough and dedicated member of the school's wrestling team, he graduated in 1930 and his drive to fly took off. He promptly left home to pursue a bachelor's degree in aeronautical engineering. This journey led him to attend the University of Washington in Seattle where his military train-ing began; by the time he left he would be a cadet captain and a member of the Army Reserve Officers' Training Corps. University didn't slow down the ever-competitive Boyington either, and he made a name for himself on the wrestling and swimming teams, for a time even holding the Pacific North-west Intercollegiate middleweight wrestling title.

It was also during this time that his boisterous personality would begin to come into its own and with that, his drinking. Despite all the hard liquor, he had high ambitions for himself and worked until he was blue in the face, spending his summers in Washington at a gold mining camp and subsequently a logging camp with the Coeur d'Alene Fire Protective Association. Boyington graduated in 1934 and the first thing he did was marry Helen Clark; as a married man he accepted the highly respectable job working as a draftsman and engineer for Boeing. But Boyington wasn't satisfied with being a great engineer — he was destined for the cockpit.

After being commissioned as a second lieutenant in the US Army Coast Artillery with the 630th Coast Artillery, he then decided to apply to the United States Marine Corps. To his great surprise, and despite his incredible resume, he was rejected. Come to find out, the Aviation Cadet Act of 1935, under which he had applied, made all married men ineligible to apply. When relaying the disappointing news to his family he was jolted by what his mother decided to tell him right then and there. His biological father was not in fact Ellsworth J. Hallenback, whom he grew up calling "Dad."

His biological father was in fact a man his mother had divorced when he was an infant, a man named Charles Boyington, a dentist long gone from all their lives. Even after this truth bomb dropped on his life, Boyington refused to let bitterness destroy him. In fact, he saw an opportunity. Boyington realized life was presenting him with a unique loophole he could take advantage of to get into the Marines. Thrilled, he immediately obtained a new birth certificate — which of course had no record of his marriage — and he was able to enroll as a US Marine Corps Aviation pilot. This odd mix-up set in motion the wild trajectory of Boyington's life.

From 1935 to 1940, Boyington would go on to earn his stripes, traveling across the country from the Basic School in Philadelphia to Quantico. He began as an aviation cadet and finished as a first lieutenant. Boyington resigned from the Marine Corps on August 26, 1941, to volunteer as a "Flying Tiger" pilot for the Republic of China Air Force under the supervision of Gen. Claire L. Chennault's American Volunteer Group (AVG). The monotony of normal life was abruptly quashed when he became a flight leader and saw combat for the first time during the Sino-Japanese War in late 1941 to 1942.

Here he found the life of adventure and thrill he had always been searching for. Boyington's rambunctious, larger-than-life personality — and at times belligerent behavior — would soon get him into trouble with the commander of the Flying Tigers, Claire Chennault, and more importantly with the executive officer, Harvey Greenlaw. Laughing, Boyington reportedly said of Chennault that "he was less than pleased with some of our antics, such as shooting down the telephone lines with our .45s on the train to our billets, holding water buffalo races and rodeos in the street, or shooting up the chandeliers in a bar when they quit serving us." In an attempt at a solution, Chennault decided to place a two-drink maximum on his nights out and, according to Boyington, had spies watch to make sure he was completing his end of the bargain: to drink much, much less in exchange for not being kicked out.

In his time as a "Flying Tiger," he was officially credited with destroying two Japanese aircrafts midair and one and a half on the ground (don't ask how he did that). His issues with Chennault continued, however, and he was informed that he would be inducted as a lieutenant in the Army Air Corps once the AVG was disbanded. Boyington was not happy. He did not appreciate what he considered to be a demotion as he had been previously promised a major's commission with the Marine Corps.

In April of 1942, he broke his contract with the AVG and returned to the United States, but domestic life just didn't have what Boyington needed. The Marine Corps was in desperate need of experienced combat pilots, and in September 1942, he got what he was looking for, rejoining the Marine Corps and taking to the skies again.

In September 1943, a legend was born — this was the month that Boyington became the commanding officer of

Squadron 214, known also by the nickname of the "Black Sheep Squadron." It was during this time that his nickname took hold and never let go. First it was "Gramps" because at the age of 31, he was about a decade older than most of the Marines serving under him. The name "Gramps" was changed to "Pappy" and stuck until the end of his life.

His command of the Black Sheep Squadron is what he is best known for today. During this period of intense activity in the Russell Islands-New Georgia and Bougainville-New Britain-New Ireland areas, he managed to shoot down 14 enemy fighter planes in only 32 days. By December 27, 1943, his record had climbed to a stunning 25.

One of his most infamous feats was his leadership during an attack on the Kahili airdrome in 1943. Boyington was getting desperate for a fight, and once he'd done his job and escorted friendly bombers to a nearby base, he turned back around to go have some fun in the clouds.

"It was our duty to protect the bombers, but there was nothing in the rules saying that we had to land with them," Boyington said in his autobiography *Baa Baa Black Sheep*. He and 24 of his fighters circled the field where 60 hostile aircraft were based and goaded them into sending up a large force.

"The enemy ground-control radio had our frequency and decided to join the little game. They were pretending to be American pilots on a mission in our locality. But we were willing to gamble on just who was going to [out] fox whom." Boyington practically died of joy when he tricked the radio-operators into sending their squadron into a vulnerable position. A formation of 30 "Zeros" floated into the sky, but instead of striking fear into the Black Sheep, they were like fattened pheasants flying onto the dinner table.

"As we eased down, getting closer and closer, a thought that maybe I was hoggish and our prey might get wise ran through my mind. But no. Almost everybody in the squadron got a shot on our first pass." The aluminum Zeros disintegrated like paper-mache from the hurricane of .50-caliber rounds. The whirlpool of destruction, though it had felt a lengthy operation, took only thirty seconds — and Boyington relished every moment of it. All said and done, 20 enemy aircraft were shot down. The Black Sheep Squadron returned to their base without even one loss.

At that point his squad got so confident that they offered to down a Japanese Zero enemy plane for every baseball cap sent to them by major league players in the World Series. They received 20 caps — 20 planes and then some were shot down. On January 3, 1944, he tied World War I ace fighter Eddie Rickenbacker's record of 26 enemy planes destroyed. But every streak comes to an end, and his ended during his last mission on January 3, 1944, when 48 American fighters, including 4 planes from the Black Sheep Squadron, were sent on a sweep over Rabaul, New Britain.

Boyington was tactical commander of the flight, and finding approximately 10 Japanese fighters, he and another pilot let loose their gunfire. From above, they breathed a sigh of relief as they thought they saw Allied fighters swooping in to join the fight. They were not Allies, however, they were Japanese, and Boyington was now in the middle of a swarm of 20 hostile fighters. Boyington's fellow pilot was lit up and bleeding smoke, so Pappy climbed behind the planes that were shooting him to try and take the pressure off. The sky was so thick with Japanese fighters that Boyington didn't even use his electric gun sight — he just sprayed every plane he could to give his friend a chance to bail out or dive to safety.

Despite his suicidal efforts, he couldn't save the other pilot — in fact, he couldn't even save himself. The gunfire against the armor plate of his plane made sounds like a hailstorm on a tin roof. His plane became a pinata filled with lead, nose pointed down and dropping like a stone. In Boyington's autobiography *Baa Baa Black Sheep*, he wasn't sure whether his canopy was torn off or if his body rocketed upward so hard that he blew it off himself. A painful jerk told him that his parachute had caught wind, and an instant later he cannon-balled into the water.

His inflatable vest didn't seem to be pulling its weight; looking closely at it, he realized it was more of a collection of bullet holes — dozens of them — than it was a survival aid. Hours went by as he grew weaker and weaker, and each time he felt some strength leave him he ditched a piece of sodden clothes to compensate. Soon he had no choice: He had to use his survival raft now or drown, even though the raft was as likely to get him strafed by a plane as it was to save him. Hauling himself onto the raft, he realized for the first time what kind of shape he was in. Pieces of his scalp hung around his eyes; his left ear was half torn off; his arms and shoulders were shredded with shrapnel; and a 20-millimeter cannon had destroyed his ankle.

Yet there was a ray of sunlight. Though naked and afraid, he had clutched in his hand a small card that had been sent to him from a Catholic nun from Jersey. It displayed a lady with a baby in her arms and a boat on a stormy sea.

"I truthfully wondered why a Higher Power might be saving a bum like me. I look back now and realize that this was the first time I had ever prayed without asking for something, the first time I had ever prayed honestly, or properly, in my entire lifetime," Boyington reminisced in his autobiography. Eight hours passed like molasses, but when it ended, he wished his float had continued. A massive shape surfaced in the water — not a whale, but a submarine. He gawked at the Imperial Japanese Navy submarine *I-181;* this would be his last moment of freedom for nearly two years.

During his time as a prisoner of war, he bought the works when it came to corporal punishment, getting cigarettes put out on his neck and shoulders when his answers to the Japanese captors' questions proved unsatisfying. It took 10 days for his horrific wounds to get so much as a glance by a doctor; not even the Japanese expected him to live.

Every day for weeks he was tied up, blindfolded, and interrogated — every night they'd put handcuffs on him, making sleep a distant possibility. He finally was able to bend a nail, keeping it hidden in his mouth, to unlock his bindings, but there was no such luck finding a trick to fix his malaria. Even when the malaria seemed to be killing him, he still wasn't allowed to close his eyes and rest during the day, and received fearsome beatings when he was caught with drooping lids.

He was sporadically flown around to several other bases, once getting caught right in the middle of an Allied air raid and only surviving due to an interpreter named Suyako who threw him and the other prisoners in a ditch. They were mere feet away from the explosions; the Japanese were astonished they were still alive.

He ended up in the naval camp Ofuna, where Boyington made a realization: the booze he'd been killing himself with for much of his life had finally drained out of him. It was a miserable experience — going cold turkey and becoming a POW in one fell swoop — and yet he continued to look on the bright side. But life as a prisoner was a roller coaster of ups and downs, for it was also in Ofuna that he received his most brutal beating of his life.

He had just regained his ability to stand without a crutch, finally able to do something other than lie in an infected heap of his own stinking wounds. But instead of freedom of movement, he broke an arcane rule, one that was never made clear. Boyington was taken out to the yard where one guard beat his backside with a wooden bat till he was so tired he couldn't swing it anymore. Then a younger, fresher guard took his place and beat him some more. "When they were through pounding me, my accuser drew a small circle in the dirt, about two feet in diameter, and told me in Japanese to stand at attention in this circle until nightfall," Boyington said of this experience in *Baa Baa Black Sheep*.

Months later, he would receive the best-worst news of his life. An intelligence officer pulled him into a room and showed him a paper with big, bold letters plastered across it. "Major

Gregory Boyington, United States Marine Corps, awarded the Congressional Medal of Honor ..." He stiffened up, proud yet mortified. If the Japanese found out he had been in the Flying Tigers, killing their pilots over China, he was as good as dead. However, this intelligence officer spoke English, and to Boyington's immense surprise, he let him off the hook.

"Whenever people ask me today about the Japanese, I rather suppose I am expected to hate them, all of them, and largely because of what was done to us captives there in the camp of Ofuna. ... I must say, though (and I could take what confidence I could get out of it), that heretofore I had not been treated badly by any Japanese who spoke good English."

Though he would come to feel no particular hatred for the Japanese, that small ray of optimism for humanity was little consolation after the grueling 20 months spent as a captive. He watched helplessly as the young captives barely held on and the older ones died off. Finally, B-29s flew over the base, bombarding the prison into the ground. It was terrifying times, yet he and all the others couldn't help but feel elated by "the Music" of the B-29s, their explosive payloads, and the clarion calls of the base's alarms screaming. "The Music" was the melody of their ultimate liberation.

Boyington had been declared missing in action after a very determined but ultimately futile search. As he was never accorded official POW status by the Japanese, and therefore his captivity not reported to the Red Cross, the hunt for him proved useless. He returned to the United States on September 12, 1945, where he was met by former squadron members from VMF-214. That night, *LIFE* magazine covered the party for him at the St. Francis Hotel in downtown San Francisco. This was the first time the magazine had ever shown people consuming alcohol.

After his return, Boyington was asked to Washington to receive the nation's highest military honor. The Medal of Honor had been awarded to him after his MIA status in March of 1945 by President Franklin D. Roosevelt. Boyington was also

the recipient of the Navy Cross from the Commandant of the Marine Corps for the Rabaul raid. On October 5 of 1945, "Nimitz Day," Roosevelt's successor President Harry Truman presented Boyington and other Medal of Honor heroes with their medals at a ceremony at the White House.

Boyington (lower left) with pilots of VMF-122. (National Museum of the US Navy)

Colonel Robert L. Howard

US ARMY

Medal of Honor
Distinguished Service Cross
Silver Star
Defense Superior Service Medal
Legion of Merit (4)
Bronze Star (4)
Purple Heart (8)
Meritorious Service Medal (3)
Air Medal (3)
Joint Service Commendation
Army Commendation Medal (7)

July 11, 1939–December 23, 2009 (70 years)

Wounded fourteen times. Nominated for three Medals of Honor. Said to be "the most decorated service member in the history of the United States." Robert L. Howard proved time and time again he was unkillable. His legacy is indescribable; it can only be expressed through the inspiration he instilled in the men he led. Nevertheless, we all owe Robert L. Howard an attempt to give his story the recognition it deserves.

It was November 1967, and a Special Operations Group team led by Johnnie Gilreath discovered an opportunity too good to pass up — a massive North Vietnamese ammunition and food cache in the mountainous plateaus of southeast Laos. Gilreath held tight, keeping the prize under surveillance while MACV-SOG command assembled a search and destroy unit, a Hatchet Force, to deploy and destroy the valuable stockpile. Enter Robert L. Howard, the square-jawed, soft-spoken soldier from a small city in Alabama.

The first chance he got, Howard volunteered for a recon

team to lead the company from the landing zone to Gilreath and keep a watchful eye out for any approaching North Vietnamese soldiers. They soon discovered, however, that their plan was completely unsuited to the reality on the ground. Immediately upon arrival, three helicopters were heavily damaged by weapons fire. Despite the grave loss, Howard still managed to lead the Hatchet Force through enemy ambushes to make contact with Gilreath's team.

The rest of the Hatchet Force set off to demolish the stockpile while Howard took it upon himself to bring the fight to the enemy's front door. A Viet Cong security patrol of four immediately engaged him. But the Viet Cong had no idea who they were dealing with. Howard cleanly dispatched them with a single magazine of ammunition like the consummate professional he was. Just then, seemingly out of nowhere, a harrowing barrage of gunfire erupted from a machine gun cleverly camouflaged within a bunker, pinning down the rest of his team and threatening their very survival. Howard crept cautiously toward the deafening pangs of gunfire and skillfully put to eternal rest an NVA sniper who attempted to thwart his advance.

Finally, as described in his citation, "pinned down directly outside the strongpoint blazing a machine-gun barrel only six inches above his head, he threw a hand grenade into the aperture of the emplacement, killing the gunners and temporarily silencing the weapon." Unfortunately, where there's one Charlie there are always more, and other enemy soldiers rushed to take control of the gun. With steeled nerves and the lives of his men never leaving his mind, Howard picked up a LAW rocket launcher and aimed it at the heart of the enemy gunfire. As his citation reads, he "stood amid a hail of bullets, fired his weapon and completely demolished the position." This devastating one-man counterattack proved so crippling to the Viet Cong that they abandoned their positions, leaving the Hatchet Force alive, and allowing the full-on destruction of the tons of rice and ammunition.

World War II had taken a grave toll on the family, Howard noted in his interview with the Library of Congress Veterans History Project. None of his four uncles nor his father — all paratroopers — would return home from World War II. His father and one uncle perished in combat, while the other three uncles suffered grievous injuries that eventually led to their deaths.

As a child, Howard recounted how his mother worked in a textile mill in Opelika to support their fatherless family. He and his sister were raised by their grandmother. "So my childhood was really rewarding to me but it was quite difficult, as I look back and compare it to nowadays. I didn't realize that it was difficult at the time. But I've had to work all of my life. It seemed like life has been a tremendous struggle just to survive." Despite the heavy price paid by the Howards to help with the defeat of the Nazis, a deep love and respect for his grandmother and the armed services welled up through the cracks of his hard life. "She taught me never to have hate in your heart. And she taught me how to read out of a bible."

Howard's hometown of Opelika, Alabama, sat near a highway where he watched wide-eyed as military trucks sped back and forth to Fort Benning. In his straight-talking manner, he told the interviewer from the Veterans History Project, "And I'll never forget that one time I was standing on the side of the road and a bunch of young paratroopers were going by, you know, and they were hollering and wavering. And I can remember seeing the glider patches on their hats and all that stuff... And so then I finally realized what paratroopers was later, so I said I'd like to be a paratrooper."

The outstanding small-town athlete eventually turned down a scholarship for higher education and enlisted at age 17. Instead of walking the halls of universities, he would follow in the footsteps of his forefathers, donning the silver wings of the paratrooper. Instead of scoring touchdowns on the gridiron, he'd jump out of planes, coordinate surprise attacks, and apprehend strategic objectives. He would accomplish more than he imagined, witnessing the paradigm shift of modern warfare firsthand and going on to become one of the greatest special forces legends in history.

After shipping out to basic training where the grueling drills were designed to separate the wheat from the chaff, the depth of this man's soul and his love of his fellow man instantly became clear to those around him.

Howard was a powerhouse athlete, and watching the less fortunate struggle was difficult, but ultimately rewarding. Here, he got his first taste of leadership and the camaraderie in the armed forces that cannot be found or bought anywhere else on Earth. "And so that was the most, probably the best part of the training was trying to assist the weaker ones ... I kind of catered to the underprivileged, so to speak, whether they were weak physically or whatever. And I think it was because of my childhood, you know, with being poor but not really realizing it, not being able to eat three meals a day."

After helping those around him through the trials and tribulations of basic training, he and 4,000 other troops stepped onto a ship and headed off for 'Nam. A couple of problems became instantly apparent as they stuffed themselves on board — namely that these 4,000 men were on a ship designed to carry only 2,000.

Thirty-one days on that cramped vessel was the experience of a lifetime. After 17 days, they'd run out of fresh water and had to ration small amounts for drinking; there was salt water for bathing. Everybody was sick. If you didn't get sick fast, you'd get it slow; it was coming for you. Also, for lack of space, the men had to eat standing up. There was one massive upside to the whole affair — "I was eager to go to war, to get off that ship."

Out of the frying pan, into the fire. Howard — then a staff sergeant — was made to believe they'd be making an amphibious landing on a potentially hostile beach. It was an unmitigated shitshow — not Howard's choice of words but that was the truth of it. Troops were falling off the ropes into the 12-foot-deep water, many nearly drowning, weapons and equipment lost to the murky, violent waters. "[T]here was no enemy soldiers, there was no firing ... Thank God, if there had been an enemy there they'd killed us all because we were trying to keep from drowning and getting on the beaches."

For two weeks, a general state of confusion raged through the rank and file as reality set in. The war of their fathers was not this, not Vietnam. There were no clear enemy formations waiting for them on the other side of the hills or tree lines. Instead, sporadic mortar fire wore away at the men's spirits. The disarray caused by this harassment was palpable; a mortar round would go off, which would start a "friendly" firefight — the greener Americans were known to shoot at each other while guarding the perimeter at night. Arguments between the non-commissioned and commissioned officers ensued, with the frustrated men wanting — needing — to find and fight the enemy instead of staying put and self-combusting. Their wishes were eventually granted, but contrary to "needs," war wasn't exactly an improvement.

The American soldiers began making contact with the enemy in the form of nasty ambushes and snipers lying in wait within the impenetrable walls of the jungle. Luckily, Howard hadn't gone into the military blind — he'd read up on his military history and knew about the area and the French's colonial defeat at the hands of the locals. This caused Howard to grow wary, as all the maps he was given appeared to be completely wrong. "We were always confused in what area we were in. We really didn't know where we were at."

It was around this time that Howard received his first combat wound — the first of 14 over his 54 months of active duty. Night had draped heavily over the landscape of the Quin Yuan province where they had cleared out a battalion-sized camp. That was when the Viet Cong struck.

It was chaos. While mortar rounds showered the area, Howard was among the scramble to get a squad of soldiers together. Darkness was their greatest enemy; the enemy wore black fatigues that made them nearly invisible at night. Confused Americans were shooting each other. Howard had a keen mind for combat even as a greenhorn, and knowing this situation was untenable, he rushed to his platoon leader for clear orders that would cut through the confusion. His mission, as given to him by the higher-ups: secure the area and hold tight until daybreak.

An order can lead to order. Howard pulled his squad together and began securing the ground. ... And then a bullet struck his head, penetrating his face and blowing out his jaw. Thoughts cascaded around his skull as he tumbled to the earth: had his head just been blown off? Was he still alive? When he finally impacted, he found himself in a grave, eye to eye with a decaying Vietnamese who'd been buried upright per their Buddhist customs. The Americans had set up camp in a cemetery!

"And I can remember the stench and the maggots crawling all over me. And, you know, as I moved around the decaying body, it was getting it all over me, and it made me sick. ... And that hurt worse than being shot in the face." There was not much else he could do but wait, blood pouring from his face and shock strangling his body. For three hours, Howard laid in that grave with a corpse, stunned and sickened, waiting to be rescued. Eventually, as the company commander made his rounds, taking stock of the deceased and the wounded, they found Howard and managed to evacuate him to a hospital in the province.

"And in the process of going through the evacuation, of being treated for the wound, I realized my wound wasn't that bad. I had, in fact, been shot by an AK-47 or an SWS ... And the ammunition ... is not as powerful as our ... AR-15s at that time. And so the round, it went in my face, lodged in my jaw and come out my jaw, but apparently ... it just destroyed some teeth that I had on the lower and upper part and went through my face."

The more one reads and listens to Howard describe his

experiences in the war, the more one understands that some men are just made differently. Perhaps a life of little means and the strength of character gained by the bond with his grandmother and her bible prepared him for life as a soldier, but it's hard to imagine a modern American saying that he "just" got shot in the face, that having his teeth pulverized and blown out of his head was "not that bad."

Howard took the facial-reconstruction surgery lying down, but he jumped at the chance to make something truly great of himself. In the bed next to him was a Special Forces soldier who would become a lifelong friend. One fateful day, a senior commissioned officer in charge of Special Forces operations in Korea came to the hospital on a visit to Howard's hospital mate.

"'There's Sgt. Howard, he's out of the 101st and he got shot in Quin Yuan and we need a guy like him in Special Forces,'" his friend blurted out, unprompted. This mate, the man in the bed next to him, had been evaluating Howard's character and had found both a comrade and a soldier of pristine character.

Howard took the bait and told the officer, "You know, I can train and I can fight, and we're a little bit disorganized, and we don't know what we're doing. So if you got a job for an infantry sergeant I volunteer for it." The officer took his name.

The next week, Howard was back on the front line, reporting to his first sergeant, his face bandaged like an Egyptian mummy. That's when he was hit again, this time with the best news of his whole career: he wasn't going back to the 101st; he was to head to Saigon on a special mission. His sergeant was mystified about how this man got himself top-secret clearance from a stretcher, but that didn't matter: Howard was Special Forces now.

Whatever that meant. He was sent to Saigon for an interview, and although he didn't know exactly what Special Operations was at the time — few did — it could not have been more different from normal infantry operations. After taking lie detector tests and briefing the interviewer on his history, the real training began. The emphasis was on demolitions and training, small unit patrolling, shooting weapons, and setting up ambushes. And that was just phase one.

At the time Howard joined MACV-SOG (Military Assistance Command, Vietnam – Studies and Observations Group), the organization was still in its infancy. While this carried with it some difficulties — unfilled positions, some lack of logistics support, etc. — it allowed get-it-done types to shine and make the organization their own. Men like Howard, coming in on the ground floor, were able to shape and be shaped by MACV-SOG in a way that would have been difficult, if not impossible, elsewhere.

"And the amazing thing is that within the entire compound, he was the only one who had been school-trained early in his career as a supply specialist," John Plaster noted in an interview for a biography about Robert L. Howard produced by USSOCOM History & Research Office. "So he would run recon missions, come back, and while teammates were on stand-down — blowing steam, having fun — he would be spending that week in the supply office, filling out requisition forms because he was the only guy who knew how to do it. He didn't have to do that, but he cared enough about the unit that, by golly, everybody else go have fun, Bob Howard is going to make sure we have the supplies we need."

"I was a weapons and a demolition expert by the time I finished Special Forces training," Howard admitted in his interview with the Veterans History Project.

Howard would find much success using his demolitions training to blow a hole in the North Vietnamese war machine. The Vietnam War was a petri dish for unconventional warfare, as time and experience would show that 'Nam was anything but conventional. One such ingenious operation — code-named Project Eldest Son — was an SOG program to sabotage enemy munitions with faulty, exploding cartridges.

When the NVA attempted to vaporize American troops with mortar shells — as they had done to Howard's fresh-off-the-boat comrades — or AK-47s, they'd instead find themselves on the wrong end of a lethal explosion directed from their own weaponry.

Howard put his own spin on Project Eldest Son. As told in John L. Plaster's book *SOG*, Howard took an aged footlocker, painted it bright red, and filled it with around 80 pounds of TNT. Now, being an expert in demolitions, he rigged the risky payload to explode with a short-delay detonator and left his devious trap on what was to be his team's landing zone. After circling around in the jungle, they returned just in time to see the fireworks.

"[P]eople were coming from everywhere, running out to get that footlocker. And I actually think some of them were in the process of opening it when it went off. I mean, that bastard blew a hole in the ground, it blew shit for a quarter of a mile, that's how much TNT we had in it," John Plaster described via an interview in his book.

SOG also undertook missions to increase fellow soldiers' chances of survival. They gathered intelligence. On one such mission, Howard scoured the hostile landscape for 19 days, exploring the nooks and crannies of the wild mountain passes of North Vietnam's panhandle to map out the best escape routes to Laos. Such was the versatility of the man often cited as the most decorated American soldier of all time.

Many, if not most of the heroic actions performed by the members of our armed forces are not earned by being in the right place at the right time. To the contrary, the greatest valor emerges when men of war find themselves in the most dangerous place at the worst time. Through such moments, the best and bravest show their stripes. Howard was a man who often found himself at the wrong end of enemy rifles, explosives, and ambushes, but somehow he managed keep his cool, or his "intestinal fortitude," as he called it.

This was no accident or anomaly; men like Howard are

wired differently than the rest of us, able to perform astounding feats of bravery consistently, time after time. He was "Leonidas reborn" as a great nephew described him, referencing the Spartan king who led 300 Spartans in defense of their lands, taking down 10,000 Persians before succumbing to an honorable death in combat.

Within a one-year period, Howard was recommended for the Medal of Honor three times in succession, an unheard-of accomplishment. Unfortunately, two of those commendations were downgraded due to the top-secret nature of his missions and possibly, as fellow soldier John Plaster alleged in his book *SOG*, politics and jealousy. However, Howard was a humble man at his core, a soldier's soldier, and while these downgrades may have created some consternation within the man himself, they caused anger among his comrades who saw him as a one-of-a-kind inspiration, time and time again risking everything for his country and his brothers-in-arms.

One such action that had been recommended as grounds for the Medal of Honor, and subsequently downgraded to Silver Star status, took place over several days in November of 1968. Howard and his platoon were on an operation deep within enemy-held territory. In the middle of a ground insertion, heavy enemy fire opened up from all directions. Howard leapt from the still hovering craft and began laying down covering fire, providing desperately needed protection and diversion to avoid as many casualties as possible to the dismounting troops. Spotting two enemies at the edge of the tree line and sensing weakness, he charged the hostiles and dispatched them both. The landing zone was cleared and disaster avoided.

Also in November, on the 16th, Howard's leadership kicked into high gear when his platoon was outnumbered and under attack by a company-sized force. Howard went to each platoon member, offering them personal encouragement and directing their fire all the while exposing himself to barrages of bullets. "He was a man of action. When it was time to do something and no one stepped up to the plate, he would step up to the plate. And by force of personality he dragged everybody with him," Dan Ster, fellow MACV-SOG soldier said of Howard in a biographical video produced by the USSOCOM History & Research Office.

Two days later, his unit was outnumbered. Two North Vietnamese companies against one platoon. With masterful maneuvering, Howard drew his men back and forth, in and out, catching the enemy in deadly crossfire and unraveling the ambush. The sun fell and rose again and the threat grew ever larger. Howard took point in the platoon when he observed the beginnings of another ambush, this time battalion-sized. While companies are typically made up of platoons, battalions are composed of multiple companies. Plainly put, they were staggeringly overwhelmed.

Howard suffered a wound in the initial exchange of fire, yet continued to expose himself to the aggressors' line of sight, the better to be at the perfect striking point for counterattacks. Ducking and weaving from position to position, he administered life-saving first aid to wounded soldiers. Then he began setting up a landing zone for evacuation. As the first ambulance helicopter rushed in, machine gun fire struck metal and the vehicle burst into flame. Howard was hit a second time. He was unstoppable, running a hundred and fifty meters to the crashed ship and pulling the trapped pilot from the wreckage's inferno. After the entire crew was freed, he led them back to the platoon, providing covering fire en route. This continued for three hours until another helicopter was able to arrive, land, and evacuate the casualties. Still, Howard refused to leave — he had a duty to lead.

The following morning, now suffering from two wounds, Howard spotted three North Vietnamese soldiers headed their way. Howard saw them before they saw him, and he shot first, killing all three.

From everything thus far, anyone with a pair of eyes could see that Robert L. Howard was fluent in the language of courage and armed to the teeth with the type of fortitude and cunning that is so essential for life on the battlefield. But what follows is a different kind of story — a firsthand account of Howard's actions the day he earned his Medal of Honor.

Laos, December 30, 1968. The war in Vietnam was at its midpoint, America having ramped up its presence significantly during Johnson's escalation, with 1968 proving to be the single deadliest year in the conflict for American troops. Howard was now the first sergeant of a reconnaissance company for the Forward Operational Group 2, headquartered at Kon Tum.

"[W]e had sent a team into Laos. And they went in to locate an enemy force that we had been watching for a number of days," Howard recalled in his interview with the Library of Congress. But the mission had gone sour. The team in Laos broke radio silence — the first sign of the dire nature of their situation — to report that they were surrounded, soldiers were disappearing, and there was nothing they could do. Working at top speed, the colonel in charge put together a platoon-size operation and a squadron of helicopters to strike fast and recover the captured team of six. Howard was a senior non-commissioned officer with the most combat experience of anyone at hand, thus the colonel offered Howard a role assisting Lt. Sheridan to bring the Americans back.

Six helicopters came in hot to the last known communication location and received a greeting of heavy enemy gunfire. Some of the helicopters dropped to the ground more than landed, with the rescue team taking casualties on the insertion. A lieutenant turned to Howard and said, "Bob, we need to secure this LZ, and I want you to get a couple of men and secure the exterior of the LZ. And we need to organize and get off the LZ and move toward our target area."

Maneuvering around the clearing, the rescue team had to fight for their lives just to get some distance from the helicopters. As they made a break for cover, an entire platoon of NVA soldiers came down on them like an anvil. "I can remember in one accident, here is a platoon of NVA soldiers coming toward me and I got three men behind me, and I can remember being fired at. And I fell backward and they killed three men behind me. And I'm firing and killing the North Vietnamese that's trying to kill us. And so, I finally said, 'There's no way we're going to secure this LZ.' So I made my way back to the lieutenant after finding out that two or three people that was with me got killed and I told him that the LZ was completely surrounded."

One of the remaining six helicopters then made a meteoric impact with the earth, killing all troops onboard; the rescue had devolved into a catastrophe. The sergeant updated the forward air controller of the urgent situation and requested immediate termination of the mission. There would be no help arriving by air — at least not soon enough to save their lives. They needed to move, and it would be on foot.

After the smoke cleared and all survivors accounted for, they discovered that the 37-strong force had been whittled down to 28. This was a devastating decision for any soldier, but the remains of the helicopter and the deceased soldiers inside would be left behind. They pushed forward even as enemies gathered at their flanks.

Howard was responsible for bringing up the rear as the platoon powered forward up an incline toward higher ground. Around that time, the wolves on their heels began to pick them off, firing on the men from the perimeter. As Howard recounted in the Veterans History Project, he made his way to the lieutenant at the front to tell him they needed a better plan "because the enemy knew where we were at and they were following us. And we were all going to end up captured ourselves." He didn't get the chance. Just as he neared the lieutenant the jaws of the trap closed shut. They had walked right into an ambush.

"And so when I come to I was blown up in a crumple on the

ground. And my weapon was blown out of my hand. And I can remember seeing red, and saying a prayer, hoping I wasn't blind; I couldn't see." Hands wracked with pain, Howard realized he couldn't get up — and all his thoughts were consumed by pain. Finally, his vision crept back to him; blood pooled in his eyes. Feelings other than just pain materialized, but his hands were burnt and mangled, and his weapon was lost to him.

"Part of my web gear was blown off. And I was blown up, and the front part of my legs was blown up." There were bullets sweeping the ground from every direction — more than that, there were flames and smoke flooding over him. An enemy soldier with a flamethrower was blasting the casualties. Howard's consciousness came rushing back to him in this moment of ultimate despair and he struggled to grab his web gear nearby. He had decided he would not burn to death today, or ever — he would rather blow them both to kingdom come. He palmed his grenade, but the pin required a dexterity that his damaged fingers could no longer manage, his one hand consisting of hanging fingers and a useless thumb. His teeth would have to do; he pulled the pin with his clenched teeth.

"I got the pin out of that grenade, and this guy's standing there ... And he's looking at me, and he's got that flamethrower, and he's just burned a bunch of people that was in the kill zone. He didn't burn the lieutenant. The lieutenant was about five feet away from him, and he's laying face forward ... I knew he was hurt ... And the guy looked at me ... and then I looked at him. And I guess I looked so bad and pitiful he decided not to burn me up. He just turned and walked off."

So there he was with a live grenade in his hands in a field of burning bodies. There was no way he could put the pin back in. He looked around and lobbed the grenade in an area clear of bodies. Crawling toward the limp body of the lieutenant, Howard got a hold of him and started pulling him backward down the hill. Lt. Sheridan was six-foot-four, 200 pounds, but

Howard wouldn't be stopped — he used what was left of his hands to drag the man down the hill to safety, telling the lieutenant to hang on to his life, to not give up. Then, he noticed a sergeant behind the cover of a log with an operable weapon at his side. The sergeant was alive — his heart beats — but he is broken. The trauma has left him weeping and with no will to fight back.

"And so, I get up against this log and I'm pulling the lieutenant, and I'm screaming at him, help me get the lieutenant, come on, get me — help me get the lieutenant. But he wouldn't move. ... And here I am, begging him to help me because I can't walk to drag the lieutenant back down."

The sergeant would not give up his primary weapon, but when Howard continued to plead with him, he reached into his holster and handed Howard his .45 handgun. Being intimately familiar with the handgun — likely the Colt M1911 — Howard knew there would only be seven rounds in the magazine. The place was crawling with enemies; seven rounds was almost as good as nothing. Howard wants to tell the man to give him more magazines, but the sound of running interrupts any further discussion.

The NVA are already on top of Howard and the Americans, bayonets gleaming, fixed to stick the wounded soldiers. Howard blows one away. The corpse piles on top of Lt. Sheridan, but there are more Vietnamese soldiers following closely behind. The sergeant whom Howard had been arguing with — nearly fighting with — comes to his senses, gets up, and pulls the trigger, killing enemy soldiers.

A torrent of bullets also hit Howard, this time striking the magazines full of ammo in his gear. The magazines explode, blowing Howard away for the second time that day. Moments pass and Howard puts himself back together, figures he can still move, and starts crawling back to the lieutenant to continue his rescue mission. The sergeant is keeping the fight alive, running around unleashing bullets at every enemy he can see. Howard notices other Americans now, stuck in the same state the sergeant had been in before, alive but not firing their weapons — shocked and traumatized and motionless, seemingly waiting to die.

Howard dragged himself back to Lt. Sheridan, but the sergeant got there first. "... And I said, 'Well, I can't get him any further. You know, I'm really hurt,' I said, you know, that this time when I was blown up, it tore a part of my leg out right in my thigh right here." Howard was in no position to drag a 200-pound man. Fortunately, any semblance of the broken man Howard had argued with before was gone. The sergeant had made the transformation into a hero. He grabbed the lieutenant and went into a sprint. Howard watched as bullets caught the lieutenant in his torso and blood began to gush out of his mouth.

Howard's emotions began to well up again, thinking about the soldiers behind them, too shell-shocked to fight, but he soldiered on. Finally, he and the sergeant made it to a position where surviving friendlies were fighting back. But, while trying to talk with a Vietnamese Special Forces officer, the officer is shot right in front of him. Three or four enemies pressed on with their attack. Howard, barely hanging on to his own life — let alone his gun — fired his weapon and then heard the click of an empty magazine. That click was the last thing Howard remembers.

Until consciousness returned and he found himself at the bottom of the hill with a medic, a sergeant named Brown, who was shot up but still breathing, still fighting.

"'Is the lieutenant still alive?'" Howard asked.

"'...Yes. ... I've got an IV in him, but I don't think he's going to make it.'"

"Make him make it. You keep that lieutenant alive. ... I want you to get every live person that we've got that's able to fight, I want to talk to them right now.'" According to Howard's interview with the Veterans History Project, the sergeant propped him up and placed a radio in his hand. Howard was going to tell it like it was — this is where they sank or swam, gave it everything or gave up.

"And so he kind of propped me up ... And so, [over the radio] I said, 'We're going to establish a perimeter right here, and you're going to fight or die.'"

Howard asked for and received a weapon, and they set to work holding the perimeter. Simultaneously, the radio came to life with the voice of the forward air controller, their only connection to outside support. As darkness fell, Howard explained their situation: there were a lot of soldiers scared to death, a few that could fight hard, and a whole lot of enemies. The FAC told him that they needed strobe lights. Without those blinking lights cutting through the darkness, there was no way in hell any rescue operation could take place.

Gathering all the men — a small handful of Americans and eight or ten South Vietnamese allies — they were able to scrape together three working strobe lights. Howard, propped up because he was unable to stand, instructed Sgt. Brown to array the strobe lights in a triangle to create a clear signal visible from the sky.

"I've got your strobe lights," the FAC said. With their position locked down, the cavalry would finally have a chance to arrive. The cavalry in this case was 'Moonbeam,' a Fairchild C-119 Flying Boxcar equipped with two M61 Vulcan 20 mm cannons — enough firepower to keep the enemies off their backs through the night.

"And he says I want you to know — and we used code names at that time ... [current commander] Gen. Singlaub ... says that we'll get you out."

Soon after, the C-119 flew overhead and started pumping rounds around their position. The FAC came back over the radio, asking Howard if it was effective, if the enemy had attacked again. Howard was in the middle of explaining that they were still being saturated by small-arms fire when he saw the enemy positioning to strike, but "by the grace of God" from across a creek.

"And so then in my own mind I said they will attack us, but as long as we got that water obstacle between us and the enemy and we can keep the air force putting fire around our position, we'll be okay."

By that time, the 37 survivors of the insertion had been reduced to about a dozen, but they were putting up a stalwart defense, receiving no additional casualties. The NVA kept probing the position with bullets, the Americans and South Vietnamese kept receiving gunfire, and the air support continued to spray the surroundings with ballistics every time the enemy gave away their positions with muzzle flashes. Howard was stuck relaying information back and forth between the ground and the air, his only weapon an empty Colt M1911 and his own determination. Still, a feeling of doom hung in the air; as well as they were doing, as proud a fight they were putting up, they might not make it through the night.

"And I can remember, you know, jokingly telling the forward air controller, if you've got a weapon up there, if you could throw it out the window of your aircraft, I'd appreciate it, you know."

The brotherhood is strongest between soldiers when the war is at its worst, and Howard recalls fondly the big heart of the forward air controller who kept reassuring him at every moment.

"And he kept talking to me, a great guy, an Air Force captain, and saying we're going to get you out, don't you worry, we'll get you a weapon." Hours passed like this, the soldiers hanging on. The strobes were beginning to die out and six hours still until dawn. Without the strobes, the Americans knew they didn't stand a chance. The enemy knew it too. Howard didn't have a gun, but he could still change out those strobes, which he managed to do before they were plunged into darkness.

New developments livened up the radio and the spirits of all the men left standing. Aviators from nearby had agreed to pilot helicopters and attempt a rescue in the dark.

"And even though it was dark, they agreed to do that. And that's the first time, I think, historically in Special Operations that you had a bunch of aviators that were willing to die to come in and get us. And I was told this later; I wasn't told this at the time."

Whatever divine spirit drives men to risk death for one another, while perhaps rare in the world at large, was plentiful there in Vietnam that day. Problem was, the C-119 needed to be replaced every few hours and would need to be replaced before the rescue helicopters could swoop in and save them. That C-119 was their lifeline. Howard alerted Sgt. Brown — his link of communication with everyone on the ground — that the replacement was happening.

The communication did not go unnoticed. The enemy always sensed the lull in the battle when the Air Force pulled a C-119 out, and they would press their attack as soon as the weakness presented itself. This night was no different. The enemy fell upon them, threatening to shatter the remaining Americans. Howard took a stern look at the situation and made an astounding call. He told the FAC to blow the entire situation — friend and enemy alike — off the face of the earth.

"... Just kill us — kill us and the enemy because I don't want to be captured, I don't want to blow my own self up, just bring it in."

Bullets plowed the ground right between Howard's feet, the firepower from on high so intense that ricochet hit him in the face. All at once, the helicopters soared in out of the night. They had somehow managed to replace the C-119. Hope shone through the darkness and the thrill of rescue was palpable. But they weren't saved yet — those choppers would have to fly through overwhelming firepower to reach them.

Howard never forgot watching that inbound helicopter fly in among the gunfire. The FAC told him to get everybody together for the first load, but Howard wanted to get the dead lifted out first — not standard procedure. The pilots hesitated, but Howard wasn't backing down: No soldier would be left behind.

The helicopter was only about twenty meters from him, but it felt like a mile with Howard dragging a dead soldier, nearly a dead man himself. The crew was running around, gathering up the soldiers and loading them into the helicopters. Howard was adamant that he'd be the last one on, after all the dead and wounded. At one point, Howard watched, horrified, as two bodies slid off the helicopter as it was taking off and hit the ground. He carefully placed those soldiers back on the next helicopters and made damn sure such a disservice didn't happen again.

Finally, after the crews had run their routes, making sure everyone was aboard and new helicopters had been rotated in, Howard's job was done. He got onto the aircraft, his duty completed.

"And so we finally got on a helicopter. And the dead soldier that I was next to was the lieutenant that I had drug down the hill. He had finally died. ... He was also one of the ones that had fell off the helicopter that took off initially. And so he ended up back on the ground. And — and that hurt me worse than being shot up, seeing that lieutenant die."

While the spectacular heroism that earned him the Medal of Honor would be the end of most stories that go like this, Robert L. Howard is no normal man, and this was no normal Medal of Honor. In fact, he was nearly killed before he received his much-deserved award. Howard was in the middle of an enemy attack while in the Central Highlands region of Vietnam. The North Vietnamese were invading South Vietnam — and they were about to wrest control of the city of Kon Tum away from America and her ally.

In a camp just across the Dak Bla River, Howard and his men were getting mercilessly pounded by mortar shells. There's Howard, setting up a perimeter, when a non-commissioned officer approaches him. Howard goes to meet him when a bullet hits him in the foot.

"... You know we got Gen. Westmoreland on the [field telephone?] He wants to talk to you."

Gen. Westmoreland was the chief of staff of the army at the time, and Howard was flummoxed.

"And I said, 'Well what does he want to talk to me for?'"

"He says he's got a special message for you."

Howard made his way back to the field telephone, his foot bleeding from the bullet wound.

"Bob, how're you doing?"

"Well General, the situation's not good here, but how're you doing?" Howard said, laughing as he remembered one of the strangest Medal of Honor notifications in history.

Problem was, Howard's men were in a fight for their lives, and medal-be-damned if he was going to up and leave his soldiers to fly to Washington. His colonel assured him he'd take over — going back to Washington, DC was more of an order than an offer, anyway. After giving back the phone, Howard went back outside to continue the fight.

The next morning, Howard set off to the airfield to hitch a ride back to America. Problem was, enemies were crawling everywhere. "... We almost didn't make it to the airfield."

They came to a bridge that had been secured by the enemy. Howard and the sergeant driving the truck looked at each other, said screw it, and stepped on the gas. Remarkably, they made it across, the truck taking all the bullets for them.

"I didn't want to leave and go back to Washington and receive a medal," Howard said. He had the utmost respect for the Medal of Honor: within it was the reflection of all the men who made it and those that didn't. It was a beacon of the freedom that they fought and died for. The reason he didn't want to go back to Washington was that he was a fighter, surrounded by enemies, who hated the idea of leaving before victory was won.

But Howard followed his orders, survived the enemy fire on the way to his transport, and earned a Purple Heart for getting shot in the foot on his way to his award ceremony. Truly, a hero quite like Robert L. Howard may never exist again, but in his legacy lies an aspiration for every man, woman, and child who ever looked up to the values of freedom and hard work and seeks to carry that legacy forward.

"... Everybody's important. Regardless of what background you come from," Howard told the Veterans History Project. "But if you're willing to work hard, there's still an opportunity in America to move ahead. ... Freedom. that's inherent in everything we do. It's worth fighting for. ... freedom was the underlying reason I guess that I survived every battle that I was ever in in Vietnam. Because I didn't want to lose that freedom."

After receiving his Medal of Honor, Howard visited the Tomb of the Unknown Soldier. Those family members of his that had never made it back home — having been left in unmarked graves on battlefields strewn across Europe — he wore the Medal of Honor for them, too.

"And so when I received that honor, I felt that I was sharing it with members of my family that had sacrificed their lives in the Second World War and my family knew that. ... I was thinking about grandma and I was thinking about my dad and I was thinking about my uncles."

Robert Howard at the Old North Church in Boston, Massachusetts, 2009.
(*The Boston Globe,* December 26, 2009)

Sergeant First Class Eugene Ashley, Jr.

US ARMY

Medal of Honor
Purple Heart

October 12, 1930–February 7, 1968 (37 years)

Sgt. 1st Class Eugene Ashley Jr. charged five times against dug-in NVA forces and four times he was rebuffed. He persisted through the excruciating pain of a bullet in the chest and on the fifth charge, his actions would go down in history. He would become one of the few and proud bearers of the highest American military decoration in existence.

Mortar rounds began pounding the Lang Vei Special Forces compound on the morning of February 6, 1968. They stopped, then started back up again with full force at 1800 hours. Sixty more rounds hitting the camp, wounding 10 soldiers, and all but demolishing two bunkers.

Lang Vei served as a base from which a detachment of the 5th Special Forces Group of the US Special Forces trained indigenous Civilian Irregular Defense Group (CIDG) forces. This was all about to change, as the North Vietnamese Army (NVA) began to descend upon the encampment with quick and blistering firepower. Around midnight, Sgt. Nickolas Fragos spotted something even worse headed toward them over the horizon: Soviet-made PT-76 amphibious tanks were busting through the barbed-wire perimeter fences and storming toward them. By dawn, Lang Vei was completely overrun by the potent combination of armored tanks and dedicated NVA manpower.

Capt. Frank C. Willoughby — trapped inside the compound — had called down ferocious artillery and air strikes on the enemy, but it had not been enough. NVA tank crews had driven up and fired point blank into protective bunkers. The M-72 rockets fired by the Americans had either missed completely, jammed, misfired, or simply failed to knock out the enemy tanks. Now, the remaining allies found themselves holed up in the command bunker and under constant grenade attack. It seemed as though all was lost. But at this most dire moment of the Battle of Lang Vei, Sgt. Eugene Ashley Jr. entered the fray.

Ashley was born in Wilmington, North Carolina. He had joined the Army in 1950, serving in the Korean War. By 1968 — the year the North Vietnamese had chosen Lang Vei as the grounds to stage their first effective use of armored vehicles — Ashley was an accomplished veteran serving with the 5th Special Forces Group. He wasn't about to sit idle while his comrades were blown to smithereens.

Ashley had been nearby when the attack on Lang Vei began, and he pulled out all the stops to quickly assemble and equip around 100 Laotian soldiers. The plan was to launch not only a rescue operation but, if possible, recapture the base. Ashley formed the Laotian soldiers into a loose skirmishing line and made his way toward Lang Vei, radioing the forward air controllers stationed overhead to direct strafing runs and soften up the enemy.

At this point, Gen. Westmoreland of Military Assistance Command Vietnam, Col. Ladd of the 5th Special Forces Group, and Maj. Gen. Anderson of the 1st Marine Aircraft Wing were putting together another plan to airlift the survivors out of Lang Vei. That plan would never get off the ground without Ashley — he needed to take the fire pressure off the base. The Laotians were understandably reluctant to face the superior NVA force, but Ashley levied his superior leadership abilities to rally them forward into an offensive. He led the charge, attempting to break through the North Vietnamese lines, even as they were met with a downpour of grenades and volleys of machine gun and automatic weapons fire.

Beaten but not broken, Ashley would go on to lead four more charges against the devastating firepower of the NVA. Every bunker that Ashley tried to take control of was booby trapped with explosives and blew up in his face. Relentless, Ashley regrouped and charged for a fifth time, determined to make this his last. He adjusted the air strikes such that they would fall nearly on top of his assault element. They were putting themselves in mortal danger, but the gambit worked. The enemy withdrew in the face of the wild courage of the American-led force and the hellfire of the air strikes. Ashley had taken the hill.

The five charges into the heart of Lang Vei had exacted vengeance upon the NVA; this pressure proved absolutely critical for diverting the enemy and carving a path for the remaining survivors to escape the grip of their attackers.

During the violent madness of this final attack, Ashley was struck by thunderous machine gun fire to the chest but continued to lead the assault despite his wounds. In the end, though, his gambles against fate in the service of rescuing his comrades came at a grave price. Ashley lost consciousness, his body giving up long before his will ever would. As he was carried away, an artillery round found its mark and ended Ashley's life — but not his memory.

Under the cover of Ashley's attacks and US air strikes, the survivors of the Battle of Lang Vei escaped to relative safety and were whisked away to freedom by Marine helicopters. Sgt. Eugene Ashley Jr. was posthumously awarded the Medal of Honor on December 2, 1969, by Vice President Spiro T. Agnew, and was buried at Rockfish Memorial Park, Fayetteville, North Carolina. Ashley's name lives on in the spirit of Eugene Ashley High School, established in 2001 in Wilmington, North Carolina, which was christened in honor of the all-American war hero.

Poolaw during the Korean War.

First Sergeant Pascal Cleatus Poolaw

US ARMY

Distinguished Service Cross
Silver Star (4)
Bronze Star (5)
Purple Heart (3)

January 29, 1922–November 7, 1967 (45 years)

Poolaw served alongside his father, brothers, and sons across multiple wars and generations. A one-man army, Poolaw is the most decorated Native American in United States history.

For Pascal Cleatus Poolaw, war was a family affair. The year was 1942, and with the German wave crashing over the Soviet Union and the Japanese dominating the Western powers in Asia, the threat of the Axis powers loomed over the entire world. Pascal Poolaw had just volunteered for the war, leaving behind his wife of two years and his hometown of Apache, Oklahoma, for a battle-torn Europe. However, Poolaw did not go into this war alone; at his side in the western front stood his father and both his brothers. "He has followed the trail of the great chiefs," his wife said, and indeed, over the course of Poolaw's life, he and his family would prove just how much fight they had in them.

It didn't take long before Poolaw had his first brush with death — in 1944 he was wounded in a bloody fight against the Nazis, his bravery winning him the Purple Heart. But Poolaw was just getting started: he would ultimately leave the military with 42 medals and citations. After making a full recovery, Poolaw and the Company M 8th Infantry would fight the battle of their lives against German forces near Recogne, Belgium.

It was September 8, 1944, and Nazi machine guns and mortars were giving the Allies hell. Poolaw, now a sergeant, took an offensive role in support of a nearby rifle company. With an open field between his squad and the objective, his chances for survival were slim. But slim chances are where heroes shine, and Poolaw led his squad into the bloody-but-beautiful Belgian fields looking to win. Even with heavy mortar and small-arms fire raining down on them, Poolaw's natural talent as a leader shone through as he stormed across the killing field with minimal casualties to his squad. But from his new position, Sgt. Poolaw spotted something that would strike fear into even the most combat-hardened soldier: the Nazis were coming, in full force, to stage a devastating counterattack.

Standing steadfast as the Statue of Liberty, Poolaw held, unflinchingly, as machine gun fire hosed down his position for five full minutes. And for five minutes, Sgt. Poolaw responded with a vengeance, hurling grenade after grenade into the enemy lines until the fearsome explosions broke the back of the German host, sending the survivors into a panicked flight. That day, one man had held off the Nazi tide, and it was due to his extraordinary actions that the battle was won and many of his comrades were saved. After word reached command about this one-man army, his display of courage and his warrior spirit were deemed in line with the highest traditions of military service and the Silver Star was promptly pinned to his chest.

But the Poolaw family's relationship with war wasn't over yet. The year is now 1967. The Grateful Dead and marijuana teamed up to create the summer of love, Vietnam — and the protests against it — were heating up, and Pascal Cleatus Poolaw had finally retired, having accrued two more Silver Stars and another Purple Heart in the Korean War. Following in his father's footsteps, Pascal's son, Pascal Jr., was serving in Vietnam — until tragedy struck.

It was a normal, humid February day in Vietnam when

Pascal Jr. was critically wounded in both legs by one of the deadliest, most horrific weapons of the day: land mines. In 1965 alone, 65 to 70 percent of US Marine Corps casualties were caused by mines and booby traps. Vietnam holds the dubious honor of being one of the only nations in the world with land mines from three different countries: old French mines from the '50s, American "toe-poppers," and Vietnam's own homegrown variety of "mosquito mines." Needless to say, land mines are a living nightmare to soldiers and civilians alike and continue to plague Vietnam to this day.

The entire Poolaw family felt the blast from the land mine that day. Pascal Jr. had to have one of his legs amputated below the knee, Pascal Sr. was devastated, and to add to the family's fears, Poolaw's other son, Lindy, was drafted and set to deploy to Vietnam. Having just been through a parent's worst nightmare, Pascal Sr. wasn't ready to lose another son. In an act of valor, he rejoined the military after over a decade of retirement to take his son's place. Pascal Sr. rushed to the West Coast, but he arrived too late; his son had shipped out just one day before. His plan had failed but not his resolve. He put on the jungle fatigues, picked up his service rifle, and followed his son into Vietnam; for the Poolaw family, war had always been a family affair.

On November 7, all sides involved in the First Battle of Loc Ninh were beginning to wear out after nearly a week of bloody brawling between the Viet Cong and the South Vietnamese and American forces. While other troops were consigned to hold and secure the town of Loc Ninh, 1st Sgt. Pascal Sr. was deployed on a search and destroy mission. Search and destroy was to Vietnam what Blitzkrieg was to World War II, with new technology — helicopters and tanks — being the driving force of change. Central to the American strategy in Vietnam and based on the new power of "air cavalry," search and destroy was a tactic of inserting ground forces into hostile territory, searching out the enemy, destroying them, and then withdrawing immediately.

At least that's how search and destroy is *supposed* to go. Just after Poolaw and his men were inserted behind enemy lines, they were ambushed by the Viet Cong. The last thing Poolaw did that day puts to rest any questions about the character of this hero: seeing a downed soldier, he swam into open water and put him onto his back, even as the bullets were soaring. Swimming back to shore, bullets tore through both him and the man he was saving.

His actions were more than emblematic of the bravery of the American warrior; in that moment he was a symbol of the proud warrior traditions of his Kiowa Native Americans back home. "This is patriotism from the Indian people, of Kiowas, this family. They weren't afraid to go," Poolaw's sister Evalu Russell said as recorded in the book *Kiowa Military Societies: Ethnohistory and Ritual*. In the days of old, the highest honor of any Kiowa man was to be a member of the elite Dog Society — those warriors of the highest caliber for whom eventual death in combat was all but guaranteed. In 2014, the publishing date of *Kiowa Military Societies*, talk was made of reviving the Dog Society, and most Kiowa said that more than anyone, Pascal Poolaw exemplified the courage, service, and selflessness of the Kiowa military ethos.

1st Sgt. Pascal Cleatus Poolaw would enter the history books as one of the best-of-the-best and was awarded a monumental fourth Silver Star after his death. Despite Poolaw losing his own life, Lindy, the son he followed to Vietnam, would make it out alive. Across three wars, across generations, Poolaw and his family served like few others have.

Pascal Cleatus Poolaw. (www.goldstarfamilyregistry.com)

Jeannette Guyot. (*The Telegraph*)

Jeannette Guyot

Legion of Honor
Distinguished Service Cross
George Medal

February 26, 1919–April 10, 2016 (97 years)

When France buckled under the pressure from German forces in WWII, many begrudgingly accepted their fates as captives to the Nazi overlords. Not Jeannette Guyot. She took up the mantle of resistance at age 22, working day and night to save all those she could, even surviving capture and months of interrogation by the Gestapo. When she finally retired at war's end, she would go down in history as one of the war's most decorated women.

It was February 8, 1944, and Jeannette Guyot leapt from the British RAF bomber into the bitterly cold night sky above occupied France. She was not afraid — she had earned her parachute wings — but the mission she undertook was drenched in danger. She had already been captured once; if the Germans got their hands on her again, her life was over.

Jeannette Guyot was a French resistance veteran without peer, fiercely fighting against German occupation for four long years. Even after being captured and interrogated for three months, her patriotism compelled her to return to France despite the threat of more torture and execution rising with every passing day.

"I landed pretty heavily as the wind was strong, got rid of my gear and found myself in the bright moonlight," she later wrote in a letter to a superior. Suddenly, a man appeared out of the darkness. If this was an Englishman, she was well on the way to success. If this was a German, she was dead.

"All right, old chap?" he whispered to her. As he leaned in closer, he corrected himself, taken aback.

"Oh sorry, this is the first time a woman dropped on us."

Guyot was born in Chalon-sur-Saône on Feb. 26, 1919, and defiance ran thick through her family's blood. When the Nazis invaded, her father, Jean-Marie, joined the underground Forces *Françaises Combattantes* (FFC). Jean-Marie paid the ultimate price for his bold opposition to the Germans; he was captured and deported to Germany in 1943, where he perished. Her mother, Jeanne, also participated in the FFC, and was arrested 10 days after her husband. She was sent to a concentration camp in Ravensbrück, Germany, where she would remain until the end of the war.

When her country was torn asunder by Nazi Germany, 22-year-old Jeannette did not hesitate to join the Resistance. Instead of running away or submitting to the invaders, she took advantage of her hometown's proximity to the relative safety of Vichy France to escort refugees and intelligence agents across the Saône River.

In 1941, Guyot joined the Confrérie Notre-Dame resistance network where she continued her courier work, but it wouldn't be long before disaster struck. In 1942 she was arrested by the Gestapo, and three harrowing months of interrogation followed during which a single misspoken word would've meant the end of her life. But Guyot was a determined professional, and she never broke under the extreme pressure; she left imprisonment with her cover story intact and went right back into her work with the Allies.

This all changed, however, when the resistance network was infiltrated by German intelligence. In June of 1942, Pierre Cartaud sabotaged the Resistance from the inside, leading to the arrest of many of its members and placing Guyot in mortal danger.

Betrayed and under immense threat of capture, she was forced to flee to Lyon in Vichy France. But that, too, proved to be a sinking ship. In November 1942, Germany rolled into

Vichy, stomping out Resistance elements and forcing Guyot to make one of the hardest decisions of her life: she needed to immediately leave France or face inevitable death at the hands of the Gestapo. On May 13, 1943, a British squadron discretely landed in a pasture in central France, and Guyot hastily boarded, putting her fury at the Germans into the back of her mind — for now.

Instead of succumbing to defeat, the moment she touched down in Britain she joined the French Free Forces. She worked against the Germans from London for half a year before her stubborn bravery urged her into taking a more direct approach. She underwent more intelligence training, earned her jump wings, and parachuted back into France as part of Operation Sussex. Guyot and her team would perform pivotal and immensely risky intelligence missions from behind enemy lines in the buildup to the D-Day invasion.

After her landing in Occupied France, she made her way to Paris, where she walked into Café du Reseau with the intention to make an ally. Recruiting assets into resistance forces was a dance with the devil: recruitment was an absolute necessity to building intelligence networks, but every new recruit came with the possibility of bringing a German plant into the ranks. In this case, Guyot's grit paid off. Madame Goubillion, owner of Café du Reseau, whose husband had been taken prisoner by the Germans a short time before, was ready to go to any length to get back at the Nazi invaders.

"I remember she came into the bar," Madame Goubillion told *The Observer* in 1988. "I knew she did this sort of work, and when she asked me, I agreed without the slightest hesitation." Even though the Gestapo had an office just down the street, Goubillion felt no fear; she had a duty to fulfill for her husband and her country.

At one point, Goubillion was hiding seven men and a cache of weapons in her tiny cellar when a German soldier marched in. "If he had been any trouble, I would have knocked him on the head and pushed him down the well," Goubillion said, "but all he wanted was a glass of white wine and a chat about his wife and children."

The French suffered deeply for their resistance to the Nazi occupiers. Guyot's fellow Resistance operatives were routinely captured, tortured, and executed for their "crimes" against the Germans. Even worse was the collective punishment perpetrated by the Nazis, in which random French civilians would be killed to punish the Resistance. By the time the war drew to a close, 30,000 French hostages had been shot to intimidate defiant members of the Resistance.

This never stopped nor even slowed the indomitable Guyot. From the moment German boots stomped into her hometown, to the Allied victory in 1945, Guyot risked her life to fight against the Nazis who had enslaved France. She continuously set up airdrop zones and safe houses up until the Allies liberated the area.

Guyot's exceptional resolve earned her three of the Allied Powers' top military awards: France's Croix de Guerre avec palmes, America's Distinguished Service Cross, and the British George Medal. Guyot reunited with her mother after her release from a concentration camp and married one of her fellow Resistance fighters whom she'd fought side by side with.

Jeannette Guyot left the Resistance in honor, able to retire with the knowledge that she'd spent every day doing all she could to sabotage the Germans in her home country. She ended the war as one of France's most highly decorated agents and will forever serve as a model for fearless resistance fighters standing up to the forces of fascism.

A British soldier guards a beach in southern England, October 7, 1940.
(Imperial War Museums)

Boatswain's Mate First Class James Elliott "Willy" Williams

US NAVY

Medal of Honor
Navy Cross
Silver Star (2)
Legion of Merit
Navy and Marine Corps Medal (2)
Bronze Star (3)
Purple Heart (3)
Navy and Marine Corps Commendation Medal (2)

November 13, 1930–October 13, 1999 (68 years)

James E. Williams hardly needs an introduction — he is well known for having one of the most impressive careers in the history of the US Navy. He was an honorary chief boatswain's mate whose service spanned almost 20 years, most notably serving in both the Korean and Vietnam Wars. Williams is one of only 32 Native Americans to have earned the Medal of Honor.

James Elliott "Willy" Williams was so determined to get into the US Navy that he faked his own birth certificate. He was only 16 years old at the time, but already an ardent young man with a dogged determination to serve his country. More than 50 years have passed since President Lyndon B. Johnson presented Williams with his Medal of Honor, yet he is still considered the most decorated officer in the history of the Navy. Williams is one of only seven men in US naval history to have earned the Medal of Honor, the Navy Cross, and the Silver Star.

Williams was born on November 13, 1930, in Fort Mill, South Carolina. Shortly after, his Cherokee family moved to Darlington, South Carolina, where he grew up and graduated from St. John's High School. In those days, you had to be 18 years of age to enlist in the Navy, but Williams had no interest in waiting. At 16 he convinced a country clerk to change his age on his birth certificate so he could enlist early. "I thought there was nothing better than servin' my country and gettin' paid for it," he told *All Hands Magazine* in 1998.

His first day in the Navy was August 8, 1947, and he completed basic training in San Diego, California, in November of 1947. After numerous assignments in the US, including a tank landing ship, a receiving station, and the destroyer USS *Douglas H. Fox*, the call to duty finally came down. In June 1952, he was deployed to Southeast Asia to fight in the Korean War. His assignment was just off the Korean coast, where he led raiding parties into enemy territory with small boats detached from the destroyer.

When he returned to the United States, he served on the USS *Thomaston*, the minesweeper USS *Direct*, the light cruiser USS *Little Rock,* and spent time with Air Transport Squadron SIX and the Fleet Training Center. These appointments all provided him with invaluable experience for his next assignment: the Vietnam War.

Williams earned his Medal of Honor on the Mekong River in the Republic of Vietnam on October 31, 1966. He was boat captain and patrol officer aboard the River Patrol Boat 105. On this particular day, he and his team were navigating through the waters of the Mekong River as they'd done so many times before when suddenly, and seemingly out of nowhere, the patrol came under fire from two Viet Cong sampans — a relatively flat-bottomed type of boat common in East Asia. Williams instantly ordered his men to return fire. The entire crew of one of the enemy sampans was killed, the other turned back to take refuge in a nearby inlet. It was an ambush. As they pursued the fleeing boat, they encountered heavy, close-range, small-arms fire from a hidden Viet Cong sampan.

Then bad went to worse. As Williams led his men through

an intense and nonstop counterattack, they were suddenly confronted with a stunning enemy force: two enemy junks and eight sampans armed with heavy automatic weapons. "Looking at the map, I could see where he had to come out, I turned hard right to wait for him. As I did that, lo and behold, we found a big staging area. All I could see were boats and people," Williams remarked much later in an interview.

A ferocious fight initiated. What Williams did next cemented his place in Naval history. With utter fearlessness, he directed a precise counterfire to buy time until their backup of armed helicopters arrived. That's when he discovered an even more alarming concentration of enemy boats. "We got through that and I am trying to zigzag, I go by a couple more corners and turn into this area. Lo and behold, we hit the second staging area." But Williams's motto was "Lead from the front" and this is precisely what he did — he coordinated a savage counterattack in the treacherous Mekong Delta that destroyed or damaged 50 sampans and seven junks. When the armed helicopters arrived, he then organized the attack on the remaining forces.

By this time, it was dark. His patrol was still in danger, but he was not about to surrender. Williams ordered the search lights turned on and cautiously and meticulously directed the patrol to shore. It was pitch black; he was working against the clock; the stores of ammunition were quickly running out, and despite all these forces working against him he successfully disabled the enemy ashore, brought his team to safety, and won a tremendous victory for his country.

His exceptional leadership led to the patrol destroying 65 enemy boats and inflicting nearly 1000 enemy casualties. It was for this day that on May 14, 1968, President Lyndon Johnson presented Williams the Medal of Honor for "his extraordinary heroism and exemplary fighting spirit in the face of grave risks inspired the efforts of his men to defeat a larger enemy force, and are in keeping with the finest traditions of the US Naval Service."

Williams retired after 20 years of active service and was made honorary Chief. He received an honorable discharge from the Navy and went on to work as an instructor at the Federal Law Enforcement Training Center in Glynco, Georgia, and then the US Marshal Service Headquarters in Washington, DC, before retiring from Federal Government Service in April of 1967.

Williams passed away at the age of 68. His Medal of Honor citation is proudly displayed on the *James E. Williams*'s mess decks, providing sailors with a daily reminder of his legacy and to *always do your best and be your best.*

USS *James E. Williams*.

Master Sergeant Raul Perez "Roy" Benavidez

US ARMY

Medal of Honor
Purple Heart (5)
Defense Meritorious Service Medal
Meritorious Service Medal
Army Commendation Medal
Texas Legislative Medal of Honor

August 5, 1935–November 29, 1998 (63 years)

He was never supposed to become a soldier, having grown up an orphan living a life filled with alcohol and violence. He was never supposed to walk again after a mine shattered his spine. He was never supposed to survive Vietnam or come back to life after being put in a body bag. But he did do all those things, and showed the world what true heroes look like.

The lights fell harshly over the stage where Roy P. Benavidez stood on February 24, 1981. President Ronald Reagan and the Secretary of Defense stood at his flanks as cameras flashed, then Reagan turned and presented Benavidez with a flowing blue ribbon that ended in a golden star, one of only about 3,500 ever made.

"If the story of his heroism were a movie script, you would not believe it," the fortieth president of the United States said.

As President Reagan placed the Medal of Honor around his neck, Roy Benavidez recalled in his book *Medal of Honor,* how the floodgates in his mind broke and the memories washed over him with great and terrible strength.

"The blood flooding the floor of the helicopter and gushing out the doors as we banked and ran from that Cambodian jungle. The sights and sounds of my six hours in hell. The agony of the wounded and dying kept repetitively flashing through my mind while I watched the honor guard and heard the president, my commander-in-chief, read the details of the award. I was not ashamed of the tears that blinded my eyes."

This is the story of a man who faced defeat throughout his whole life, and who never seemed to learn the meaning of the words "give up."

Over his life people used a hundred names for what Roy P. Benavidez was: Mexican, Mexican American, Hispanic, Chicano ... and those were the nice ones. But Benavidez viewed it differently. He was American. And like all other Americans, he had a heritage — Mexican and Yaqui Indian.

As Benavidez told it, the Yaqui were about the meanest family of Indians that ever lived. In the ancient times of the Aztecs, whole armies were eaten and destroyed by the "wild men of the desert," holding out against the great hordes of the Aztec for hundreds of years. When Cortés conquered Mexico, his men marched north and met the Yaqui masters of the desert, proclaimed "victory," then got the hell away, never to return.

"If there is a crazy, never-give-up, never-quit side of me, I believe that it comes from my Yaqui ancestors," Benavidez says with pride in the pages of *Medal of Honor*.

World War II was raging during his childhood, and he fondly remembers going to the theater to watch newsreels of paratroopers jumping from planes. Afterward he and his friends would sneak into the cotton gin, climb into the loft, and leap into the cloud of fuzzy cotton seeds below. These dreams of becoming airborne would come to life later at Fort Bragg when he would make the 34-foot jump from a jump tower.

That "crazy, never-give-up, never-quit side" would be needed in the fight to come, not just the fight to survive Vietnam, but also to survive his childhood.

Back in those days, nature was still untamed in much of the country, and the dark tide of tuberculosis rolled over the countryside, killing countless men and women who eked out their lives on the land. He lost his father to tuberculosis first and soon his mother followed.

The pain of losing his parents caused Benavidez to carry a chip on his shoulder for a long time. Hardly a day would go by without him getting into a brawl, only a few of them happening within the ring at Golden Gloves — and even some of those legit matches looked more like a street fight than a sportsman's spar. By age 15 he was living the life of a typical high school dropout, working odd jobs and riding the fast track to prison.

Luckily, Benavidez had two guardian angels who helped him see the light. The first was his uncle Nicholas, who stepped into his life to tell him: "*Dime con quien andas, y te diré quien eres.*" Translated, this means "Tell me with whom you walk, and I will tell you who you are." Benavidez was hanging around troubled boys who would drag him down — he needed to become a man who could stand on his own two feet and make something of himself.

With help from Uncle Nicholas, he met his second guardian angel, Art Haddock, the bookkeeper at the neighborhood Firestone tire store. Haddock was looking for someone good and dependable to help at the store. Benavidez was neither of those things, but by the time he left Haddock's tutelage, he would be.

"Art was different from any Anglo I had ever met at that time," Benavidez says in *Medal of Honor*. "He wasn't Catholic like we were, but he was an ordained minister. His Bible was always on the desk next to the ledger books, and he often found occasions to read it to me. If he heard me say a curse word when I was trying to loosen the lug nuts on a tire, he would summon me." After a year, Haddock had taught him what it meant to be a man. It wasn't about beating his fists over the head of anyone who gave him a dirty look, it was about responsibility and strength of character. In the presence of honest men doing honest work, he finally began to understand what his uncle Nicholas had been trying to teach him for so long.

After whipping himself into shape with the help of his guardian angels, Benavidez joined the Texas National Guard and found a place he was proud to call his home. Soon after, he took it a step further and joined the Army.

After a tour in Korea, he was assigned to Vietnam in October 1965. There, he'd learn that his military training so far had not prepared him for guerilla warfare in the deep jungles of Southeast Asia.

"Say, mate, just keep eating, don't look up, we're not alone," Dickey, a wily Australian vet who'd served in Malaysia, said under his breath.

The food in Benavidez's mouth turned to ash, as he recalls in *Medal of Honor*. He was on his first combat patrol in south central Vietnam, six kilometers out of the city of Tam Kỳ, and so far the jungle had been quiet. That peace disintegrated as a burst of rifle fire rang out over the canopy. Benavidez dove face first for the cover of a massive tree, rolling over and bringing up his weapon, ready to return fire. Benavidez's eyes darted to Dickey; his head was tilted upward deep into the canopy. Dickey wore a lopsided smile — cracking branches gave way to something tumbling down on top of Benavidez. An AK-47 crashed near his feet. Then a body careened out of the foliage and hit the ground with a sickening crunch.

"'Sorry about that, mate, had to shoot a little early but he had bloody well sighted in on you. Have to keep your ears open out here, mate, if you want to stay alive,'" Dickey said with the cool professionalism of an expert — a master survivor. Benavidez remembers in *Medal of Honor* a little voice in his head responding: *Stay close to this man, he's gonna make it out of this war.*

Benavidez learned many hard lessons early on about how to survive, and most of those lessons centered on not sticking out as an American — the Viet Cong and NVA would always go for the "round eyes" first. Sleep on your stomach so as not to snore — the Vietnamese don't snore. When the mosquitos are eating you alive, just let them feast — the Vietnamese ignored them. Walk like the Vietnamese, squat like them, eat like them, and dress like them; that's how you'd make it out on a boat or a plane instead of a body bag.

One day, Benavidez broke his rule of making every move like the Vietnamese. They had stalked into a deserted village and hanging from a post was a bag with a little puppy inside. It was squirming and whining. Benavidez wanted to rescue the poor animal left behind in the evacuation, but Dickey rushed in and stopped him. Sure enough, the puppy had an explosive attached to it that would've blown him apart if he'd tried to save it.

Sometime later, Benavidez was returning to a village the Americans had helped clear just days before. Walking into the village, he found children who had been crucified, grieving grandparents at their feet utterly devastated by the despicable act of cruelty. Benavidez realized that day that evil was a real force in the world, and that America, with all its faults, was a place worth fighting for.

"Every time I thought I was getting a handle on what was going on and why, something else would pop up and convince me I knew no more than a flea on the backside of a dog. Wherever that hound decided to go, I was going along for the ride," Benavidez wrote with the insight only a soldier can muster.

Today was no normal day, as today Benavidez was the point man on patrol. The point man is the most dangerous position to be in — you're first in and last out, and your injury, or more often death, is there to serve as a canary in the coal mine, an alarm to tell everyone else to run for cover. Benavidez had run his mouth the day before; he'd been shooting the shit with his colonel and had told him he was part Indian. The colonel, having watched too many movies, figured that Benavidez had to be the Lewis and Clark, Sacagawea sort of Indian, tracking game through the forest with footsteps as light as feather falls — and that's how he ended up point man.

It was his last mission in the region, and unfortunately, that's also the last memories Benavidez had of this expedition. He stepped on a mine. The mine failed to completely explode, yet hunks of metal jumped up like a rocket and smashed into the bottom of his spine, twisting and squishing it like it was made out of cheap Chinese plastic. Benavidez was out cold, out of the war, and out of hope to ever live a normal life again.

"Benavidez, how you doin' today? Time to go back."

"Doc, y'all got things messed up here, these pegs don't fit in those holes."

The year was 1966, and for two months Benavidez had lain like a vegetable in a hospital bed. Finally, whole words sprang out of his mouth — nonsensical as they were — and within hours everything came bursting back to him. Benavidez had been part of the first wave of veterans coming back from Vietnam with horrific combat trauma. It was still a new thing in the States, though it wouldn't be for long. Benavidez, while alive and reunited with speech and his memories, had a mind that was wild with confusion, terror, and despair.

The army had been his life for 11 years: it was his job, his pride, his future. Now his future would be collecting checks while sitting on his porch, living the life of a retiree as a man of barely 30. This look into the future was unthinkable to him — the loss of the place he'd earned through hard work was as excruciating as the pain, maybe worse.

The doctors were ready to discharge, but Benavidez begged and pleaded that they not give up on him. They were only human, but even that could only go so far for so long. The doctors and the army were running out of reasons not to send him home.

Benavidez responded in the only way he knew how: he prayed and he kept his chin up, deciding to work his ass off to get his ass up. At night he would roll out of bed with only his arm strength, paying as little attention as possible to the crunching sound that would echo across the room when he landed. At first the other patients didn't get it — they heard him fall and they called for the nurses.

"Shut up, you guys," he groaned. "This is my therapy, leave me alone."

That first night he didn't even make it to the wall before the nurse came in and chewed him out like he was a man-sized toddler crawling out of the crib. The next night he was able to drag himself to the wall and sit against it — he got that far before the nurses came in, dressed him down, and plopped him back into his bed.

On the third attempt, another patient gave him a hand by putting two nightstands against the wall. When Benavidez made the long crawl to the wall, he used the nightstands to pull himself up so that he could hang there. He tried to put his weight on his legs, but the pain hit him like a Mack truck and he collapsed. The nurses came back to finish the embarrassing, nightly ritual.

This continued every night, and every night he inched forward through the agony. The nurses were at an impasse: they could either ignore him or tie him up, and since they had hearts in their bosoms, they chose to ignore him.

"Night after night, I bailed out of bed, crawled for the wall at the head of my bed, and pulled myself up. I pushed the nightstands ahead with my arms, pressed my feet against the cold tile floor, and dragged my dead body along until my arms were under me again. Then I'd start all over again. Finally, I was moving about two tiles at a time. Every night, I got knocked down. Every night I got back up again."

For the other patients in the ward, he was the star attraction — the only attraction in the otherwise dreary life they led.

"'Hey, look at that Mexican. I'll bet you a beer he falls.'"

At first, he fell so hard and so often that gambling on his success wasn't much good for peanut gallery fun and profit. The patients might've been bored but they weren't stupid, and nobody was crazy enough to bet on this lame horse. Pretty soon the odds shifted, however, and it was anyone's game. *He was going to get out of there one day,* murmured some in the ward.

"Finally, I could stand. In unbearable pain, I could lock my dead limbs under me and they would hold my weight," he stated with conviction in his book *Medal of Honor.*

One day an officer came in to give him the news nobody else had had the guts to: you're not walking again, and you sure as hell don't have any place in the army outside of a desk job. It was cold, but the officer was right. On the field you have to be in tip-top shape or you're putting everyone else's lives at risk. There's no place for participation awards in war.

Benavidez stammered his disagreement, hurled the covers off his legs and rolled himself off his bed. Keeping one hand on the bed for balance, he shuffled along the floor, keeping a stiff upper lip against the furnace of pain burning in the base of his spine. The officer wasn't impressed. Nothing he saw changed the fact that Benavidez's future was in the seat of a chair for the rest of his life.

The other patients in the ward erupted.

"'Give the guy a break.'"

"'Come on, Colonel, listen to him.'"

"'Don't kick him out yet. I've got two beers bet on his walk tonight.'"

"'Yeah, Colonel, fix him up so he can go back and get zapped the next time.'"

It was impossible to shut them up. They were all fighters in that ward, and they'd found something to fight for in Benavidez. The colonel slammed his file shut without saying another word, absolutely furious with these clamoring veterans. But Benavidez and his platoon of bedridden warriors had won the day. He was not discharged.

And he continued to get better. His strained relationship with his wife started on the path to normalcy. His eyes slowly opened to see just how lucky he was; compared to a lot of the other guys surrounding him, he was in great condition.

Within a couple of months he was back on his feet — in constant pain that he wouldn't mention for fear of getting the boot, but up nonetheless. He was fit for limited duty. Pulling a few strings, he tucked himself into the lineup taking the jump test. His first jump was embarrassing, but by his third he was performing clean jumps from a thousand feet in the air like he was born with wings. He was finally a soldier again — he finally felt alive again. "The sound of the parachute silk popping in the air was still music to my ears. I was finally home."

When he should have still been in physical therapy, now he was training physically for the Special Forces, the elite of the elite. He gained his Alpha code: Tango Mike/Mike.

"I am as proud of my second name as I am of my first name. The second name was bestowed on me by my brothers-in-arms. They were all the bravest men in the world and I loved them."

The date was May 2, 1968, the day Benavidez would earn his Medal of Honor while face to face with 1,000 NVA soldiers. The following story is compiled in Roy P. Benavidez's book through the accounts of Benavidez himself as well as Roger Waggie, Bill Armstrong, and Jerry Ewing, who were all involved in the mission.

Armstrong, the pilot, zigzagged, dipped, dodged, and dived the helicopter to make his destination impossible to predict for any enemies who had eyes on them. The helicopter finally landed in the thick of the jungle, and at lightning speed, the team had jumped from the chopper and the aircraft had left, leaving no trace that American forces had ever touched this little corner of Vietnam.

The men took a moment to make absolutely sure they were clear and undetected. After they achieved certainty, Wright took point and O'Connor brought up the rear, every soldier loaded up with special equipment — cameras, food, lots of ammunition — and made their way through the sticky heat. As they hacked through the dense overgrowth, point man Wright broke through to a hidden, well-trodden trail cut through the jungle. They had just discovered a likely enemy pathway, and Mousseau did reconnaissance for the team; he returned quickly, confirming their suspicions. There were enemies nearby, and they were coming down the trail.

Wright gave the order to return to their positions, and O'Connor, the man positioned furthest back, would be the one to lead the retreat if the situation warranted. O'Connor sat, stared, and sweat in the eerie quiet of the jungle — but the calm didn't last.

A small scream broke out through the flora, followed by the cracks of a burst of gunfire — O'Connor immediately recognized the cadence of an AK-47. But he was a fine soldier, and he waited for the order before so much as twitching. The order came, and he began the quick retreat backward, paying no heed to the vines that reached out from the jungle to trip and scrape at them, until they reached a gorge.

The relative safety of the gorge allowed Wright the time to let all the men know what had happened: Mousseau had slit the throats of two woodcutters who were clearing the way for more NVA to come pouring through, but one of the woodcutters had managed to get a shot off into the brush. The bad news hung darkly over the men. Someone had likely heard those shots, and one could only guess how many enemies were behind the woodcutters. Even worse, their request for emergency extraction had been denied. They were to return the great distance back to their original landing zone.

They got most of the way back to the LZ before they heard the sound of machetes chopping through the foliage and calm NVA voices rumbling just beneath their ability to make the words out. Wright desperately tried to contact command again; first he failed, and the voices neared ever closer. He tried again and received the orders loud and clear: keep your head down and complete your mission.

They left the area with haste, coming across a small clearing. One by one they made their way across the clearing to the safety and cover of the treeline on the other side — and ran face first into a dozen or more NVA troops.

Both the Green Berets and the NVA were equally taken aback. The Green Berets hatched a plan without hesitation; the Americans buried their faces in their maps while the interpreter and the allied South Vietnamese Special Forces with them convinced the NVA that they were on the same side. When the NVA began to let their guard down, the Green Berets took action and turned on the hapless NVA. But before they could pull their triggers, the interpreter barked out words that turned the Green Beret's blood cold: "They know!"

That small clearing turned into a gunfire-fueled bloodbath. Most of the NVA fell into the dirt, peppered with bullet holes, but one of them managed to lob a grenade with his dying breath. The grenade lit the treetops up like a flare — everyone within a mile would be crawling all over them.

Wright tried again to call for extraction. This time it was accepted.

While the men were shooting and dying on the ground in some patch of jungle west of Loc Ninh, Benavidez was at a church service. A chaplain managed his service with meager means, using the hood of a jeep as a makeshift altar. Suddenly, the radio came alive with noise: metallic sounds of weapons clattering around and desperate cries for help.

At that moment, Benavidez saw Michael Craig, who had been on the first rescue team headed for the Green Berets. As soon as Benavidez laid eyes on him, he knew Michael was going to die. He was nineteen; Benavidez knew that because they'd celebrated his birthday two months prior. Craig had been a little brother to everyone, always so eager to serve, eager to please, and full of life.

"Oh, my God, my mother and father ..." he said as Benavidez held him. He passed away right there in the arms of his brother.

Benavidez whipped around to the co-pilot of Craig's chopper.

"Who's in trouble down there?" When the co-pilot told him it was Wright and his men, his mind seemed to explode at the seams; those were his men out there, and from the sounds of it, they were doomed to die without any chance of rescue.

The beat-up helicopter was quickly repaired and one of the pilots, Larry McKibben, announced he'd be going back in. The area was alive with the conversation of different crews, comparing what they'd seen. Each man claimed to have seen more enemies in the jungle than the one that came before.

When the chopper's engine started and the rotors began to spin up, Benavidez jumped in. He wasn't exactly sure what he was going to do; all he knew was that he wasn't going to sit and listen to his friends die over the radio.

Benavidez heard the onslaught before he saw it. While he was promising the pilot that he would jump down so long as the helicopter could get him where he needed to go, a strange feeling came over him. He described it as going into autopilot. Maybe it was that crazy, never-give-up Yaqui side of him coming alive. Maybe it was the years of training. In actuality, though, it was *everything*. Everything he'd ever done, ever lived through in his life, had led up to this point. Once a troubled, orphaned kid, Benavidez had become a hero.

The pilot dodged gunfire as best he could while soaring straight into the heart of the battlefield. Benavidez performed the sign of the cross, tossed a medical bag out the open door, and rolled out of the helicopter with a calm, determined mind.

It was only seconds before the first bullet ran through his leg, but Benavidez was pumped full of adrenaline and furor and whatever else courses through the veins of soldiers when they commit to doing the undoable. He found Mousseau first, rounds having blown his eye out of its socket and pierced through his shoulder. But Mousseau was still alive, firing his weapon and not giving an inch.

He found O'Connor next, who motioned to him that there

were still a couple other survivors. "We're going to live. We don't have permission to die yet. Not here," Benavidez told him. O'Connor and another survivor began dragging themselves toward him, but bullets cut through the air. It was then that Benavidez took his second hit, now in his thigh. Benavidez released the green smoke signal to show the chopper where to land.

Everyone who was able to make it to the location did — everyone except O'Connor and the interpreter.

Benavidez sprayed the enemy ranks with fire from his AK-47 while making his way to O'Connor. He reached the two men and asked O'Connor what supplies Wright had had on him before he'd died. O'Connor responded saying that he had sensitive materials that could prove disastrous if they fell into enemy hands. Benavidez made up his mind: he would retrieve that intelligence. It was not a choice; it was a fact.

Benavidez picked up his dead friend Wright and hauled him back to the chopper — a third bullet soared into his back. He dropped Wright and reeled over in pain. He no longer had the strength to carry him.

He was out cold for a time. He woke up, rolled over, and powered through the pain, rising up to stand. Dazed, looking around for the helicopter — their only possible saving grace — all he saw was a wrecked mass of smoke and fire billowing out of the metal corpse. The pilot was dead, the co-pilot had a blood-red branch sticking out of his head.

O'Connor and the interpreter hadn't made it — or at least that seemed to be the case. When Benavidez and an allied Vietnamese soldier went to retrieve O'Connor's radio, however, they found him, still breathing. Five had survived that devastating crash, including Mousseau, and they still somehow managed to return fire from the chopper's tail, but the machine was dangerously close to giving out in a final, lethal explosion.

Benavidez needed to get them out of that deathtrap. They split into two groups to set up a perimeter, and Benavidez used the precious seconds of downtime to dispense morphine from his medical kit. As they steeled themselves for their last stand, Benavidez called for heavy air support. By chance, two F-100 supersonic jets were deployed to drop heavy ordnance on a nearby area. When they heard the call for assistance, they rerouted toward the dying men on the ground.

The fighter-bombers arrived, flying so close the men could feel the heat of the afterburners from the ground. The massive payloads were released and it seemed like the whole nearby jungle splintered into slivers of wood, metal, and body parts.

Benavidez was reminded of the Book of Revelation: the sky turned black with locusts as more and more air support poured in.

One helicopter touched down about 25 meters away, and everyone knew they were looking at their last chance of salvation. They loaded the last of their ammunition into their weaponry and took their final shots of morphine. This was the end of the line — do or die.

They were surrounded on all sides by enemies they couldn't see, hidden as they were in the cover of the jungle. Later it would be discovered that along with hundreds of NVA, there were thirty machine gun emplacements set up around the area in a bristling wall of death.

One more attack from the air cavalry stopped the hail of gunfire for a few moments, moments enough for that single chopper to fully land. Everyone had come to help, Benavidez thought. "What I saw was the American fighting man at his best."

The men carried as many of the wounded as they could, but withering gunfire was aimed at everyone who was trying to power their way up into the chopper. Benavidez was losing sight from the congealing blood on his face, blood that had poured out of shrapnel wounds on his head. The chopper was taking hits like a champ, but it could only take so much, and the bullets were turning it into a pincushion. Waggie and his co-pilot were firing their .38 pistols out of the empty space where the windshield had been moments before, and the door gunners, Darling and Smith — who were officers, not door gunners, but had volunteered for the job — were rapidly acquiring targets and saturating them with bullets from their M-60s.

Benavidez went back for another trip to get Mousseau. What he didn't see was the NVA soldier getting up off the ground behind him, delivering a blow to the back of his head with the butt of his rifle. Benavidez turned around — both men were shocked, shocked that Benavidez was still staring at him in the face. Before he could fire, the NVA soldier smashed the butt in his face again, and hell went dark.

But only for a second. Benavidez's hand felt the grip of his Special Forces knife as the NVA soldier wound back to stick him with his bayonet. Benavidez used his last ounce of strength and struck his knife into him — the man crumbled to the ground. Benavidez left his knife where it was.

A final bullet tore through Benavidez's insides, exposing his intestines. He clutched them in his hands, keeping them from hanging to the ground. He then found Mousseau lying on the ground, looking up at him with his one good eye. They clasped hands.

From there, Benavidez's memories are tattered. He was lying on the ground listening to the sound of a body bag being snapped closed; his eyes were blinded; his jaw was shattered; his body punctured thirty-seven times; his intestines outside his skin.

Jerry Cottingham recognized his face before the body bag was fully shut.

"That's Benavidez. Get a doc!" he screamed. The doctor leaned in to check his heartbeat, quite sure that the man in the body bag was a corpse. Benavidez spat into his face. The doctor changed his condition from "dead" to "likely dead." From there, he was evacuated to Fort Sam Houston's Brooke

Army Medical Center where he miraculously recovered. He received the Distinguished Service Cross and four Purple Hearts for his "Six Hours in Hell" fighting an entire enemy battalion.

It wasn't until 1973 that Special Forces Lt. Col. Ralph R. Drake would become aware of more evidence of Benavidez's heroism and insist that he receive the Medal of Honor. The time limit had, unfortunately, expired, and Roy Benavidez was not allowed to receive his medal. An appeal to Congress was made that an exemption for Benavidez be granted, but the Army Decorations Board denied the upgrade. An eyewitness account from someone present during the action was required, and it was believed there were no more living witnesses to the "Six Hours in Hell."

As luck would have it though, there was: Brian O'Connor, the former radioman of Benavidez's Special Forces team in Vietnam. In 1980, O'Connor was on holiday in Australia when he read a newspaper account of Benavidez that had been picked up by the international press. He immediately contacted Benavidez and gave him a 10-page report of the encounter, confirming what others had already said. The Distinguished Service Cross was promptly upgraded to the Medal of Honor.

In 1969, Benavidez was assigned to Fort Riley, Kansas, and in 1972, he was assigned to Fort Sam Houston, Texas, where he remained until retirement.

Benavidez had choice words for those who looked upon wounded soldiers.

"My buddies didn't want pity; all they needed was a little understanding. I vowed that I would try to make other people aware of how such men feel.

"I would say, 'When you see that guy on the street don't pity him. He doesn't want that. Don't help him either. He's a man and just as proud of what he can do as you are. Just treat him like a man and try to understand. Try and understand that he got that way fighting for you and for your way of life.

"'Maybe it was ten thousand miles away, and maybe it was a stupid senseless war, but he was there. He didn't choose the time and place and the situation. When he was called, he served. And he sacrificed, without question, for you.'"

Master Sgt. Roy P. Benavidez (center) at his 1981 Medal of Honor presentation ceremony with United States Secretary of Defense Caspar Weinberger (left) and President Ronald Reagan.

236

Harry M. Beal

US NAVY

August 16, 1930–January 26, 2021 (90 years)

Harry Beal was at ground zero to watch the previous era of Navy frogmen become the world-famous SEALs. From his humble beginnings as a milk-delivery boy to traveling the entire world at the behest of rapidly centralizing military, Beal never met an obstacle he couldn't overcome.

Harry Beal and his best Navy friend Harry Williams glared at each other in a Virginian classroom in 1962. President John F. Kennedy had come calling with a new idea to implement a special forces unit called the US Navy SEALs. Every man in the room was fully aware that the United States was going to war in Vietnam; this decision was no peacetime affair — it had deadly serious implications.

They were wondering who would pull the trigger first, signing the clipboard and agreeing to "go anywhere in the world at any time and do things that were needed in a moment's notice." Beal recalled Williams taunting him in an interview with *Cumberland Times-News* on November 30, 2015.

"You don't have the guts to sign that," Williams jeered. But Beal had never met a challenge he couldn't handle, and this one was no different. He strode up and signed the paper. Williams, not to be outdone, signed it right after. When pen left pad Harry Beal had not just become the first official SEAL, but also one of the shortest, standing just five feet tall.

But Beal's journey into the history books had started long before that fateful day. In the 1940s, he was a highschooler who worked the graveyard shift delivering milk from midnight until the first bell rang in school at 8 a.m. "I didn't sleep much in those days," Beal said in his interview with the *Cumberland Times-News*. "I could do a one-arm pull-up. It was because of delivering milk and pulling the crates off that truck." His father had ideas about Beal working in the coal mines after high school, but he had no interest in grinding away underground. Instead, Beal talked his father into letting him enlist as a 17-year-old.

Beal wasn't convinced this "kiddy cruise," lasting for only three years and requiring parental permission, would bloom into a lifelong career or start him on the path to the history books. Nevertheless, he sailed off to the Korean War, serving as a gunner's mate on the USS *Shenandoah*. "It was the best thing that ever happened to me," Beal said in an *AP News* article on May 25, 2019.

But the USS *Shenandoah* never saw combat, and he was left wanting more. His previous plan to return home after three years to marry the girl next door changed in the face of the ongoing war; the government decided to keep him longer, and he reenlisted afterward.

This was the era before the Navy SEALs had come into being, but its experimental predecessors had been thriving since World War II: the Amphibious Scouts & Raiders, the Naval Combat Demolition Units, the Sino-American Cooperative organization, and the Underwater Demolition Teams (UDT). In 1955, Beal found his true calling, becoming a Navy frogman for UDT.

"They start with 100 candidates. After Hell Week, half of them would be gone. ... It was tough," Harry Beal said. Though Beal began his career in the Navy as a gunner's mate, he had now achieved the status of a specialist — one of the best when it came to underwater demolition — and this rarified toolset is exactly the kind of qualifications John F. Kennedy was looking for when he created the SEALs.

"He [JFK] was talking to us just like I'm talking to you," Beal told the *Cumberland Times-News*. "He said, 'We want 50 guys in each team. SEAL Team One will be on the West Coast and SEAL Team Two on the East Coast.'" The ballsy personalities making up Beal's group weren't pleased with the West Coast contingent being named SEAL Team One while their East Coast received the label of Team Two.

"If I may sir, the sun comes up over here first, we thought we would be SEAL Team One," Beal's frogman comrade said. The man said right to JFK's face he'd "take a bullet for him," but that he was disappointed with the president. "We thought he had just got a ticket right out of the Navy, but Kennedy just laughed it off," Beal reminisced.

UDT training had been brutal, but the regiment for the newly minted Navy SEALs was downright mad. Every branch had their paws in the pie, Beal recounted to *AP News*. The Army showed him the ins-and-outs of jungle warfare, foreign weapons, and plane-jumping. The Air Force gave him survival lessons, and the Marines headed the training for escape and evasion tactics. When the underwater section commenced, one course had the men dropped to the bottom of a 15-foot-deep pool with their feet and hands tied together. Whoever grabbed the face mask that sat at the bottom of the pool got a weekend pass. It was sink or swim, and Beal made it look simple by clenching the mask between his teeth.

All that training proved invaluable almost immediately; before the year was up, he'd be in Vietnam, teaching the South Vietnamese underwater warfare tactics. Mack Beal told *taskandpurpose.com* that his father was given the simulated rank of lieutenant because the South Vietnamese officers didn't give a damn what enlisted US troops had to say. Beal remembered in his interview with *AP News* how the South Vietnamese were terrified of poisonous white sea snakes in the waters. And hammerhead sharks.

"The snakes were not aggressive, and they were often more afraid of humans than humans were of them," he said. "Oftentimes big fish brushed up against us in the waters and they could have been sharks. On a dark night you could see underwater if the moon was out."

Harry Beal would go on to serve 20 years in the Navy from 1948 to 1968. JFK's recruitment demand of men needing to "go anywhere in the world at any time and do things that were needed in a moment's notice" proved exceedingly true; Beal would see South America, Europe, Southeast Asia, and the Caribbean Sea, including Cuba, during his time with the SEALs.

As with all the Special Forces greats, the vast majority of adventures Beal underwent will have to be left to our imaginations.

"I was on him year after year to try to get some interesting stories out of him," Mack Beal told *GoErie*. "He said 'I swore an oath.' Nothing that you could really put out for public. Everything was classified for him. He wasn't giving anything up even in his 90s." By 1963 he had returned stateside to his family and became a well-respected SEAL instructor for five more years until his retirement. He was even part of the team that fished astronaut John Glenn out of his waterlogged space capsule following his historic orbit around Earth.

Beal's son Mack recalled to *taskandpurpose.com* the times when early astronauts would work with SEAL teams to learn how to use breathing apparatuses; his father, ever the consummate professional, never asked to have his picture taken with any of the famous people that surrounded him.

"When [John] Glenn and the other guys came to us, we didn't think the program was going to work," Harry had told his son. "He said, 'We figured they'd get into that rocket; they'd light it off, and that would be the end of the program because it would blow up.'"

"Most kids go to the comicbook store to see superheroes. I just walked out on base," Mack Beal told *Erie Times-News*. "In my opinion they were real superheroes," he said of military personnel he saw on base in his youth.

"It's been a wonderful life and I wouldn't change anything," Harry Beal told *AP News*, looking back on his lifetimes of hardships and history-making. "Some things in life are more difficult than others but we all have to keep going and keep the faith. Sometimes I wonder why I am still here, but the good Lord must have a reason," he said. "Maybe it is just because I am supposed to represent a generation of men who loved their country, their families, and one another. My heroes have always been firemen and policemen, our American presidents, and Jacques Cousteau."

Mack Beal stated to *Erie Times-News* that the inclement weather on the day of his father's funeral — he died on January 26, 2021 — was a far more fitting conclusion to his father's life and legacy than any sun-drenched day would be. His father would often say that when people retreat from storms to seek warmth and comfort, that's when he'd go to work.

Command Sergeant Major Patrick J. Tadina

US ARMY

Silver Star (2)
Bronze Star (10)
Vietnamese Cross of Gallantry (3)
Army Commendation Medal (4)
Purple Heart (3)

August 16, 1942–May 29, 2020 (77 years)

Patrick J. Tadina was the longest continuously serving Ranger in Vietnam. He is one of the godfathers of the Army Rangers and is a legend within the Special Forces community to this day.

"We were beside the trail, right on the border there. We had the art of hiding down so good. I'd already counted 25 of them passing. Hardcore [North Vietnamese]. I could barely move, except my eyes. Here came another column, brush all over them, really sneaking along — scary stuff. We had to stay so still. They were only three or four meters away now, long files of them. Just the slightest movement, and they would detect us."

In a split second, a 5'5'" American warrior and his five brothers-in-arms burst out of the brush like a pack of vicious wolves — but wolves armed with explosives. After the smoke cleared, these demons of the jungle melted back into the leaves, leaving a once-disciplined fighting force turned upside down and inside out, scattered and wondering just what paranormal entity had blown their columns into mincemeat.

But these men weren't ghosts, nor were they fiction. They were Army Rangers, and they were led by the lionhearted legend Patrick J. Tadina.

In 1985, shortly after the release of *Rambo: First Blood*

Part II, Don Tate of *Stars and Stripes* got one of the only long-form interviews of Tadina on record, comparing the big screen's "Rambo" with the real thing. When Sylvester Stallone — bare chested with bowie knife clenched between Hollywood-white teeth — depicted Rambo on the big screen, he was acting. Patrick J. Tadina was doing his duty for his country and his comrades. The real Rambo stood at 5'5"', weighed a buck twenty-five, and spent 60 months of continuous service in one of the bloodiest wars in American history. And not a single man under his command — not one — ever fell in the line of duty. As it often turns out, fact is far wilder than fiction. Patrick J. Tadina, the soft-talking Hawaiian made out of steel and forged in the jungle heat of combat, puts his fictional counterpart to shame.

A young man growing up in Hawaii, Tadina saw the writing on the wall: get out of Dodge or be left on the wrong side of the law by teenage hooliganism.

"I was living in Hawaii. And one of the reasons why I came in is because a lot of my friends that went to school were getting in trouble, so it was better for me to leave than to get in trouble," Tadina said matter-of-factly to an interviewer for the Library of Congress Veterans History Project.

"It's good for any young person to spend at least a couple years in the service ... it taught me a lot of things, you know, and how to be self-sufficient in your own way. How to do a job well without people being on you telling you what to do all the time, and you took responsibility for your actions. You did the best you could."

After joining in 1962 (behind his sister, one of the first women to join the Army), Tadina and a whole batch of Hawaiians were shipped off to basic training. This would start Tadina's damn-near mythic career toward holding a permanent place in the Ranger Hall of Fame.

Tadina would never walk on the red carpet like Stallone, and he'd never win an Oscar, but at the end of his 30 years, one month and 14 days in the service (he counted), he'd achieved more than any tuxedo-clad theater major at an awards ceremony could ever dream of. Tadina earned himself two Silver Stars, 10 Bronze Stars (seven with valor), three Vietnamese Crosses of Gallantry, four Army Commendation Medals (two for valor), and three Purple Hearts. Maj. Bob McKensie of the 3rd Infantry Division called him the most decorated enlisted man of the Vietnam War.

But what was it that made this 5'5"' man a goliath on the battlefield? Well, his appearance for a start. Tadina had told fellow soldier Mir Bahmanyar he was of "Filipino-Chinese-German-Irish-Hawaiian descent or some exotic cocktail mix like that."

"I looked like them," said Tadina in his interview with *Stars and Stripes*. "They would see me in the middle of these big, regular-looking Americans, and didn't know what to do. It gave us the edge. We knew what to do." His slight build and dark complexion let him blend right in with Viet Cong soldiers on the long patrols deep into the Central Highlands of Vietnam, where he always made sure to lead from the front in the point position. Citations describe him walking within feet of known enemies waiting to ambush and leading an enemy patrol into a trap. Guerrilla warfare was supposed to be the Viet Cong's game, but Tadina outplayed even the wiliest of the North Vietnamese combatants, making the infamously sneaky enemies look like amateurs dropped into the pro leagues.

One can only imagine the confusion among the North Vietnamese upon seeing Tadina decked out in the company outfit — sandals, black pajamas and the AK-47 — popping out of the misty jungle hills of the Central Highlands and giving them a full metal jacket surprise. Being the best of the best, however, takes more than just a good disguise.

"We also had patience," Tadina relayed to Don Tate of *Stars and Stripes*. "The American soldier is not always noted for his patience. So we learned how to outwait them. How important attention to detail was. We also knew how to deal with them in the jungle in the dark. Dark was when Americans normally pulled inside their perimeters. Everyone said, 'The night belongs to Charlie.' Night was when they attacked. But, for us, it was easier at night. If you had your stuff together, you could really do it to them at night. They didn't expect Americans to come at them at night."

And just who, or what, were these Army Rangers? "[T]he units I was assigned in were all combat units. ... And we're in the field and behind enemy lines and usually what our missions call for is we spend anywhere from two days to six days in the field and then we get pulled out after we accomplish our mission ... unless we get run out by the bad guys. We were the intelligence people at that time during Vietnam." Tadina's brothers-in-arms of the 173rd Airborne were almost always outnumbered in the field — that's the odds you're up against when you're neck-deep in hostile waters. Two dozen to one was just standard practice — but they were always one step ahead of their killer competition. By the end of his five-year streak of jungle dominance in Vietnam, he'd personally sent at least 136 enemy combatants to the afterlife, always quick to cite his men's lives as the fire that powered his engine of war. The actual toll is undoubtably higher — keep in mind that the Rangers were experts at pinpoint airstrikes and artillery bombardments against any Viet Cong unlucky enough to run into them.

One story told by Mir Bahmanyar on his blog, originally told by Roy Boatman (a deceased Ranger who served in Vietnam) was that Tadina snuck into an enemy hospital to attempt to break out a POW. He quietly took out a guard with a silenced .22 but found the hospital deserted. "Talk about balls and trade craft," Mir Bahmanyar said breathlessly.

Even though Tadina was like a guardian spirit to his men, never letting a single one come to lethal harm, he himself felt the sting of bullets more than once.

"I was shot three times, man. The first time I was shot right in the middle, about halfway up my back." But as the enemy's sights locked on to Tadina, he was able to dance behind a tree and use it as a makeshift shield.

Speaking during his Library of Congress interview: "... the reason why it did not damage me too much is because I seen the guy aiming at me and there was a tree right close to me. So I jumped behind the tree just as he was shooting, and then he shot again, and the bullet went through the tree, but the tree was a good, maybe eight inches around. By the time the bullet got through the tree, it kind of mushroomed out. So it did not penetrate into my back."

Tadina's time with the Rangers was full of close calls like that, and while once might have been luck, the Hawaiian's ability to risk everything and come away still breathing was a matter of skill, not dice rolls.

"And the second time I was shot, I was shot while I was running. Trying to get outta an ambush, you know, and I was shot in the back, again, not in the back, but in my butt. ... He shot me right in, you know, one of my butt cheeks and just knocked me down like somebody gave me a stiff kick."

The third time he was shot earned him not only a Purple Heart, but a Silver Star as well, as he put himself in extraordinary danger to protect his men at any cost.

As the point man, Tadina was within the kill zone when his Special Forces senses told him something was wrong, but the enemy, apparently confused about who he was, didn't immediately fire. After spotting the enemy, Tadina pulled the trigger and warned of the ambush to his teammates before hitting the ground and being shot in both calves. His Silver Star citation reports that he refused medical aid and continued to command until the enemy retreated.

"The last time I was shot, I was in an ambush, and they were waiting for us. I shot the first two, took the first two out, then the rest of 'em, there were about eight of 'em. All of 'em start opening fire on me and two bullets, one through each leg behind ... One of 'em cracked the bone in my left

leg, but the other one, the bullet just kind of cut my calf. ... When I cut my pants off, patched myself up, I looked at it and my calf was hanging down around my ankles. Oh, then I'm bleeding real bad, so I tied it up with a rag, and then I got some albumin, blood expanders and took that so I wouldn't bleed out."

Not all the wounds from war are physical, however. During the war, his brother joined the many brave soldiers memorialized on the Wall of the Vietnam Veterans Memorial. This loss, far from defeating Tadina, only pushed him to fight harder, and while he lost his brother, he still had his Ranger family.

He always seemed most at home with his "Ranger family," his daughter said in an interview with the *Together We Served* blog. "He was my dad, but he belonged to so many other people," she said.

His final statement in his interview with the Library of Congress showed his faith in God and of his Ranger brethren. "Airborne all the way, and the big ranger in the sky is always with you. We always think about the big ranger in the sky. He will always take care of all of us."

250

Colonel Charles A. "Chargin' Charlie" Beckwith

US ARMY

Distinguished Service Cross
Silver Star with Oak Leaf Cluster
Legion of Merit
Bronze Star
Purple Heart

January 22, 1929–June 13, 1994 (65 years)

The father of Delta Force, Charles Beckwith was a Promethean figure who spent his entire career — suffering many political defeats on the way — transforming the American Special Forces into the greatest unconventional fighting force the world has ever seen.

In military history, from ancient to modern, from Sun Tzu to George S. Patton, one trait comes up time and time again as perhaps the most important quality that defines a leader for whom men will fight and die: the ability to fight from the front. Col. Charles "Chargin' Charlie" was a man born for the front lines. He pushed forward the cutting edge of Special Forces tactics and was always charging ahead to secure a better future for America and for those who risk their lives in the name of freedom.

While studying at the University of Georgia, Charles Beckwith was offered one sure path to fame and fortune, and one tougher path that could lead him anywhere from dignity to death. He was drafted by the Green Bay Packers, but his dreams led not to the football field, but to the battlefield. He joined the US Army and was commissioned as a second lieutenant in 1952.

For six years Beckwith would learn the trade of war and experience the life of a soldier with the 7th Infantry Division in South Korea, and later the 82nd Airborne Division. His direction shifted in 1958 after completing the tough-as-nails, 62-day Ranger School. Tactical expertise and leadership sharpened to a fine point, Beckwith received his Ranger Tab and joined the 7th Special Forces Group. Beckwith and his battlewise brothers deployed into the simmering conflict between Communist and Democratic forces that would soon become the Vietnam War.

Enter Operation Hotfoot. Operation Hotfoot was a clandestine military training mission in Laos, whereby Beckwith and those serving with him donned civilian clothes and worked with the French military to train the Royal Lao Army to be the best it could possibly be.

"I found nothing but a rabble ... with no discipline and no organization to speak of. Equipment was in terrible shape ... it was just awful," Brig. Gen. John A. Heintges was recorded saying by US Army Special Operations Command History Office. They were to work for the Programs Evaluation Office, a US covert paramilitary operation, as a training arm, teaching Laotian soldiers the use of the M1 Garand, Browning Automatic Rifle, M1 Carbine, bazooka, M18 recoilless rifle, and both 60mm and 81mm mortars. French instructors in Laos would teach tactics, while the American trainers would teach technical subjects.

For all its efforts, the Special Forces and their Laotian allies could not quell the specter of Communism that was expanding rapidly in Southeast Asia. As the war escalated, the conventional warfare that once had proved so successful struggled to keep its footing against the cunning guerilla forces fighting against them. The Special Forces desperately needed to evolve, and Beckwith would be the man to do it.

In 1962, Beckwith went across the Atlantic on a cross-pollination mission with the British Special Air Service (SAS): they would learn from and teach one another. Beckwith soon discovered that he had little to actually teach his friends in Great Britain, but a lot to learn from them. The SAS was a much older institution, and the wisdom he gained from studying its inner workings would be the foundation for Delta Force, the US military's "tier one" special units tasked with performing the most complex, covert, and dangerous missions directed by the National Command Authority.

Beckwith landed on Britain's shores a cocksure Green Beret with the strict standards of conventional American military training drilled into him. "Straight lines, square corners, yes, sir, no, sir," as Beckwith put it in his book, *Delta Force*. That kind of straitlaced behavior was not how the SAS officers operated. The mess hall looked like a high school cafeteria after a food fight, the barracks seemed like more of a locker room. In his book, Beckwith recalls nearly losing his mind when trying to reprogram his brain to call his superior by his first name when off the field. But beneath the nonchalant, rebellious appearance, there was a trained force of hardened operators who, at the time, blew American Special Forces out of the water.

For the first exercise, he was dropped into nearly impenetrable terrain with a map that only showed the major landmarks. Where the instructors at Fort Bragg would give an hour of explanations to the men, the Brits only gave them a sentence or two. If a trainee didn't make it to the rendezvous on time, he'd be left in the wild for a day without food. If he got lost, his superior would toss him in the river along with all his gear, and for a day or two he'd work soaking wet.

Beckwith realized he'd misjudged these men. They played hard, but they worked harder, and their drills were far superior for breeding independent warriors than what he'd gone through to get his Ranger Tab. When he received his sand-colored beret, just like when he got his nickname "Chargin' Charlie," he felt had earned it — it hadn't been handed to him.

Beckwith went back to the US and submitted a report advocating for an SAS-like unit. He submitted and resubmitted the report. Since no one was interested, and as he'd been assigned to the 7th SFG(A) as an operations officer, he took his training ideas to the Green Berets.

"Before a Special Forces Green Beret soldier could become a good *un*conventional soldier," Beckwith wrote in *Delta Force*, "he'd first have to be a good conventional one. ... Because I had commanded rifle and weapons companies, I was appalled on arriving in Special Forces to find officers who had never commanded conventional units." Beckwith essentially rewrote the book on training, implementing tough standards that would result in the contemporary Special Forces Qualification Course, or Q Course.

In 1965, he volunteered to return to Vietnam and was put in charge of a high-priority unit called Project Delta. The setup had not been ideal. Beckwith was frustrated with having been assigned a bunch of drunks and prostitute addicts instead of real soldiers. He took the ax to most of them and started again from scratch. After months of recruitment — putting up signs asking for only the best of the best — he had something resembling a fighting force. Project Delta's first mission was to rescue besieged allied forces from Plei Me.

As they circled around in a gunship, analyzing the proposed landing zone, one of the helicopter's rotor blades flung off its axis. This caused the hull to fall, becoming a massive, lethal falling fireball. Beckwith looked upon the accident grimly. "A bad omen," he thought to himself. But an omen would not stop the first Delta force from pushing into the headwind and achieving victory.

After landing safely, they began to creep cautiously toward a small Vietnamese village. The settlement was deserted but the cooking fires were still smoldering; it was clear that the civilians had been rounded up and taken by the North Vietnamese just a short time before. This thoroughly spooked the whole team, especially the South Vietnamese. Beckwith was already expecting trouble, so it didn't make him flinch.

The single file of hard-eyed American and Vietnamese troops stretched through the jungle, guns at the ready for the worst. One shot rang out through the trees; a second followed soon after. Beckwith described in *Delta Force* charging forward and finding an enemy killed by American bullets — but a second North Vietnamese soldier had managed to disappear into the impossibly dense undergrowth before Americans could react. Maj. Tut, the leader of the South Vietnamese embedded with Project Delta, was shocked with what he found; this man was a North Vietnamese Army (NVA) regular, not a Viet Cong guerilla fighter. They were nearing a bona fide hornets' nest of enemy activity, and they might be in way over their heads.

Later that day, they neared their objective of Plei Me, a South Vietnamese camp. They knew they were close as they could hear an orchestra of gunfire playing out over the canopy. Night loomed over the men, and Beckwith put himself in the shoes of the South Vietnamese within the camp's borders. If they approached now in the low light, they might be taken for enemies, and Beckwith wasn't going to lead his men into a trigger-happy catastrophe of friendly fire. "I radioed back to Pleiku and informed Bill McKean that I would enter the camp at dawn," Beckwith stated in *Delta*.

As dawn broke over camp, they made their way in. Tangled up in the interior barbed wire was a mass of dead Montagnards (the name the French gave to the allied native people of central Vietnam). "There were about 60 other dead Montagnard soldiers stuffed into body bags and stacked up like cordwood. ... Outside the barbed wire there were a hell of a lot of Communists."

The fighting immediately reached a hellish peak. Beckwith and his combat-savvy cadre — Tommy Thompson, Bo Baker, Bill DeSoto, and John Pioletti — touched base and all concluded that they'd need a lot of luck, and more than a little grit, to get out of the deadly rat's nest alive. Mortar and recoilless rifle fire crashed over them in waves. Occasionally an enemy would pop out of the jungle gloom and charge the perimeter, throwing live grenades. As night fell, the explosions threatened to shatter the base into pieces. Beckwith recalled in *Delta Force* his worries about the men manning the guns on the perimeter breaking and running.

In the early morning Bill DeSoto caught a spray of hot slugs from a heavy machine gun. It "nearly tore his arm off." Beckwith calculated the immense size of the enemy from the volume of fire. Beckwith wrote: "When I reported I thought there were at least two, maybe three, large forces of regimental size surrounding the camp, I got some people in Pleiku really shook up." Command gave the besieged soldiers priority on all airstrikes, and with Maj. Thompson's direction, the Americans began to give as much as they got, slowly blowing holes in the hordes of NVA surrounding them.

"They hit the enemy with napalm and 250- and 500-pounders all day long." That night they received a telegram via radio from President Johnson: "We're thinking about you. Hold out there as long as you can. God bless you all." The Delta Project could only hope that those kind words would not be the last they ever heard from the States.

Nights were far worse than days. Mortars and recoilless rifle fire pounded harder; new bodies were added to the old; rats would come alive and crawl over the ruins of the camp, unaware or unafraid of the men and havoc.

Beckwith, in *Delta Force,* recalled Maj. Thompson growing manic and hollering, "I like it! I like it!" as the fury of the airstrikes came so close they sprayed scraps of metal into the allied men's faces.

Capt. Moore wanted a photograph despite Beckwith's warnings to keep his head down. A scrap of smoldering bomb shrapnel tore half his shoulder off. They were running out of men who had the energy to hold the perimeter, so Beckwith trained a couple of unauthorized newspaper reporter stowaways how to fire .30-caliber machine guns.

"They did a first-class job for us," Beckwith stated with pride in *Delta Force*. God bless those civilians. Meanwhile, the South Vietnamese were really pulling their weight; armored columns fought to reach the camp despite facing crippling ambushes. Pusser, an American captain, had been shot dead outside the moat of barbed wire and his body needed to be recovered. "The Vietnamese," Maj. Tut told Beckwith, "will get his body for you."

In fact, the open graves piled with dozens and dozens of rotting bodies were deteriorating morale. When Khoi, a Vietnamese pilot, arrived in his helicopter, Beckwith thought he was out of his mind flying into the maw of hell. But Beckwith was fond of the Vietnamese Evel Knievel. Khoi could get in and out of tough spots he'd never seen American pilots even dream of attempting. "You know, Boss," Khoi said in pitch-perfect English, "your problem is you worry too much." He loaded up as much dead as the aircraft could handle and flew out of there, taking a few bullets as he left.

One morning the 2nd Battalion, 1st Brigade, from the 1st Cavalry Division was dropped into Plei Me, and Beckwith was asked by their liaison officer where they should deploy the unit. "Around and beyond the north slope there were a lot of dead enemy soldiers and the stench was terrible. Landing there would be an instructive introduction for the 1st Cav, which had only arrived in the country a short time before. No better way to let them know war is hell. After the battalion landed, because his people were throwing up all over themselves, their CO asked if they could move somewhere else."

After days of bloodbath, rescue finally became a reality. The women and children in the camp, then the dead, then the living were lifted out. The perimeter of the camp looked like the surface of the moon — a pitted and cratered, napalm-blasted wasteland with 800 or 900 dead North Vietnamese regulars spattered all over the place.

All was said and done, Project Delta had been a success — they'd saved the camp and killed a helluva lot of bad guys.

It was January of 1966, and Project Delta has been making waves. Beckwith agreed to team up with the 1st Cavalry and head out on Operation Masher. It went like this: they'd sweep the coast, drive the Viet Cong up the mountains, and slam the lethal jaws of the trap shut. In Beckwith's book *Delta Force*, he describes Project Delta's role as the operation's eyes and ears, allowing the 1st Cavalry to have perfect information on enemy locations.

Three teams dropped into the An Lao Valley, an emerald, double-canopy jungle surrounded by rugged peaks. It was one of those rare-as-unicorns quiet nights where most everyone sleeps well. The sun rose and broke the peace; some of the forward operators were surrounded and in dire straits, encircled by Viet Cong and taking heavy fire. Although the monsoon season had passed, heavy rain poured out of the sky, making it impossible for air support to swoop in for the rescue. When the walls of falling water finally thinned, Beckwith jumped into a chopper, and they headed toward the team in distress. The weather forced them to stay low, nearly buzzing the foliage. The team's location was easy to recognize because they started receiving heavy fire. "Almost at once a .51-caliber machine-gun bullet comes through the helicopter. It goes in one side of my abdomen and comes out the other. I pass out."

.50-caliber rounds were invented to kill aircraft. With proper aim, .50-caliber rounds took out tanks in the World Wars. A basketball player holding one of these tank-killers would appear to have a hand the size of a child's. These things don't kill men, they slaughter them; get hit by one of these anywhere on the body and the shockwave of force will cause neurological damage.

It split Beckwith like a smashed pumpkin. The few things he recalled in *Delta Force* is a shot of morphine — then darkness. Thoughts bubble up to the surface of a helicopter ride, vague hints of a hospital.

"You're in bad shape, Boss." There's movement of people running around.

"'He'll bleed to death before we can do anything for him.' They agree, I'm not worth fooling with. I'm not going to make it. I grab the big nurse, she's closest, 'Now let's get one thing straight here. I ain't the average bear, and I didn't come in here to pack it in.' That gets the two doctors' attention." Beckwith's gallbladder and twenty-one inches of intestines are cut out, he's split down the middle from his sternum to his groin. But Beckwith was proven right — he was no average bear; he was "impossible to kill," as the *Washington Post* described him.

That evening a young Hawaiian man was rolled into the ward from the operating room.

"'Major, this boy next to you is in a bad way,'" the nurse commented to Beckwith. His gut, shoulder, hip, and leg showed bullet wounds, leaving him barely clinging on to life.

"It's up to you," Beckwith told him. "If you want to make it you can. It's all in your mind." Beckwith squeezed the young man's hand as hard as he could. "If you want to quit you'll be dead by morning. If you're strong, you'll live. Goddamn, son, make up your mind." Beckwith felt the slightest pressure from the Hawaiian, squeezing his hand back and telling Beckwith he wanted to fight in the only way he could. As it turned out, he was up and out of the hospital long before Beckwith.

Time sped up over the following years. Beckwith had decades of Special Forces experience under his belt, Vietnam had tired him out with politicians going half-assed on it near the end, and global terrorism cast an ever-longer shadow over the world. Delta Force, all these years later, was still just a jumble of thoughts in his head and a pile of papers on his desk.

The Delta Program had been a success, but Beckwith had not been able to realize his dream for the American Special Forces to be the best in the world. The Pentagon and Washington, DC, are massive, labyrinthian machines that can be tough to change at best and impossible to budge at worst. Beckwith worked his entire career to get his vision in front of the top brass, and he would never have been able to do it without help from a dozen other high-ranking men that he'd convinced and befriended over the years.

Plus, Beckwith had earned his damn stripes — he was a full colonel now. They'd ignored his ideas about American Special Forces before; he was a lot louder now, and a lot harder to dismiss. And, he had a hundred brothers-in-arms who believed in him.

"I don't want to lose when we go to Washington. We're going to get their attention only once and once has to be enough." That was Gen. DePuy as recorded in Beckwith's book *Delta Force*. And though his words were harsh, they were wise.

Col. Tom Henry got him to rid his briefing of most of the praise of Brits — it had to be all-American. Gen. DePuy got him to work all branches of the military into the deal, making sure he loaded them with praise first, but ultimately pointing out that there was a hole in the military that needed filling. So many other allies of Beckwith did their part, making sure the brief was in front of the right person at the right time.

Now he was at the end of the line: the briefing room at Fort Monroe. It was do or die. If he didn't impress the bigwigs now, his entire life's project would go into the garbage. Early in his career, when others hadn't understood his grand plan for Delta Force, Beckwith had come off as hot-headed. Now they had the sales pitch down to a science. Their presentation, their data, their arguments — flawless.

"Well, I'm not totally satisfied," Beckwith remembers DePuy saying in *Delta Force*, "but I think we're probably as far down the road as we can go. I'm going to go with it like it is. The packaging is good, so let's move it forward. By the way, what should we call the unit?"

"Delta," Beckwith said. "Call it 1st Special Forces Operational Detachment — Delta [SFOD-Delta]."

On November 17, 1977, Delta Force was born.

Three years later, in 1980, President Jimmy Carter gave Colonel Beckwith and his Delta Force their most complicated mission yet: they were to rescue American hostages from the

United States Embassy in Tehran, Iran. It would be the worst day in Beckwith's life.

The mission was doomed from the start by internal turmoil by bureaucrats who had no idea of the realities of high-risk missions. The forces that took part in the mission — Army, Air Force, and Marines — had not trained together properly. Even worse, the chain of command had tangled itself into a knot trying to tackle this joint-operation.

Beckworth's Delta Force, their skills sharpened to a fine point, never even got a chance to strike the enemy or rescue the hostages. Three of the eight helicopters needed for the mission failed. One crashed in a sandstorm, killing the eight servicemen onboard.

"It was the biggest failure of my life," he stated in 1981. "I cried for the eight men we lost. I'll carry that load on my shoulders for the rest of my life."

Today, America's Special Forces is, without a doubt, the premier counterterrorism and asymmetrical warfare fighting force in the world. Beckwith spent his entire life cutting through political red tape to sculpt the military status-quo into something worthy of the future. Without men like Charles "Chargin' Charlie" Beckwith and their expansive, self-critical vision, America wouldn't be the greatest country.

Carlos Hathcock II. (*The Los Angeles Times*, February, 1999)

Gunnery Sergeant Carlos Norman Hathcock II

US MARINE CORPS

Silver Star
Navy Commendation Medal
Purple Heart

May 20, 1942–February 22, 1999 (56 years)

Snipers are first and foremost about precision, secondly about skill and experience. Carlos Hathcock had all that and then some; his service was so legendary that a rifle was named after him: the M25 White Feather.

The world is made up of two kinds of men: the ones who spend time deciding who they want to be in the world and the ones who were born knowing. Carlos Hathcock II knew from a very early age what he wanted to become. He wanted to be a soldier; he dreamed of fighting for his country.

Hathcock was born in Little Rock, Arkansas, but grew up closer to Memphis in Wynne with his grandmother. His favorite pastime was shooting. When he visited family in Mississippi, he'd go into the woods alone with his dog to play soldier and hunt imaginary Japanese soldiers with an old Mauser that his father had brought back from World War II, all while daydreaming of becoming a Marine.

In 1959 at age 17, he pursued this dream and enlisted in the US Marine Corps. His uncanny talent as a marksman was quickly recognized by his superiors at the rifle range while he was in recruit training at Camp Pendleton.

After completing basic training, Hathcock was sent to Hawaii as part of Company E, 2nd Battalion, 4th Marines, where he easily won the Pacific Division rifle championship. As if that wasn't proof enough of his inherent skill, while at the Marine Air Station in Cherry Point, North Carolina, he set the Marine Corps record, scoring 248 out of 250 points on the "A" Course. No one has broken that record to this very day, decades later. His extraordinary talent was then recon-firmed in 1965 when he outshot more than 3,000 other ser-vicemen to win the Wimbledon Cup at Camp Perry, the most prestigious prize for long-range shooting.

In 1966 Hathcock was deployed to Vietnam and worked as a military policeman, but destiny had a different job in mind for him. Capt. Edward James Land had convinced the Marines to employ snipers for every platoon, then began recruiting Marines who had set records in sharpshooting. Impressed with Hathcock's achievements, he quickly asked him to join. Hathcock completed his training with more ease than most and was immediately sent on assignment. He very quickly became enemy number one for the NVA. He ran up a kill count so high that eventually a $30,000 bounty was placed on his head. To put this in perspective, the usual reward for US snipers was between $2,000 and $8,000. Hathcock was different; he and his rifle proved so destructive that the NVA believed it crucial to kill him for the sake of its own troops. He was in a league of his own; every single marksman who made an attempt on his life ended up a corpse.

The Viet Cong and the PAVN gave Hathcock a nickname: Lông Trang or "White Feather" because of the white feather he kept on his hat. It's said that he wore the feather as a taunt to the Communists to come find him. At one point, a platoon of Vietnamese snipers was sent to hunt him down. In response, other Marines in the area also wore white feath-ers in their hats so as to confuse the counter-snipers. These Marines were aware of the impact Hathcock's death would have and took it upon themselves to make sure they didn't lose him. It worked.

As a result of Hathcock's impeccable record, he was re-cruited twice for covert assignments. One was a mission to kill a Frenchman working alongside the North Vietnamese and torturing captured American airmen, which made Hathcock understandably furious. He took the man out with one round from his revised Winchester Model 70.

Before the next covert mission, he was told very candidly by his superiors that his survival chances were slim to none. This time the target was a North Vietnamese general. A difficult feat for most, but not for Hathcock. The general was swiftly killed from 800 yards by one of Hathcock's bullets.

His precision was unreal, almost unnatural. In one absolutely unprecedented incident in the jungle near Hill 55, southwest of Da Nang, an enemy sniper known as "Cobra" was sent to kill Hathcock. After a long, drawn out game of cat and mouse between Hathcock, his spotter, and the enemy sniper, Hathcock shot the final round from 500 yards which flew right through the enemy sniper's rifle scope and penetrated the man through his eye. Before he considered the mission completed, however, Hathcock seized the enemy's sniper rifle as a trophy and took it back with him to be turned over and tagged. Mysteriously, however, the rifle was stolen from the armory not soon after.

In 1967 Hathcock set the record for the longest sniper kill. He killed a Viet Cong guerrilla using an M2 .50-caliber Browning machine gun mounted with a telescopic sight at an impressive range of 2,500 yards. There was only one instance during his whole career in which Hathcock took off his white feather. This was during a volunteer mission only a few days before the end of his first deployment and he was not told any specifics of the mission until he had accepted the challenge. He was to shoot and kill a PAVN general.

This took a grueling four days and three nights. No sleep, barely any food — just crawling. He had to crawl over 1,500 yards, slowly, inch by inch. He said that at one point he was almost stepped on while he lay camouflaged in a meadow just before sunset. Later, a bamboo viper nearly bit him, but he still managed to keep up his position. Hathcock fired a single shot as the general was exiting his encampment and got him right in the chest, killing him on the spot.

That was his last mission before he returned to the US in 1967. Yet he couldn't stay away for long; he missed the Marines too much. Hathcock returned to Vietnam in 1969 and took command of a platoon of snipers. This tour changed his life forever.

On September 16, 1969, he was riding in an LVTP-5 armored vehicle along Highway 1 just north of Landing Zone Baldy, when the vehicle struck an anti-tank mine. Recovering first from the devastating explosion, Hathcock pulled seven Marines from the flames and consequently suffered severe burns on his face, arms, and legs — some of which were third-degree. A fellow soldier pulled him out and dunked him in water. He and the seven Marines he saved were then evacuated by helicopter and taken immediately to the hospital ship USS *Repose,* then to a naval hospital in Tokyo, and they ultimately ended up at the burn center at Brooke Army Medical Center in San Antonio, Texas. Hathcock received a Purple Heart while in recovery from the tragedy, but it was not until 30 years later that he received a Silver Star for his actions on that day.

His Silver Star citation reads: "With complete disregard for his own safety and while suffering excruciating pain from his burns, he bravely ran back through the flames and exploding ammunition to ensure that no Marines had been left behind in the burning vehicle. His heroic actions were instrumental in saving the lives of several Marines."

After discharge from the burn center, Hathcock returned to active duty and was instrumental in establishing the Marine Corps South Sniper School in Quantico, Virginia. The pain from the injuries constantly hounded him, but his fortitude and dedication to his trade kept him teaching sniper recruits up until his health failed. Hathcock was diagnosed with multiple sclerosis and, in 1979, was granted permanent disability separation and received 100 percent disability pay.

During the Vietnam War, Hathcock racked up 93 confirmed kills. Kills had to be confirmed by the sniper's spotter and by a third party, who had to be an officer. But snipers usually did not have a third party present, making confirmation impossible — especially when the target was behind enemy lines. Hathcock himself estimated that the real number was between 300 and 400 enemy personnel.

He once said that he survived his work because of his ability to "get in the bubble" and put himself in a state of "utter, complete, absolute concentration." After the war was long over, a friend read Hathcock a passage written by the great Ernest Hemingway: "Certainly there is no hunting like the hunting of man, and those who have hunted armed men long enough and like it, never really care for anything else thereafter." He copied Hemingway's words down on a piece of paper and said, "He got that right, it was the hunt, not the killing."

In *White Feather: Carlos Hathcock, USMC Scout Sniper,* he said, "I like shooting, and I love hunting. But I never did enjoy killing anybody. It's my job. If I don't get those bastards, then they're gonna kill a lot of these kids dressed up like Marines. That's the way I look at it."

In retirement, Hathcock taught counter-sniper techniques to police departments and select military units, including the SEAL Team Six. He died in 1999 in Virginia Beach, Virginia, from complications from multiple sclerosis and was buried at Woodlawn Memorial Gardens in Norfolk, Virginia.

To this very day Carlos Norman Hathcock II remains a veritable legend. He was one of the few men to utilize the M2 Browning machine gun as a sniper. The success this weapon had in the sniping context led to the adoption of the .50 BMG cartridge as a viable sniper round. Springfield Armory designed a version of their M1A Supermatch rifle with a Mc-Millan Stock and match grade barrel and named it the "M-25 White Feather." The rifle had a white feather logo marked on the receiver.

He is also honored by the Marine Corps League which every year sponsors a program with 12 award categories, one being the Gunnery Sgt. Carlos N. Hathcock II Award presented "to an enlisted Marine who has made an outstanding contribution to the improvement of marksmanship training." There is also a sniper range named after him in Camp Lejeune, North Carolina.

On top of all that, Turner Saddlery also honored Hathcock by creating a line of leather rifle slings embossed with Hathcock's signature. On March 9, 2007, the rifle and pistol complex at Marine Corps Air Station Miramar was renamed the Carlos Hathcock Range Complex.

There have been many mentions of Hathcock's impressive career in popular culture, most notably in the 1998 movie *Saving Private Ryan,* in which a shot "through the scope" was reproduced; a great movie scene imitating an even greater real-life man.

Carlos Hathock in the room he calls his bunker. (Bill Ballenberg for *The Buffalo News*, October 10, 1986)

Sergeant Joe Ronnie Hooper

US NAVY
US ARMY

Medal of Honor
Silver Star (2)
Bronze Star (6) w/ "V" Device
Purple Heart (8)
Air Medal (5)
Army Commendation Medal (2) w/ "V" Device

August 8, 1938–May 6, 1979 (40 years)

While Sgt. Joe Hooper at times played the role of antihero, after finding his place with the legendary Delta Raiders, he completed the full transformation into hero. Hooper was an indomitable warrior who was wounded eight times in Vietnam, yet after every injury he ran right back into the thick of battle. His valor and prowess was an inspiration to his comrades, and continues as a model of battlefield bravery to this day.

Rockets bombarded the riverbank while machine guns and automatic weapons fire punctured the thick mists of that cloudy February day in Vietnam. The Delta "Raiders," the name given to Company D, 2nd Battalion, 101st Airborne Division, were stuck in the mud; overwhelming firepower was keeping them from pushing past the river, but their duty and the courage burning in their bellies stopped them from retreating. This was no minor jungle skirmish — they were knee deep in the Tet Offensive of 1968, and the fate of the war felt like it rested on the success or failure of the day.

Past the river, the rockets, and the fortified bunkers was the ancient city of Hue. Sitting smack dab in the middle of Vietnam, Hue and the highway running through it were too valuable to allow the Viet Cong to hold on to. American and

South Vietnamese troops would suffer a month of heavy casualties trying to regain control of the city in what would become one of the longest and bloodiest battles in the Vietnam War. While morale waned among the soldiers who saw their deaths waiting on the other side of the riverbank, Sgt. Joe Hooper felt no such trepidation.

Sgt. Joe Ronnie Hooper was at the front lines of the bloodbath north of Hue, and he was tired of the Viet Cong doing all the shooting. As squad leader, Hooper gathered a few of his best men and made the call that they would storm the riverbank and take the fight to the enemy. He would ensure victory for himself and the men of the Delta Raiders even if he charged through hell to do it.

The Raiders were an extraordinary rifle company, largely populated by mechanics, cooks, clerks, and other noncombatant specialists rather than trained infantrymen. The infantrymen they did have were scrapped off of other companies that used the opportunity as an excuse to offload their least attractive prospects. Some of the Raiders had disciplinary records longer than their limbs; others came straight from the stockades. In the rush to build up manpower for deployment to Vietnam, this kind of unconventional recruitment was deemed necessary for the war effort even though conventional wisdom would say that such a group of men would make poor soldiers.

That conventional wisdom couldn't have been further from the truth. The non-traditional infantrymen who had originally been trained in specialties other than fighting led to a company of men that was sharper than average, and that extra intelligence made training faster and easier than elsewhere in the Army. And train they did; while others rested, the Raiders practiced night operations. James R. Kearns, who would later join the Special Forces, said in *Looking for a Hero: Staff Sergeant Joe Ronnie Hooper and the Vietnam War*, that when things got rough "what would get me through was just remembering that I was a Delta Raider. I thought everything after that is downhill and nothing else could be that hard, and there's no sense in quitting because you never did then."

For his part, Hooper fit into the Raiders like a hand to a glove, blending hero and antihero perfectly. The steel-nerved soldier who busted bunkers and carried wounded soldiers to safety also had a pair of lips tattooed on his buttocks, in commemoration of the fact that "everyone can kiss my ass." This contrast between savior and troublemaker traced all the way back into his childhood. Hooper was a loving older brother, teaching his sister how to drive the family pickup, play baseball, and helping with her homework. But he also felt stifled by normal life, choosing gambling and hustling over a regular job, and women and alcohol over school.

In *Looking for a Hero*, Hooper's biographer speculates that Joe was trying "doubly hard" to compensate for what he considered the failure of his father and brother to act like men. His father was a long shot from a good role model: absent, drunk, and in-and-out of jobs. Hooper would spend his teenage years fighting desperately to liberate himself from the shadow of what he saw as a deadbeat dad.

By 1956 Hooper had finally burned through all the adventure to be had in the secure and serene town of Moses Lake, Washington, and he dropped out of high school and walked right into the local naval recruiting station. Striking off on his own to control his own fate, he left Moses Lake with nothing but a burning desire to leave the quiet life behind. After a stint in the Navy, Hooper gave the civilian life another go, doing factory work in Glendale, California. By 1960 he told his childhood friend that "he was bored and he didn't have a good job and he didn't know what he wanted to do." He set off to reenlist in the Navy, but just as he arrived at the recruiting office, the Navy recruiter went home. So instead of waiting a day, Hooper walked straight to the nearby Army recruiter and became a soldier rather than a sailor, simple as that. The thrill of jumping out of planes and the adrenaline of combat made Hooper a perfect fit for the Army — in theory.

"He'd have been in the stockade, probably still sitting there, or in Fort Leavenworth," Capt. Charles Wayne McMenamy, the man in charge of the Delta Raiders, said of Joe Hooper. Described as "a hell-raising son of a gun" and "the kind of guy who would bite off more than he could chew and proceed to chew it," he hardly looked the part of the reserved, rule-abiding man often associated with professional soldiers. Yet Hooper and the other "undesirables" found a home in the Delta Raiders, and the unique composition of their company resulted not in a disorganized band of ne'er-do-wells, but in one of the bravest and most effective fighting forces of the war. Where some saw a troublemaker, the men of the Raiders had found Joe Hooper, the six-foot redhead with the slanted smile, to be a father figure, braver than most by a mile.

In 1968, with the Tet Offensive and American involvement in Vietnam burning red hot, while drenched in mud and assaulted by gunfire from across the river, the Delta Raiders would find Sgt. Joe Hooper to be more than just a fatherly soldier or a brave warrior; they would come to realize that they had a hero in their midst.

As the Delta Raiders sat across a river from a bunker complex, most of the men didn't see victory waiting for them on the other side, they saw suicide. River crossings are where soldiers go to die — from Ancient Rome to Vietnam, rivers have always presented a deadly obstacle to military operations. One wrong move could get you stuck waist deep in water and mud with a bullet between your eyes. Yet Hooper sensed a fleeting opportunity, and he began the charge across the river to execute a counterattack. And when Hooper sprinted across that river, he blazed a trail for others to follow.

"I know a lot of men were awfully afraid to go forward since the enemy fire was terrific and they had bunkers on every side," Sgt. Pettit said, an eyewitness to Hooper's heroism. "But the reason no one lagged behind was because Sgt. Hooper was always out front, and it kind of shamed them and made them feel more confident at the same time." As soon as Hooper and his men began wading through the water, the Viet Cong opened fire from their bunkers on the bank of the river.

The intense fire wielded against them would have stopped an ordinary man from continuing, but not Hooper. He masterfully maneuvered his squad into a superior position, and now it was the Viet Cong who found themselves at the wrong side of the Raiders' guns. Watching Hooper and his small squad turn the tide of the battle, more Americans flooded into the water to join the fight, emboldened by this act of suicidal — yet effective — courage. A couple of men didn't make it, the total lack of cover making them clay pigeons to Viet Cong shooters, and they went down without a chance to fight back. "Leave no man behind" isn't just a phrase, it's a code of ethics, and one that Hooper followed to the end.

Sgt. Hooper braved the enemy gunfire, bringing one soldier back, then two, sustaining a wound in the process, all while mud and blood mixing together in the chaos of battle. Next, Hooper surveyed his surroundings to decide what the best next move would be. He soon found what he was looking for: nearby, S.Sgt. Thomas was pinned down by gunfire from an unknown position, and it was only a matter of time before one of a hundred bullets got lucky and ended his life right then and there.

Hooper instantly sprang into action — calling out to a soldier ahead of them, he communicated that there were hidden shooters and that the soldier may be able to locate them from his position. The moment the soldier took one step out of full cover a bullet tore through his leg. Because of his leg wound, he was now fully pinned down and enemy fire was getting closer and closer to finishing him off with every passing second.

Hooper was not about to have anyone killed under his watch; taking drastic action to prevent further injuries to other soldiers, he navigated around to the left flank, right into the kill zone of hostile bunkers. Nobody knows exactly how he was able to survive this reckless charge, but those who witnessed Hooper on the battlefield understood that he didn't just survive the chaos of combat, he thrived in it.

Now Hooper was behind enemy lines and had gotten an idea. There were three bunkers that had been stopping their advancement, all connected by a single trench. Hooper was only one man, and he saw only one way to go forward — he would go it alone or die trying. His plan of action solidified, Hooper got up from his position and charged the first bunker. Pulling the pin of his grenade with a "click," he tossed it into the bunker, then followed up with a volley from his rifle. When the dust settled, nothing but bodies remained, and every enemy around knew there was an American in their midst. They reacted too late — Hooper opened fire from one bunker into another and left no survivors.

Hooper then climbed on top of the third bunker, this time with an NVA radioman running out to meet him. That radioman never got a transmission off, though he did catch a bullet from Hopper. After the radio operator dropped, not a soul stirred in those bunkers — none except for Hooper. Most of the American soldiers were still on the riverbank, not too keen on pushing forward into what seemed to be certain death. But Hooper appeared through the jungle, and seeing this hero, wounded but alive, their spirits lifted and they stood and marched onward to follow him.

Just as the men reached the top of the bank, a group of three Viet Cong burst out of the bamboo, firing off their AK-47s straight into the Americans. The chaplain went down, and terror froze the rest of the soldiers mid-march. Terror does not freeze one as fiery as Hooper, though, and he alone fired back, dropping two of the ambushers instantly and leaving the third to flee in fear. Without missing a beat, he performed first aid on the wounded chaplain and got him to safety. After returning, he led the men in a sweep to the three bunkers he had cleared earlier, and with the newfound support of his troops, they quickly overran the remaining bunkers on the flank.

"As I was trying to inspire the men on the field I found that Sgt. Hooper's amazing bravery was the greatest inspiration possible and made heroes out of timid men as they attempted to follow his example," Chaplain William Erbach, whom Hooper saved, said in his eyewitness statement. "I cannot help but believe that much of the company's success was directly resultant from the gallantry and heroism of Sgt. Hooper."

Although the constant danger had made the day feel more like a year, the fight was far from over. Hooper was determined to lead his men to victory. He moved ahead to assess the situation, and while on the move witnessed three snipers running into the cover of a house. Only two of them made it to safety, as Hooper made quick work of the slowest one with a well-aimed shot.

Not wanting to enter a house where an ambush was all but guaranteed, Hooper had a better idea: He picked up a LAW rocket launcher, steadied it, and fired the rocket into the building. The two remaining men and the house itself were demolished. Immediately after, his ears picked up more gunfire and he realized the enemy was holed up in other houses and were peppering his men from their cover. The LAW made quick work of those huts just as it had the first.

Even after having reduced what seemed like half a village to rubble, there was still more gunfire aimed at his men, this time from a shrine. Sgt. Hooper grabbed two other soldiers and hit the ground, slowly crawling toward the enemy holdout. After reaching their position and saturating the enemy with fire, they quieted their weapons and listened. For the first time that day, silence reigned over the jungle, a silence owed to the heroics of Sgt. Hooper. The momentary peace was sweet, but it wasn't the end. Hooper and his men had to carry on despite their injuries and their physical and mental exhaustion.

Continuing to sweep and clear out the bunkers that infested the countryside, Hooper and his men made steady work. One of these bunker complexes proved particularly dug in, and Hooper decided to get on top of the structure in order to gain the upper hand. As he reached the top, an NVA officer appeared out of nowhere, his iron sights locking with Hooper's head. Then there was a click.

A soldier's worst nightmare turned out to be a miracle for Hooper that day, as the gun about to kill him jammed. Reaching for his own gun, he found that the reality of the situation was more far-fetched than a Hollywood script — Hooper was out of ammunition. The two men tossed their weapons aside, the officer making a run for his life and Hooper sprinting after him. Hooper proved to be the swifter runner; a bayonet put an end to their brief chase.

Returning to the rest of his men, he found them pinned down once again by heavy weapons fire from a house. Everyone was taking cover — everyone except for Hooper, who sneaked around the back of the house. After kicking the back door down he was instantly fired upon. Onlookers were stunned, watching the torrent of bullets miss him by millimeters or less. The Viet Cong inside would not get a second chance at killing Hooper; the American responded to the threat with a fearsome blast of gunfire and a grand finale of grenades, the total effect being the deaths of all those inside.

Thus far, Hooper and company had been fighting in the outskirts; now they were hitting the last line of defense and the resistance they came up against was fighting with the ferocity of a cornered animal. Hooper, having already done one suicide mission today, was ready for seconds. Dashing through gunfire, he jumped into the trenches connecting the bunkers with another soldier in tow. Hooper tossed a grenade into the back of each bunker he passed while his companion would spray fire inside, making sure there were no survivors.

When they got to the last bunker in the trench, they took cover inside and used it to fire upon the enemy farther down the line. The NVA were quick, ducking for cover before they could get shredded. Hooper ran and climbed on top of the bunker, dropping a grenade into it while continuing to fire at other Viet Cong nearby. One witness described Hooper in this moment as "awfully effective."

But all was not well — he had just seen an American soldier wounded in the trench near the bunkers he'd been spraying with fire. As bullets continued to sweep across the field, Hooper put his own life on the line and rushed to help the man out of harm's way. When he reached the soldier, he sat his rifle down; he was out of ammunition anyway, and it would just get in the way. S.Sgt. Thomas threw him a .45-caliber pistol in case he needed it. Just when he got his arms around the wounded soldier, an NVA fighter came out of nowhere and pointed his rifle at Hooper's skull. Before the trigger was pulled, Hooper whipped out the pistol and blasted him — all while carrying a wounded soldier on his back.

"Sgt. Hooper in one day accomplished more than I previously believed could have been done in a month by one man," Sgt. George Parker said, who witnessed his heroism. "And he did it all while wounded." As the Vietnam War drew to a close, Hooper would go home as one of the most decorated soldiers of the war, credited with 115 confirmed enemy kills in ground combat and winning the Medal of Honor for his heroics during the Battle of Hue.

Back in the US, Hooper began work for the Department of Veterans Affairs. But he polarized those he worked with. On the one hand he connected with other veterans as easily as family: "Some you feel like a brother to, some you feel like a father to and most you feel like a comrade," he said in *Looking for a Hero*. On the other hand, he fit as well into civilian bureaucracy as a bull in a china shop. In addition to his discomfort with a peaceful, civilian life, the anti-war sentiment that enshrouded America in the '70s weighed heavily upon him, and he used alcohol to combat his disillusionment with a society that quickly forgot — or even spurned — veterans.

"It's sort of like the war itself, now," Hooper is said to have told his friend Rick Anderson in *Looking for a Hero*. "So many people wanted to forget it when I was fighting it. Why would they want to remember us now?" On May 6, 1979, Hooper passed away at age 40, his life tragically shortened by excessive use of alcohol. He was buried in Arlington National Cemetery. Sgt. George Parker once said about him that more than the enemies killed and positions overrun, what stood out the most about Hooper was "the fantastic inspiration he gave every man in the company," and that inspiration shall never be forgotten.

Sgt. Joe Ronnie Hooper (US Department of Defense)

Sergeant Major Billy Waugh

US ARMY
CIA

Silver Star
Legion of Merit
Bronze Star (4)
Purple Heart (8)

Born December 1, 1929

Billy Waugh wrings more life out of a year than most get out of a lifetime. For over 50 years and across 64 countries, he's practiced his personal code of action, whether against the godless Communists of Vietnam or the relentless zealotry of jihad. Wherever smoke rises out of the barrel of a gun, Waugh is sure to be found; a bloodhound to the hunt, a magnet to gunmetal, a heat-seeking missile made of flesh instead of steel.

Contemplating the deep questions of the effects of war on the minds of men isn't Waugh's game, nor is bothering with politics or any other such armchair pursuits. Little Billy Waugh never wanted fame as a child, and he wouldn't get a sliver of it until writing his book, *Hunting the Jackal,* in the twilight of his life — 364 days out of his year are classified information anyway. He's a warrior to the core, and after getting a taste for the feeling of a knife at his throat and rifles pointed at his skull, normal life just never felt quite the same again.

As told in *Hunting the Jackal*, for his sixteenth birthday back in 1945, he got the gift of *ambition* from a couple Marines who returned to his little town of Bastrop, Texas. Those proud soldiers, veterans of WWII, wore their wounds with pride, and in their weathered exteriors Waugh saw a map for his future — a map that urged him to take the plunge into a life of adventure. He wanted to be like them; he wanted to see the world; he would serve his country as they had.

On the grapevine Waugh heard that a boy as young as sixteen could join the Marines in California, so he stuck out his thumb and set out hitchhiking his way to this fabled land of underage recruitment. He never quite manifested this destiny — in Las Cruces, New Mexico, a well-meaning police officer approached this kid with his eyes locked on the western horizon and asked him what he was doing hitching rides to California instead of high school. He could try to put on his adult voice as much as he wanted, but the officer was having none of it, especially when this kid didn't have so much as a library card for identification. Waugh wouldn't tell him where he came from — which was the first sign he'd grow up to be a fine CIA operator — but underaged silence before a police officer got him exactly nowhere, as in jail.

The Las Cruces jail wasn't the destination he'd had in mind when he walked out of his front door days prior, and eventually he wised up, told his whole story, and went back home to Bastrop. His new warden was his own mother Mrs. Waugh, who was extremely unhappy to say the least. His dreams would have to wait a couple years, but he was merely delayed, not defeated. In 1948, he joined the Army paratroopers, and this time nothing could stop him.

He first served with the 187th Airborne in the Korean War, and although Waugh didn't write much about his time there, very few of the 187th serving at that time made it out without seeing combat. After the Armistice was signed in 1953, Waugh met some non-commissioned officers on a train in Germany, where their talk of the Special Forces sounded intriguing. He volunteered, earned his Green Beret, and went on his first tour in Vietnam in 1961 to train indigenous forces for the joint Special Forces/CIA Civilian Irregular Defense Program. He found his true love in the arms of both the Special Forces and the CIA, and that romance would last the rest of his life; first though, there was the Vietnam War to fight.

The date was June 18, 1965, and America and its allies were going to blast the North Vietnamese Army right the hell out of its hiding place in the Bong Son plain before they knew what was happening. In contrast to the reactive, counterpunching actions the US had taken in September and October in Ia Drang, this time they were going to hit first. They would protect the quarter-million civilians, the plentiful resources, and knock the Communists out of a valuable transportation nexus.

Special Forces operators Billy Waugh, Capt. Paris Davis, S.Sgt. David Morgan, and Sgt. Robert Brown were leading a group of 86 indigenous mercenaries on a raid on a unit compound. They were ready to give Charlie a beating he wouldn't soon forget — or that was the plan, anyway.

That wasn't how things turned out. It is said about the Viet Cong that they were an army that was "everywhere and nowhere" all at once. Waugh and his men went in expecting a few hundred troops; they found over 4,000.

After an absolutely savage hurricane of a fight, Billy Waugh was out of ammo, out of grenades (a favorite of his), and nearly out of hope. And he was one of the lucky ones: by the end of the battle, Waugh's team would suffer a horrific 80 percent mortality rate. Waugh wrote in his book that he was pretty certain that every last one of the lucky 20 percent that had survived had crawled, not run, out of there.

Waugh had just seen green — not the green of the jungle flora, but the green of a tracer round from a Russian RPK, blowing right through his right knee. The force alone was enough to knock him on his ass, and his nerves cried out in terrific pain. He dragged his body into the trench-like cover of an irrigation canal, providing a short respite from the endless swarm of buzzing and zipping of bullets overhead. He oriented himself to the west, the direction of safety, and began the slog through the sand, dirt, and clay of the ancient loam deposited over countless years of farming.

For 40 meters he trudged forward, dirt and blood all mingled together, before the levee opened up into a mouth that spit him out into a rice paddy. The inescapable sound of supersonic tracers were now feet rather than inches from his head — he'd found a decent foxhole and relief washed over him along with mud. Waugh recalled that the relief quickly sank away, though; here he was, layered in leeches, dotted in gunshot wounds, watching any future in the military ebb away with every ounce of blood that oozed out of his mangled knee.

That moment of anguish left as soon as it had come — after all, he had to survive before getting discharged. Rolling over to look up, he froze. There was a weapon pointed at him, *staring at him*, and it wasn't designed by Mikhail Kalashnikov, it was designed by millions of years of evolution. A mean old water buffalo was staring at this witless invader with nostrils flared, and unlike its milk cow cousins, these thousand-pound bovines will charge their horned battle-helms right into a man; grumpy bulls in particular don't need any provocation to do so. Waugh had fallen right onto this guy's lawn, and the bull wanted him gone. Luckily, there was a no-man's-land of mud so thick that a de facto peace reigned over the rice paddy.

"You big son of a bitch, move over," a delirious Waugh said to the bad-tempered bovine in *Hunting the Jackal*. "You ready to fight? Let's go, big boy." At that moment a commotion of earth crumbled down into the pit as a bewildered S.Sgt. Morgan slid down to join the party. Morgan did a double take at the strange bedfellows, and Waugh couldn't help but find comedy in the absurdity. Since men have waged war, soldiers, sailors, prisoners, and all manner of folk in the worst situations have found humor in the darkest places. When the Prefect of Rome executed Saint Lawrence in a burning pit, the legend goes he declared, "I'm well done. Turn me over!"

"War is hell and all that, but sometimes it's pretty damned comical," Waugh stated in *Hunting the Jackal*. But as much as they'd love to take a break and laugh, enemies were rapidly closing in and their chances to escape that ditch while still drawing breath were coming to a close.

Waugh knew he was in no shape to make a mad dash and would only slow his friend down, so they agreed that Morgan was going to have to sprint through waves of gunfire to the rally point where he might be able to organize some aerial backup. Waugh did his part by deploying his red canvas emergency panel in the hopes that the forward air controller would notice it and call the airstrikes in that way.

Morgan leapt out of the hole in the ground and was gone. Waugh made up his mind to also move forward, crawling low and slow toward the withdrawal area. The seemingly infinite *rat-tat-tat* of bullets crashing into and over the terrain were beginning to sound more like ambient noise than shocking thunder. He didn't make it five meters into this green mile before getting skewered again. A tracer round found a particularly cruel path into and out of his body, squarely hitting him in the sole of his foot — leaving three of his toes little more than tattered meat — and exiting through the shattered bone of his ankle. Pain like this couldn't be described by even the most talented poet.

Nevertheless, there was still only one way out: forward. Through the searing pain, dragging his pile of shredded bone and muscle that was once a leg, he kept inching his way toward the cover of a bamboo stand 20 meters in front of him. It took 10 minutes to make it that 20 meters. His heart hammered against his chest from the suffering, but the bamboo now provided life-saving cover. The nearby cemetery was the next objective, but as he laid there, trembling and sweat-drenched, he knew he'd never get through the kill zone in his state — he already felt like half a corpse.

Wrangling his rucksack open, Waugh grabbed three shots of morphine, injecting himself as fast as he could. It was like a balsa wood dam set against the flood of Genesis; he needed a team of doctors, surgeons, and nurses, not self-administered triage. Taking stock of the situation, he saw what allied troops remained returning fire from the cemetery. Among them was Capt. Davis, and they locked eyes. Waugh screamed out a plea for a tactical airstrike; Davis shouted back a denial.

"The goddamn radio's shot to hell. It's got about thirty bullets in it," Waugh recalls him saying in *Hunting the Jackal*. "I'm coming to get you, Billy!" Davis yelled, charging for the wounded Waugh, the small amount of covering fire providing just enough room for him to land himself within the cover of the bamboo. After reviewing their ammo situation — there wasn't any — dread washed over the two of them, and even worse, a bullet tore through the air and ripped the ends of Davis' right-hand fingers clean off.

"Goddamn it, I can't even shoot now!"

Now there were two men up shit's creek without a paddle, but the best music they'd ever heard now flooded over the horizon. It was the dulcet tones of USAF F-4C Phantom jets and Navy F-8s coming to blow the NVA to high heavens, hopefully without Waugh, Davis, and the rest of them getting caught in the blaze. Napalm and high-explosive bombs went off in an operatic chorus, the heat from the blasts close enough that Waugh felt like he was popped into an oven.

But, while the air cavalry had slowed the advance of the enemy, it hadn't stopped them — the men were still boxed in by endless waves of gunfire.

Another bullet found its mark, tearing a two-inch trench across Waugh's forehead, blood pouring down like a waterfall.

"It sounds like the punchline to a bad joke, but you know it's a bad day when the best thing about it is getting shot in the head," Waugh said in his book. It was an odd way to get his life saved, but this finale of a wound knocked Waugh clean out of consciousness, and because of that, he looked about as dead as could be. Left knee — blown to smithereens. Right foot and ankle — a mangled mess. Left wrist — that was shot up too, the bullet having blasted off his watch. And now he looked to be brained, lying face first in the mud. For once, the bullets stopped coming at him because to anyone watching he was lying in his own grave.

Billy Waugh woke up naked and in a daze. About eight hours had passed and the NVA troops had stripped him of everything but mud and blood. But there was the sound of a chopper cutting through the air, and Sgt. 1st Class John Reinburg was crawling across the body-strewn ground toward him. The rescue turned to tragedy as one bullet pierced Reinburg's chest above the heart, then another just below. In one short moment, Reinburg had gone from savior to being in worse shape than Waugh. Capt. Davis came next, helping Waugh crawl along toward the sounds of helicopter-bound freedom. Davis hauled him inside a chopper, and with that, Waugh was finally lifted out of this half-day in the ninth circle of hell. For his leadership and heroic actions on this day, Sgt. 1st Class John Reinburg received a Distinguished Service Cross; Capt. Paris Davis received a Silver Star and a Purple Heart.

Despite the injuries, that wasn't the last Billy Waugh saw of Vietnam. His thirst to continue the fight got him out of an amputation, and after a difficult recovery, he was eventually able to rejoin the ranks of the Special Forces.

He became directly involved in the wild battle of Oscar-8 in Laos and turned Ba Kev in Cambodia into a strategically important outpost. Waugh went from being inches from death on that day in Vietnam to conducting the first combat High Altitude, Low Opening (HALO) jump into enemy territory in October 1970, a method of tactical insertion still in use to this day. He was part of both the first and last HALO jumps ever executed in Vietnam. He had devoted seven-and-a-half years of his life to Vietnam and he walked proudly out of that conflict with eight Purple Hearts and one Silver Star.

His retirement ceremony in February of 1972 was a terrible day for him. Billy Waugh is a warrior to the core, and civilian life just didn't make him feel alive after staring death dead in the eyes so many times.

"Good-bye, Special Forces," he recalled saying in *Hunting the Jackal*, as 200 of his best friends in the world sang "The Ballad of the Green Beret." He cried for his fallen brothers and the loss of the love of his life that day.

Billy Waugh went home to Texas and began a normal life, delivering packages for the US Postal Service. It was a decent job that paid well and had good benefits.

And he hated it.

After living on the edge for years in Korea and Southeast Asia, the sudden monotony was numbing him to the bone with boredom. On July 20, 1977, he got a call that offered a way out of the drudgery and back into adrenaline-pumping, world-traveling action.

"The location is overseas," the voice on the other side said, as detailed in Annie Jacobsen's book *Surprise, Kill, Vanish*. Waugh was in, without hesitation. He followed the instructions given to him — traveling to a specific hotel at a specific time — and before he even got there, a down payment was transferred into his bank account — a load of cash thicker than what he'd get in a year at the post office. That was just the icing on the cake; he felt his blood pumping again for the first time in years.

"My instinct and intuition told me this was a CIA operation," he recalled in an interview in *Surprise, Kill, Vanish*. "That the Agency was forming some kind of ground team for a covert operation in Africa. I figured this was how the CIA worked, now that covert-action operations had been curtailed."

When Waugh showed up at the hotel he was in good company: waiting with him were a band of Green Berets that he knew from his time in Southeast Asia. The skill sets of the crew ranged between medical expertise to heavy weapons mastery. Clearly this job required certified badasses and had paramilitary written all over it. A fifth man appeared, purporting to be a lawyer working for the client, and he laid out the fundamentals. They'd be given visas and headed for Libya to train soldiers for Muammar Gaddafi. Waugh figured that the whole clandestine affair was designed to give the CIA plausible deniability, but his gut told him to poke around to double-check just what the hell was going on. As told in *Surprise, Kill, Vanish*, none of his contacts had heard so much as a whisper about this whole Libyan operation.

Waugh confronted the "lawyer" over the phone, asking him outright if this was CIA. It was not; it was, in fact, a venture led by former CIA man Edwin Wilson and purportedly "all aboveboard." Gaddafi didn't want his friends or his enemies to know he was bringing in Americans to train his special forces, hence the enormous pay. Waugh hung up the phone, considering this offer that was getting more complicated by the day. He didn't have long to ponder, though; the phone rang.

This new voice immediately addressed Waugh by name and listed the identities of two CIA operatives Waugh knew personally. They should have an important meeting at a restaurant in an hour, the voice said.

"The meeting is about your upcoming travel plans to Africa," were the cryptic words used as described in *Surprise, Kill, Vanish*. He was sitting in the restaurant when a man approached, revealed his CIA credentials, and told Waugh his name was Pat. "It's not an Agency operation," Pat stated, pulling out a briefcase and setting it on the table. Inside was a 35mm camera which he slid across the table. The mission he'd been assigned by Edwin Wilson and his lawyer hadn't been real CIA business, but this one was.

It went like this: on the one hand, he'd help train Gaddafi's forces and be led around to various military facilities — surface-to-air missile sites, classified bases, etc. On the other hand, he'd be taking pictures of these same facilities for the CIA. Days before he'd been carrying parcels and avoiding dogs. Now he was a double agent for the CIA while training foreign special forces in a country whose political situation was primed to explode. Waugh was back in action.

The team of retired Green Berets landed in Tripoli and all went their separate ways. Waugh was training Libyan commandos in small arms and explosives — ambushes and sabotage. Waugh was not impressed with his students.

"Many of them were Gaddafi's friends, or people he owed a favor. Most of them ignored training or flat-out refused to be told what to do." At one point, they had been training for aquatic operations, and Waugh learned the hard way that only two of the 22 commandos knew how to swim. One man in particular believed that his scuba suit worked like a life preserver, with deadly results.

"I discovered that the commandos loved having their picture taken, and I took advantage of this," he said in *Surprise, Kill, Vanish*. He was even able to photograph evidence of Russian involvement in Libya, as well as map out regions that had previously been beyond the reach of US intelligence.

In the summer of '79, the powder keg looked ready to ignite, as Libya and Egypt engaged in a border war and Gaddafi had his plans to assassinate Egypt's president Anwar Sadat. This was the background Waugh was working in, keeping him on edge and wondering when the whole thing might come tumbling down around him.

Finally, the atmosphere, thick with nitroglycerine, went off with a bang. In November 1979, the US embassy in Tehran was stormed and more than 60 hostages were taken. Soon after, Sunni terrorists besieged the Grand Mosque in Mecca, and Iran's Ayatollah Khomeini declared to the Arab world that American and Israeli commandos were behind it. Waugh read the room: with nothing but the clothes on his back, he hailed a taxi and dashed to the airport. Waugh had nearly lost his life, but damn if he wasn't glad to be back in the "great game."

On December 21, 1975, six heavily armed militants had stormed the semi-annual meeting of OPEC (Organization of the Petroleum Exporting Countries) leaders in Vienna, Austria. Sixty hostages were taken, an Austrian policeman, an Iraqi security officer, and a Libyan economist were killed; after two days of diplomatic negotiations all hostages were freed and all terrorists walked away unharmed. Behind this siege: Ramirez Sanchez or "Carlos the Jackal."

Fast forward to December 1993, and Waugh was arriving in the airport of Khartoum, Sudan. He was entering the country without any rifles or grenades — this time his weapon was going to be a camera. He was on a top-secret gamma-classified reconnaissance and surveillance team, not to kill the Jackal, but to capture him. Waugh stated in *Surprise, Kill, Vanish* that every who's who of intelligence agencies on earth wanted him: France, Mossad, the FBI. But the CIA was going to be the one to close the jaws of the trap around him. Problem was, nobody knew what the man looked like — it had been eight years since anyone had seen him, and he was lost in a wild city of over a million people.

Immediately upon reaching Sudan, Waugh and his team noticed they were being tailed. Most of the time it wasn't even meant to be covert, but a flex on the foreigners; on the second day a Toyota pickup truck trailed a few cars back filled to the brim with soldiers packing AK-47s.

"Being in Sudan was like being behind enemy lines," Waugh said in *Surprise, Kill, Vanish*. "It's a non-permissive environment. Every step must be taken with great care."

Early on this had the feeling of an impossible mission, but all criminals make a mistake at some point, and Waugh and his team were going to be right there to spot it. Their patience finally paid off. "He decided it was time to get himself a foreign bodyguard. That was the fatal move."

The bodyguard in question was an Iraqi national called Tarek, and something was unusual about this roided up bodybuilder: he appeared Caucasian. It turns out having a white-looking bodyguard in Khartoum changed their problem from finding a needle in a haystack to finding a baseball bat in a haystack. In January of 1994, Waugh and fellow operative Greg were staking out an international hotel, a popular attraction for the professionally alcoholic Jackal. There in the lobby was fair-skinned Tarek, diligently completing a crossword puzzle.

Waugh and Greg followed the bodybuilder outside and tailed him in a vehicle, but even though Tarek stuck out like a sore thumb, he was no fool, and kept pulling U-turns. Continuing to follow him would be pushing their luck to the brink, and they were forced to let him go, but now they had a lead: he drove a 1990 Toyota Cressida with the license plate number 1049. The noose was slowly tightening around the Jackal.

The team split up to search for the Cressida, sometimes going on the hunt for 18 hours a day. In their off hours, Waugh and Greg would focus on tightening up their photo-developing skills; they were in the middle of tinkering in their film lab when their encrypted radio came alive with breaking news. Don had gotten eyes on that elusive Cressida at the Ibn Khaldoun Hospital. Waugh advised him to stay locked on, and if that four-door started moving, not to let it out of his sight.

Waugh and Greg raced out of their lab, jumped in their vehicle, and stepped on it, leaving the napping men who had been assigned to tail them in the dust. Greg snapped open the lockbox welded to the floor of the Land Cruiser and took out their weapon of choice: a 35mm Canon F-80 equipped with a 300mm lens. Minutes later they came to a stop at the hospital, pulling past Don's vehicle to an ideal spot to shoot a clean picture of the Cressida. They had a new problem, and little time to deal with it. They were sticking out like a sore thumb, three white guys just sitting in the parking lot, and relying on Tarek, the Jackal and the secret police to lack basic observational skills would be a terrible miscalculation. They needed a plan — a diversion.

Waugh stepped nonchalantly out of the vehicle and popped open the hood. Leaving it upright he jumped back in and got to work setting up the camera on the headrest of the front seat to serve as a platform for the long 300mm lens. His fingers adjusted the focus to catch a good view of the hospital exit — just as it came into focus the face of a beautiful woman walked into the frame.

It was the Jackal's second wife, Lana. As she made her way to the Toyota, a commotion erupted at a vendor on the dirt shoulder of the road nearby.

"You've cheated me!" Greg aggressively shouted at the salesman. This was their plan, their distraction; now they just needed their targets to take the bait. Unfortunately for Greg, the man he ended up getting in an argument stood up and showed himself to be about seven feet tall. Waugh couldn't keep an eye on his friend's tussle with the giant, placing his trust in Greg's ability as an actor. Staying focused on the hospital door, he was rewarded for his diligence.

"Caucasian, in his forties. Well groomed, with reddish hair, combed back. A mustache. Fat: 40 or 50 pounds overweight," said Waugh in *Surprise, Kill, Vanish*. "I spotted a leg holster near his right ankle. He wore a shooter's vest. Sleeveless and with pockets in the front." The camera clicked in rapid succession as the large man who'd sauntered out of the hospital took notice of Greg's altercation with the giant behind the counter. Waugh didn't stop until he had an empty roll of film, and now it was time to get out of Dodge before their cover went up in flames. The Cressida went one way with Don following close behind, and Waugh and Greg went the other way.

"It was the most important roll of film I'd handled to date," Waugh told Jacobsen. And this was coming from the man who'd taken top secret photos of Russian missiles in Libya. The film was sent to the CIA and the Jackal spent the following days continuing his life of debauchery, but he was an imprisoned man walking. The moment Waugh had captured him on film, he'd captured him behind bars, where he remains to this day.

Years later, a 62-year-old Waugh was jogging down the street of Khartoum, Sudan, as a wake of dust billowed up behind the large Mercedes cruising past him. As Waugh wrote in *Hunting the Jackal*, this wasn't the first time he'd seen this vehicle and its storm of dust. When it pulled up in front of the house Waugh had just passed, not a hint of surprise registered on the American's features. They locked eyes — the cloak-and-dagger Waugh and the heavy-lidded man in the driver's seat. Osama bin Laden had a habit of driving alone, like he owned the roads, and Waugh knew all about his habits.

It was 1992 and Waugh had spent 18 months keeping an eye on bin Laden, oftentimes coming within a stone's throw of the man whose name the world would come to know in a decade. Right now, with Waugh continuing his jog past him, bin Laden was not even considered a high-level assignment, but this intimate knowledge Waugh gained of the would-be poster boy of international jihad would pay off down the road. As Waugh learned more about him, his seed of concern bloomed into a garden of suspicion. More and more people would flock to his coattails, and from where Waugh was standing, it appeared like they'd do anything for him; kill for him; die for him; fly planes into buildings for him.

Waugh would eventually leave this beat to return to America, but he'd be back for bin Laden eventually, and next time, he wouldn't have a camera, he'd have a gun.

After 9/11, Waugh had one last fight in him. The men of the ODA-594, 5th Special Forces Group were sent to hunt for the notorious terrorist Osama bin Laden in the Afghan mountains outside of Tora Bora. Billy Waugh, at 71 years of age, when any thoughts of being an operator would have long passed for most warriors, was on a lethal mission one final time.

"I was 71 years old when those Towers fell, but I didn't give a good goddamn how old I was. My country was going to war, and for nearly 50 years that meant only one thing: I needed to get myself into this war also," Waugh said in his book, the warrior spirit shining through his words strong as ever. Waugh put his epic history in Vietnam, his hand in the capture of Carlos the Jackal, and his knowledge of Osama bin Laden to use, pulling all the strings to get involved in one last fight. From Waugh's recalling of events in *Hunting the Jackal,* the single most-used word in his talks with his boss was "crazy." Waugh was old and Afghanistan was "goddamn cold."

"...If having the guts and ability to track down some bastard who intends to bring harm to the United States is crazy, then I guess I plead guilty as charged." Waugh wasn't joining to inflate his ego, he had a legitimate sales pitch: nobody was better positioned to serve as an in-between for the Special Forces and the CIA. He had intimate knowledge of bin Laden, and he knew plenty about the Middle East. Even still, he'd have to familiarize himself with the M-4 Carbine, which he promptly fell in love with. Beyond the shiny new weapons at his disposal was the advanced communications gear. Gone were the ground-to-ground radios; now they bounced off satellites 22,000 nautical miles above the earth's crust and worked 24/7.

"No, we weren't in Vietnam anymore," he remarked in *Hunting the Jackal.* January 5th came around, and the team Waugh was a part of was in the area of Gardez near a meeting of the minds for the biggest big-shot Taliban leaders. Missile strikes attacked the meeting, but unfortunately, the higher-ups didn't believe bin Laden had been there, so the team continued their search. As they roamed the surrounding area, one particular region kept springing up as the focal point of their suspicion. Little Russian-made taxis swarmed back and forth over the hills on the border with Pakistan. They couldn't shake the idea that if someone didn't want to be found, that's where they'd be.

One day he stopped one of these empty taxis, asking who their normal passengers were. The Pakistani gave him some medley of bullshit as an answer. Seeing this was going nowhere, Waugh changed tactics.

"How much for a ride from those caves to the border?" he asked, pointing up to the imposing mountains. They'd found their strongest lead yet — they'd located the hideout of the world's most dangerous terrorist. Though Waugh wouldn't be there to deliver justice personally, he'd been a part of the pivotal first stage of Operation Enduring Freedom, he'd avoided being shot and falling victim to pneumonia, and he'd done it all as a 71-year-old. He left Afghanistan feeling proud of the new generation of Special Forces and knowing he'd served his country in its time of need.

As reported by the online news source *Sandboxx*, Waugh was making jumps out of airplanes into Cuban waters as an 88-year-old. Billy Waugh stands out not just as a patriot and a warrior, but as a man who can look back on his own story knowing that every single day, he lived life to the fullest.

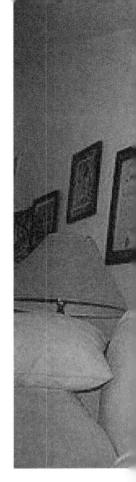

Billy Waugh in 2011. (US Air Force)

Sergeant First Class Jorge A. Otero Barreto

US ARMY

Silver Star (2)
Bronze Star (5) w/ "V" Device
Air Medal (5)
Army Commendation Medal (4)
Purple Heart (5)

Born April 7, 1937

The "Puerto Rican Rambo." "Sergeant Rock." A living legend. One of the most decorated US soldiers of the Vietnam War — Jorge Otero Barreto's story is one for the history books. Thirty-eight military decorations, 200 combat missions, five wounds in battle, and the first Puerto Rican to graduate from the US Army Air Assault School. This is a man who will never be forgotten.

Sgt. 1st Class Jorge Otero Barreto was born in the small, sleepy town of Vega Baja, just west of San Juan, Puerto Rico. His father, Eloy Otero-Bruno, was a great admirer of George Washington and decided to name his son Jorge, Spanish for "George," in his honor. Nobody could've guessed that their Jorge Barreto's destiny would lead him to fully live up to his name, becoming an American hero and icon.

After finishing high school, Barreto studied biology for three years. He wasn't sure what he wanted for his future just yet, but he did know one thing: he would marry the love of his life, Tomasa. For his mother this was an impossibility. Tomasa was not good enough for her firstborn (no one was) and she absolutely insisted that he instead go to Spain to medical school. She wanted her son to make a name for himself. Little did she know, he would, and in a big way.

Barreto was a very dedicated and thoughtful student,

and he would have made a very successful doctor. His heart wasn't in it though; he wanted adventure, he wanted action, he wanted to be a soldier. So in 1959, four years into the Vietnam War, he joined the United States Army. After completing his basic training, he was assigned to the Air Assault School in Fort Campbell, Kentucky. When he graduated in 1960, he had already made history by becoming the first Puerto Rican to graduate from this program. While he swelled with pride at this accomplishment, he still didn't have what he wanted most: to be married to his sweetheart. So that's exactly what he did. In 1961 he married Tomasa Bujana Rodriguez and then, shortly after, he went off to war.

Barreto trained in Hawaii, the Philippines, and Thailand before departing for Vietnam. "We were prepared to do whatever we had to do against the enemy," he told the American Legion. This was before the United States was officially in-country, so Barreto volunteered to help train anti-communist Vietnamese and prepare them for war. He later recalled, "They were farmers. They were trained to be jungle fighters. It's not that simple."

He worked his teams hard, mentally and physically preparing them to become "jungle rats ... We liked to be inside the jungle. I know that a person has to control his mind and body. Mental and physical courage should prepare you to take care of anything. I was willing to kill. I was willing to die. I was willing to take a cyanide pill. I am a warrior. I believed that and still believe that. I am still willing to take a pill instead of being a squealer."

Barreto's career would take him on five tours in Southeast Asia, from 1961 to 1970. He served in multiple military units, including the 101st Airborne Division and the 25th Infantry Division, or "Tropic Lightning" as it was often called. He also served in the 82nd Airborne Division and the 173rd Airborne Division. He would be a part of a stunning 200 combat missions in which he was wounded five times, which is how he got to be known as "The Puerto Rican Rambo."

Of all his citations, there are two that burst off the page with heroism: his Silver Stars. He won his first on February 17, 1968. This was the period of the Tet Offensive in South Vietnam — a massive military venture and the largest of its kind up to that point in the war. On January 30, 1968, the Viet Cong and the North Vietnamese People's Army of Vietnam (NVA) executed their plan: a series of surprise attacks against military and civilian command and control centers. The day was strategically chosen to coincide with the holidays when most of the Army of the Republic of Vietnam (ARVN) would be on leave.

On that fateful February day near Quang Tri, Barreto was serving as staff sergeant in a defensive attack known as Operation Jeb Stuart, part of a larger operation, Operation Checkers. The goal was to increase the maneuver battalions in I Corps to support the beleaguered and exhausted Marines at the Khe Sanh Combat Base, and to defeat all other enemy attacks across the Demilitarized Zones.

"Our enemy was determined, persistent and experienced. This is a fact we cannot in all honesty deny. ... The communists never worried about their losses. Every military action was as good as any other, provided their political objective could be attained," reflected Cao Van Vien, an ARVN general, in the book *The Final Collapse*.

The operation began, and immediately the gunner in Barreto's unit was wounded by enemy fire — the assistant gunner was killed outright. When Barreto stepped up and took over the machine gun, he and that machine turned into one being. Barreto single-handedly organized and covered the safe withdrawal of his platoon, keeping hope alive for his troops for one more day. While it is true that wars are fought with missiles, rockets, grenades, and machine guns, wars are *won* by men. Barreto was wounded during this fight, earning him a Purple Heart, and for his bravery, his first Silver Star.

Baretto received his second Silver Star only three months later, on May 1, 1968. This time it was during the security

Operation Carentan II in the Thua Thiên province in South Vietnam. Baretto was still with Company A, but now as a platoon sergeant. His unit was setting up occupying defensive positions near an enemy village when the North Vietnamese Army Regiment (PAVN) attacked. Three brutal wave attacks hit the unit's defense perimeter. All three failed, and the PAVN nervously retreated to the village. Barreto didn't stop to take a breath. He was not about to wait around for another enemy onslaught; they would counterattack, ferociously.

When the platoon's initial advance met vicious enemy fire, Barreto located the nearest enemy machine gun bunker and instantly killed the three men before they killed him. He pushed forward, leading his squad through three more fortified bunkers. On and on he went, from one bunker to the next, demolishing them all. Now, he could direct his squad to provide cover for the advance. Advance they did, and to safety. His actions that day allowed the remainder of Company A's platoon to move into more advantageous positions and destroy the enemy. In total, 2,096 enemy soldiers and 156 American and allied soldiers were killed during Operation Carentan II. It was a bloodbath, but partly due to Baretto's bravery, a success nonetheless.

When the Vietnam War ended, Baretto retired from his military career a heavily decorated veteran. Many other dedications followed. Among them the SFC Jorge Otero-Barreto Homeless Veterans Transitional Home, which houses and helps veterans transition to civilian society after the trauma of war.

On September 1, 2006, the *National Puerto Rican Coalition* presented Baretto with a "Lifetime Achievement Award" at a conference in Chicago. And in 2011, his hometown of Vega Baja, where he was highly regarded and known for assisting veterans — his way of giving back to his community — named the military museum after him and awarded him Civic Citizen of the Year; a great honor to him, his family, and his beloved birthplace.

Baretto is also featured in the documentary film *Brave Lords* which depicts the Puerto Rican perspective of the war in Vietnam. Jorge Otero Baretto currently lives happily with his wife Tomasa and frequently recounts war stories to his wide-eyed grandchildren.

Sergeant First Class Jerry "Mad Dog" Shriver

US ARMY

Silver Star (2)
Soldier's Medal for Heroism
Bronze Star (7) (6 with Oak Leaf Clusters)
Air Medal
Army Commendation Medal (4)
Army Commendation Medal w/ "V" Device
Purple Heart with two Oak Leaf Clusters
Combat Infantryman's Badge
Good Conduct Medal
National Defense Service Medal
Vietnam Service Medal
Vietnam Campaign Medal

September 24, 1941–Missing in Action since April 24, 1969 (28 years)

Jerry "Mad Dog" Shriver has been described as "the distilled essence of war." He was all at once an eccentric man, a fearless warrior, and a revered leader. We don't know very much about his life but what we do know is the stuff of legends.

Sgt. 1st Class Jerry Shriver inserted into the landing zone with his recon team in November 1968, and as described in his citation, they went in guns blazing. Shriver was a platoon sergeant in one of the "Hatchet Force" units, often composed of three American MACV-SOG members and 20 to 30 hand-picked locals, all trained in the art and science of unconventional warfare. The Hatchet Force's mission statement was: "probe the border areas and look for a fight."

The ultimate ambition of these patrols was to drop in and go undetected for days, allowing for the gathering of a valuable trove of intelligence before the bullets started flying. The gritty reality often failed to line up with these lofty expecta-tions, however; the majority of teams were inserted almost directly into enemy firefights, then forced into making a dan-gerous extraction within 30 minutes.

"Our [helicopter] was flying lead with the team," Sgt. Ron Winkles, who was serving as a door gunner on a chopper that would attempt to pull Shriver's team out, recounted years later in Lt. Col. Fred Lindsey's book, *Secret Green Beret Commandos in Cambodia: A Memorial History of MACV-SOG's Command and Control Detachment South (Ccs), and Its Air Partners, Republic of Vietnam, 1967-1972*. "Everything went well, and it was a beautiful, clear, sunny day. I can remember thinking when we pick these guys up in a couple days, the election will be over back in the states. ... To the contrary, we hadn't no more than cleared the tall trees of the LZ when we heard the call for an extraction."

That sunshine and optimism had proved to be dead wrong — the mission had barely begun and already an enemy battal-ion was breathing down their necks. Immediately sensing the danger, Shriver snapped into action, taking three of his men and delivering a devastating volume of fire upon the encroach-ing force, outright killing four and wounding 26. Shriver laid down covering fire for his radio operator who was urgently contacting nearby gunships. Yet, as the helicopter landed to begin the extraction, machine gun fire lit up the area. Shriver lived for risk — but never to the detriment of those under his command. He led his men to another landing zone in the only direction bullets weren't flooding in from, directing gunship fire on the enemy even as tracers cascaded over his position. Winkles's helicopter swooped in to serve as a buffer, nearly landed on top of them and startling the hell out of the NVA.

But only for a moment. An NVA soldier fired his AK-47, splintering the Plexiglass windshield and nearly blinding the co-pilot. Winkles fired back with his M-60, but immediately after, he caught a few bullets of his own. Two 7.62×39mm rounds struck him directly in the helmet. He went down and the NVA swarmed the helicopter.

Winkles miraculously was still alive: in a mad stroke of luck, one bullet had ricocheted off his helmet and the other had embedded itself within it. He had lain unconscious for around a minute before he heard a voice call out to him. "Ron, you're not hurt, but if you don't get up and start firing, you will be." Winkles would never learn whose voice that was — none among his team claimed to have spoken — but what he did know is he listened to it. He got up, started shooting and didn't stop until his 450-round ammo can ran dry. Shriver watched Winkles go down and later saw the miraculous redemption. "When you went down, about 15 NVA charged the helicopter from your side. I really think they wanted to capture it. But, when you stood up, they all fell to their death," Jerry Shriver later remarked to Winkles.

Meanwhile, a second helicopter soared overhead to extract the ground team, rope ladders unfurled, promising liberation from their would-be graveyard.

The gunship having given them breathing room, Shriver, in what would be a common theme among his citations, was last to leave, returning the bullet-point arguments of his foes with lead of his own. When all his men were safely on board, Shriver made a wild gamble. Climbing up the ladder would take too long; instead, he attached himself to the end of the ladder via his snap link. As the helicopter took off, Shriver continued to rain fire on the enemy, hanging from the ladder in a sky saturated by bullets. Then, as he climbed aboard, he felt something hit him. To Shriver's amazement, the M-9 grease gun he'd tossed over his shoulder had stopped a bullet from penetrating him dead through the back.

As happened often for Mad Dog, he and his SOG buddies had flirted with disaster but made it out alive. Shriver himself had traded in one of his dwindling nine lives for both the safety of his men and the deaths of his enemies.

Many stories of the SOG have come to light following its

long-overdue declassification, and Shriver holds the distinction of owning the most famous one. When surrounded by far superior NVA forces, Shriver is said to have radioed his worried superiors, "No, no, I've got 'em right where I want 'em — surrounded from the inside." In so few words, Shriver described himself and his ethos more succinctly that anyone has since. He was a man fully dedicated to warfare, described by some as more of a warrior than a soldier. He was a fierce ally to have and a dangerous enemy to face. US Air Force Captain and Medal of Honor recipient Jim Fleming said it best in Maj. John Plaster's book *SOG: The Secret Wars of America's Commandos in Vietnam*:

> *[T]he quintessential warrior-loner, anti-social, possessed by what he was doing, the best teammate, always training, constantly training.*

There are a lot of unknowns in Shriver's history, many in-between years where no one can account for his doings. But what we know about his early life is that he was born Jerry Michael Tate on September 24, 1941, in the resort town of DeFuniak Springs, Florida. His father, Henry A. Tate Jr., was in the Air Corps and Air Force and served in Italy during World War II. His parents divorced when he was 12 and his mother married another Air Force man, Dale L. Shriver, whose surname he and his siblings would go on to adopt.

At the young age of 17, Jerry dropped out of high school in Miranda, California, and joined the Army. He received his basic training in Fort Ord and then went on to get his 11B training. We don't know what he did for the next few years but sometime before 1961 he attended Airborne School, attained his Green Beret, and was assigned to Wildflecken, Germany, as a member of Co A, 75th Infantry, serving on a Long Range Reconnaissance Patrol team. In 1965 Shriver was at Fort Bragg attending Special Forces training and arrived in Vietnam in 1966 as a staff sergeant and was shortly after promoted to sergeant first class.

For SOG, guerrilla warfare was a way of life, and for Shriver, SOG was his life — no recon man could work the jungles better than the "Mad Dog."

"He was like having a dog you could talk to," O'Rourke explained in Maj. John Plaster's *SOG*. "He could hear and sense things; he was more alive in the woods than any other human being I've ever met." In one operation on the Cambodian border, SOG Capt. Bill O'Rourke remembered Shriver and a Montagnard comrade leaning against a tree when they suddenly bolted upright, glanced at each other, and then leaned back against the tree, at ease. "... What the hell's going on?" O'Rourke thought to himself. Suddenly, birds fly by, and a millisecond later, shotguns ring out in the distance. "They'd heard that, ascertained what it was and relaxed before I even knew the birds were flying."

Medic Joe Farrar recalls a similar incident in Lindsey's *Secret Green Beret Commandos in Cambodia*. Shriver and the team were coming back on after a rest break. Suddenly, Shriver told them all to hit the dirt. Moments later the sounds of enemy mortars launching nearby were heard by all around. "... It was really creepy how Shriver was always several steps ahead of everyone else," Farrar said.

The Vietnam War solidified the Shriver legend, and 1966 was the year his enemies' hatred resulted in the "Mad Dog" sobriquet. Shriver was a staff sergeant in the feared and highly respected Military Assistance Command Vietnam-Studies and Observations Group (MACV-SOG), a top-secret group created in 1964 by the Joint Chiefs of Staff that consisted of Green Berets, Navy SEALs, and Air Commandos assigned to carry out covert cross-border operations throughout Cambodia, Laos, and North Vietnam. It was during this time that Radio Hanoi, the North Vietnamese Army (NVA) propaganda radio station, dubbed him "Mad Dog" Shriver and wanted him put down so badly they advertised a $10,000 bounty for his head (approximately $70,000 nowadays).

Mad Dog scared the hell out of everybody. A connoisseur of the tools of war, he often looked like a human armory both in and out of battle, sometimes walking around with four to six handguns. Over the years he'd raise eyebrows kitted out with a sawn-off shotgun, suppressed M3 grease gun, 9mm Uzi submachine gun, fighting knives strapped to his leg, and satchels of explosives.

During a rare leave stateside, Shriver's biggest interest was in nabbing a lever action .444 Marlin rifle — a power-house meant to take down moose and large bears. Shriver referred to this jokingly as his "bunker buster," and the high caliber bear-killer likely terrified living enemies with the size of the exit wounds in their dead companions.

When describing Shriver, people couldn't help but be drawn to — or repulsed by — his eyes. "There was no soul in the eyes, no emotion," said Capt. Bill O'Rourke in Plaster's book *SOG*. "They were just eyes." Paul Longgrear, who served with Shriver, told *sofrep.com*: "His eyes were squinty and hollow, almost cold blooded."

The picture of the Mad Dog as a wild-eyed, stone-cold killer has its own flavor of badassery, but stories from others he served with painted a much more complex figure — an eccentric to be sure, but a mortal man who was one of the boys. Walter Jackson wrote in *Shades of Daniel Boone* that Shriver had a "shoebox full of medals" and "a ton of friends." He also carried with him a host of demons gained over three-plus years of continuous service as a Green Beret in Vietnam. Shriver often fought his demons with liquor and went to sleep cradling a rifle — sleep didn't come easily for the Mad Dog.

In addition to his buddies in SOG, Shriver had countless companions among the Montagnards, the fiercely independent tribe who lived in the Vietnamese highlands. They were known for their audacity, fearlessness, and seemingly super-human tracking abilities; during the war they were known as some of the best reconnaissance soldiers to have ever existed. Shriver spoke their language, Rade, fluently. He respected and cared for them deeply and they in turn came to revere him as their fearless leader. Shriver cared little for money and material things so everything he had after buying essentials and food, he spent on his men and their families. He would also collect food, clothing, and other donations from soldiers for the Montagnard villagers. Shriver was the only American CCS (Command and Control South) known to have lived at the Montagnard barracks. He ate with them and drank from the communal pot of Ruou can, a fermented rice wine.

Green Hornet Gunner Ron Winkles vividly recalled the respect Shriver showed to his comrades among the Montagnards, when on Winkles's first flight in June of '68, Shriver lost two Montagnards in battle and made certain they got flown back to their funerals as soon as possible.

And there could be no forgetting Shriver's undying love for his German shepherd Klaus, whom he adopted during an adventure in Taiwan. In November 1968, JJ Jensen — then a fresh recruit out of Nha Trang — got his first-ever mission from Shriver. He was to fly an important resupply mission out to Shriver's team: they needed water, and Shriver needed his dog Klaus.

"The pilot reassured me that Klaus probably had more flying time than I did," Jenson recalled in *Secret Green Beret Commandos in Cambodia*. In one legendary encounter described in Plaster's *SOG*, Shriver was out on a life-threatening mission when some men got the idea to force-feed his dog beer. Klaus, not a drinker himself, became sick and defecated on the floor. Then the men cruelly rubbed Klaus's nose in the excrement and threw him out of the clubhouse.

Shriver returned from the excursion, got wind of the abuse, and burst into the club. First, he cracked open a beer and chugged it. Next, he set one of his revolvers on the table. Finally, his dropped his pants and he took a dump right in front of everyone.

"If you want to rub my nose in this, come on over," Shriver

said. Nobody took him up on his offer, and nobody ever messed with Klaus again.

Jerry Shriver's deployment began in 1966 and for nearly three-and-a-half years he kept extending it, spending over 1,000 days on tour. He was addicted to the battlefield, so much so that he once told his superior that he was taking leave to get some R&R but instead traveled to Plei Djereng to join up with a different Special Forces team and fight with them for a couple weeks.

The 5th Special Forces Group executive officer, Lt. Col. Charlie Norton, had been watching SOG recon casualties grow out of control and became worried about men like Mad Dog, whose entire lives were spent on the edge of life and death.

Indeed, in his chiseled, wiry exterior he gave many the impression of perfect predatory ability, but having dealt so much death for so many years, he confided to his close friends that he foresaw a horrific payback looming over him.

"He wanted to quit," Medal of Honor recipient Fred Zabitosky told John Plaster. "He really wanted to quit, Jerry did. I said, 'Why don't you just tell them I want off, I don't want to run anymore?' He said he would, but he never did; he just kept running."

In the early months of 1969, while America was engaged in peace talks in Paris to end the war, scores of Americans were dying from NVA strike forces that would kill, then run back to "neutral" Cambodia. This infuriated every American involved in the war, from private to president, but the NVA's underhanded tactics came with their own weaknesses. America wasn't supposed to attack Cambodia, but North Vietnam wasn't even supposed to be there; as American bombs fell in the supposed neutral country, Hanoi had to keep its lips sealed.

With peace talks stalling out and Americans continuing to lose their lives, the order came down from on high: bomb and raid the Central Office for South Vietnam (COSVN) bunker complex in Cambodia — the headquarters of the hated and feared Viet Cong — and disrupt the NVA's influence in the region, shifting the balance of power toward America. In what would become one of the most infamous missions ever undertaken by Command and Control South (CCS), none other than Mad Dog and Capt. Bill O'Rourke would lead this motherload of raids.

Lt. Col. Earl Trabue had doubts about the mission from the moment he received his orders. He doubted that the B-52 Arc Light air strike would soften up the enemy to the degree his superiors expected; he doubted that a platoon was enough men for the colossal job. The evening before the mission, everyone, Shriver included, had played Scrabble long into the night. When they were dead tired and about to hit the hay, Shriver suddenly livened up and spoke. "I am going to get hurt tomorrow," Henry Kohn remembers him saying in *Secret Green Beret Commandos in Cambodia*. When the younger, greener men asked how he knew, he just smiled.

Lt. Col. Earl Trabue knew something the others didn't: he'd heard enough times that Mad Dog was burnt out and had finally denied him an extension of his service. Shriver was two days away from being ineligible for another mission.

As dawn crested on the morning of April 24, 1969, Shriver stepped on to the first of nine helicopters. Before they began their 10-minute flight to the target, he turned to board the helicopter and said, "Take care of my boy," referring to his dog, Klaus. Those were his last words. Within the first moments of the mission, disaster loomed large — Capt. O'Rourke and five team members were forced to abort the mission due to mechanical problems with their helicopter. O'Rourke passed on the ground commander responsibilities to Capt. Cahill and wished them Godspeed.

Patty Hopper of Omega Task Force, Inc., an organization for MIAs, conducted interviews and found that the plan was for the team to be inserted just as the air strike's dust settled. Unfortunately, the helicopters' initial coordinates took them to the wrong place, and they had to search 30 to 45 minutes for the newly blasted craters. When the position was finally located, the remaining Hatchet Force leapt off and took cover in the craters. It was a matter of seconds before the NVA unleashed heavy fire from the complex of concrete bunkers and entrenched positions. Those not already within the cover of the craters were instantly wounded or killed. Those who made it into cover were trapped.

From the westernmost crater, Shriver radioed other team members that a machine gun bunker to his left-front had pinned his men down and that he needed support. Nobody could help — they were all just as pinned down as he was. The air commander brought in the gunships for air support and their miniguns and rockets began pounding the NVA positions.

Roughly 10 to 15 minutes into the raging battle, Shriver transmitted over his radio that he and his five Montagnard soldiers were going to enter the tree line on the west edge of the landing zone in an effort to flank an enemy position. Paul Cahill observed the six men as they broke from the crater and ran across the 30 yards of open ground between the crater and the tree line. As the men raced through the low grass toward the trees, Shriver maintained radio contact with the command and control aircraft and Capt. Cahill continued to monitor their progress.

As Shriver reached the tree line, Cahill watched as he was struck by a barrage of automatic-weapons fire. Shriver crumpled to the ground and was never seen again. Cahill believed "Jerry Shriver was dead when he hit the ground."

Of the 18 men inserted for the mission and the six later inserted in support of the Hatchet Force, 10 were wounded and safely evacuated; Jerry Shriver, along with his five Montagnards, were Missing in Action.

Special Forces personnel at Command and Control North were eavesdropping on North Vietnamese propaganda made by "Hanoi Hanna" when they heard her boast that "Mad Dog

Shriver had been captured" by the NVA. Hanoi Hanna would later state "they had Shriver's ears," a twisted way of saying that Jerry Shriver was dead and the NVA had his body. In 1974, the then-Secretary of the Army gave Shriver a "Presumptive Finding of Death," and his file was permanently closed.

Shriver was posthumously awarded a second Silver Star and promoted to Master Sergeant. In June 1969, the men of Command and Control South immortalized Jerry "Mad Dog" Shriver by hanging his prized Chinese smoking jacket in a prominent place of honor in the camp's club.

Underneath the silk smoking jacket was written:

IN MEMORY OF SERGEANT FIRST CLASS
JERRY M. SHRIVER
Missing in Action — 24 April 1969

That smoking jacket was an autobiographical statement on the life of Sgt. 1st Class Jerry M. Shriver. Across the jacket is embroidered "Ogdaa," which means "One Good Deal After Another," a credo that speaks not only to his ever-burning desire to walk the battlefield, but also to the love that he felt for his brothers-in-arms and country. To Jerry Shriver, volunteering to test his mettle on behalf of his country time and time again — being part of the most elite warriors in the world — was one good deal after another.

Jerry "Mad Dog" Shriver signed up for almost every hazardous, classified project run by the 5th Special Forces Group, and due to the highly secret and sensitive nature of the missions he participated in, we will never be able to give him the recognition he deserves. His dog, his smoking jacket, and a little over one dollar constituted most of his worldly possessions. Shriver will forever be remembered by those who knew him as one of the best and bravest men to have ever worn the Green Beret. Never forget those immortal words:

"One Good Deal After Another."

Captain Richard J. Flaherty

US ARMY

Silver Star
Bronze Star (2)
Purple Heart (2)

November 28, 1945–May 9, 2015

The shortest man to ever serve, Richard Flaherty showed the world that even at 4'9", he was a "Giant Killer."

A tiny 70-year-old homeless man makes a shocking confession to his only friend, a Miami Police Officer. One week later, that man would be killed in a mysterious hit and run. The officer spent the next four years down the rabbit hole, investigating his friend's unbelievable life. From the bloody jungles of Vietnam to the dangerous streets of Venezuela, all in search of the enigmatic shadow of a man nicknamed "the Giant Killer."

On November 28, 1945, Richard James Flaherty was born in Stamford, Connecticut's Regional Hospital. Flaherty's mother didn't know at the time of his birth that her blood type was Rh-negative, which can cause serious health problems or death in a second-born fetus or newborn. Richard Flaherty's future was therefore sealed even before he took his first breath.

His doctors predicted he would only grow to the height of 4-foot-7-inches and suffer from a lifetime of physical ailments. Flaherty defied their predictions and instead grew to 4-foot-9 and 97 pounds. Relentlessly bullied, he decided to fight back one day in high school. After taking down the school's biggest bully in a classroom fight, he earned the monicker "The Giant Killer."

Coming from a family of military heroes, Flaherty also wanted to do his part and serve. Most people laughed at the idea, and all the military branches turned him down. But that didn't deter Flaherty — he spent the next three years writing letters to politicians until he finally received a medical waiver. The waiver allowed him to join the Army ... but no one really believed he would make it through basic training.

His uniforms didn't fit, the equipment was too big, and he was required to carry a backpack during five-mile-long marches that weighed almost as much as him. Because of his leg length, marching in step with the rest of his company was incredibly difficult. But Flaherty kept up. No rules were ever changed for the Giant Killer ... he would either sink or swim.

All the obstacle courses were built for average-sized men, but Flaherty conquered them all. A bully recruit, with the help of a drill sergeant, repeatedly tried to force Flaherty to quit. Five years of Karate training put the bully in his place, right in front of the other recruits. After that, Flaherty wasn't only accepted, he was revered as the platoon's fiery mascot.

Flaherty didn't just make it through basic training, he became an elite paratrooper with the 101st Airborne. The instructors, however, had to strap extra machine gun parts to his legs so he wouldn't "float away" due to his light weight.

In 1968, after graduating from Officer Candidate School as a lieutenant, Flaherty was sent to Vietnam. His baptism by fire as a new platoon leader occurred when he was sent north to fight in the bloody "Tet Offensive." He was wounded in the first week of battle by a grenade fragmentation, then received a wound to the head from a grazing bullet. As soon as he was patched up, he went right back into battle.

After several months of fighting on the front lines, many officers accepted assignments in the rear, away from the fighting, but not Flaherty. He requested a transfer to a RECON unit engaged in the most dangerous search and destroy missions, deep into enemy territory.

In one of the last battles of his tour, Flaherty's small RECON unit would be surrounded by hundreds of enemy soldiers. No help could get to him, not even resupply. All the military higher-ups were sure the unit would be overrun and killed. But Flaherty and his men gave it their all, fighting through the night, repelling wave after wave of enemy suicide charges. Every man, including Flaherty, was wounded and some were killed. They made it through the night, though, and killed close to a hundred enemy soldiers. For his actions, Flaherty would receive the nation's third highest honor. And by the end of his first tour, Flaherty would be promoted to captain and receive the Silver Star, two Bronze Stars, and two Purple Hearts for his heroics and bravery.

Flaherty returned to the US and once again achieved the impossible by completing Special Forces training and becoming an elite Green Beret. In 1969, operating out of Thailand, he led his men on top secret clandestine missions, fighting Malaysian and Burmese guerrillas.

As incredible as all his accomplishments seem, that's just the first half of his life story. After the war, Flaherty would work "black ops" for many government entities in the US and abroad, including the ATF and CIA. Some of his more notable missions were training Cuban rebels in the Florida Everglades, allegedly smuggling weapons down to Central America to resupply the Anti-Sandinistas, and recovering a stolen top secret miniature nuclear bomb called a SADM (Sub Atomic Demolition Munition).

After a lifetime of dangerous missions, Flaherty would finally succumb to his PTSD and become homeless on the streets of Miami. It was on those streets where he met his police officer friend. It was on those streets where he was killed in a shocking hit and run.

Flaherty's legacy continues today, not only opening doors for other men short of stature yet bursting with courage, but proving to the entire world that hard work and willpower can overcome any obstacle.

To learn more about Richard Flaherty's incredible life, please check out our book, *The Giant Killer,* available as a paperback, audiobook, hardcover, and eBook on Amazon, Walmart, Spotify, Barnes & Nobles, iTunes/Apple Books, Google Play, Kobo, Chirp, Scribd, Audiobooksnow, Libro, Hoopla, and most other major sites.

"The Giant Killer," an award-winning documentary, is also available on Amazon, YouTube, Google Play, iTunes, Tubi, VUDU, Roku, Xumo, Apple TV, Hoopla, and most other major sites.

Special Forces Capt. Richard J. Flaherty
AKA The Giant Killer
tMilitary Bio:

In December of 1967, was sent to Vietnam with the 101st Airborne Division. He served as a Platoon Leader with companies B, C, and D and as a Recon Platoon Leader with Echo company.

In January of 1969, he returned to CONUS and attended the Special Forces School at Fort Bragg and was then assigned to the 3rd Special Forces Group. Later that year he returned to South East Asia with the 46th Special Forces Company A-110 in Camp Pawai, Lopburi Thailand.

Captain Flaherty earned The Silver Star, 2 Bronze Stars, 2 Purple Hearts, the Air Medal, Gallantry Cross W/Silver Star, Army Commendation Medal, Combat Infantryman's Badge, 3 Overseas Bars, Sharpshooter Badge W/Rifle Bar, Air Medal, Parachutist Badge, Vietnam Service badge.

Capt. Richard J. Flaherty, AKA The Giant Killer (center).

About the Author

Born and raised in Brooklyn, NY, David A. Yuzuk attended the University of Stony Brook, then moved to Miami, FL. There, he became a 19-year veteran of the Aventura Police Department, working as a uniformed road patrolman, undercover officer, and detective. Yuzuk was awarded Officer of the Month on two separate occasions by his department and was recognized as Officer of the Month by the Dade County Chief's Association.

In 2017, Yuzuk wrote and produced the critically acclaimed documentary, "The Giant Killer," based on the epic life of his friend, Green Beret Captain Richard J. Flaherty. Yuzuk's quest was to find the answers to his enigmatic friend's shadowy life and death.

The documentary was awarded The People's Choice Award in the Silicon Beach Film Festival, Best Film in the UK monthly *Film Festival*, and was an official selection in the Rome International Film Festival and the Fort Lauderdale International Film Festival.

After five years of research, Yuzuk completed and released the nonfiction book, *The Giant Killer*. The book ran for months as an Amazon #1 Best Seller in several categories, including Vietnam War Biographies. To learn more about *The Giant Killer,* please visit www.smallestsoldier.com.

Acknowledgments

I'd like to thank Hart Cauchy and Zinzi Robles for their research and editorial skills, as well as their wholehearted assistance in helping me complete this book.

And thank you Mission Point Press for your leadership on this project, in particular Heather Lee Shaw, who also worked with me on my first book, *The Giant Killer.*

American Hero, Mercenary, Spy...

The incredible true story of the smallest man to ever serve
in the U.S. military - Green Beret Captain Richard J. Flaherty

THE
GIANT
KILLER

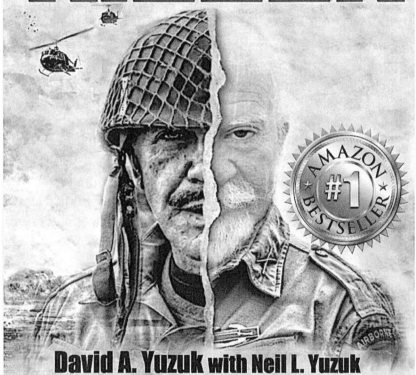

David A. Yuzuk with Neil L. Yuzuk

THE INCREDIBLE TRUE STORY OF AMERICA'S SMALLEST WAR HERO
Over 3,200 Positive Reviews on Amazon (4.6 out of 5 Star Rating)

CAPTAIN RICHARD J. FLAHERTY

He's been called spook, assassin, dope smuggler, dwarf...
but who was he really?

"Ask too many questions," said Flaherty, "and it could be
bad for your career and dangerous to my health."

Eight hours later, he was dead.

Welcome to the strange and shadowy world of covert ops,
cover-ups, conspiracies and the most unconventional man
ever to serve in the US military.

*Homeless Aventura man was secretly a dashing war
hero and maybe even a spy.* —Miami New Times

Vietnam Vet Richard Flaherty was The Giant Killer.
—Military.com

4' 9" 97 lbs
Recipient of the Silver Star
2 Bronze Stars
2 Purple Hearts

MISSION POINT PRESS

**BIOGRAPHY & AUTOBIOGRAPHY
/ Military**

ISBN 978-1-950659-47-0
90000

9 781950 659470

#1 *NEW YORK TIMES* BEST-SELLER DOUG STANTON WRITES:
"Giant Killers are among us — author David Yuzuk
walked with one and returned with this tale."

Printed in Great Britain
by Amazon

23543023R00193